The
Mystery
Hidden for Ages Past

How God Encoded a Hidden Message
Throughout the Old Testament for
Skeptics and Scholars to Find Today

VAUGHN THURMAN &
CHUCK TRESSLER

FREILING
PUBLISHING

Scriptures are taken from:

The Holy Bible, English Standard Version. ESV® Text Edition: 2016.
Copyright © 2001 by Crossway Bibles, a publishing ministry
of Good News Publishers.

The Holy Bible, New International Version®, NIV®. Copyright © 1973, 1978,
1984, 2011 by Biblica, Inc.® Used by permission.
All rights reserved worldwide.

The New American Standard Bible®, NASB. Copyright © 1960, 1971, 1977,
1995, 2020 by The Lockman Foundation. All rights reserved.

The New King James Version®, NKJV. Copyright © 1982 by Thomas Nelson.
Used by permission. All rights reserved.

Published by Freiling Publishing, a division of Freiling Agency, LLC.

P.O. Box 1264
Warrenton, VA 20188

www.FreilingPublishing.com

PB ISBN: 978-1-956267-89-1
HB ISBN: 979-8-9874834-9-7
eBook ISBN: 978-1-956267-90-7

Printed in the United States of America

Dedication

I WAS ONE of those kids who grew up in church. I believed because I was told to until I didn't. And when I didn't believe it was because I had never really been told why I should. This book is dedicated to all the people who want to know why they should believe and Jehovah, the Father, who planned our rescue and intricately pre-credentialed our Rescuer for our confident belief. This book is dedicated to the Church, the bride He loves. And to Chuck Tressler, who has helped me turn this vision into a reality. It is our hope that those both inside and outside of the church exposed to this text will understand what Jesus and the apostles meant when they explained the Hidden Mystery of the Gospel to the early believers. It is also our desire that our readers be empowered to make disciples more confidently.

Table of Contents

Acknowledgments

TO GOD HIMSELF, the one true God known as Yahweh in Hebrew, for so masterfully weaving a foreshadowing of The Gospel and the story of Jesus Himself throughout the Old Testament as powerful proof for the serious seeker.

To Jesus Christ, the Messiah, known as Yeshua ha Machiah in Hebrew, for flawlessly fulfilling all that was foretold of Him, despite knowing He would face agony and death before receiving His glory.

To the early apostles for showing us how to effectively teach believers and unbelievers alike.

To Dennis McCallum, Original Co-Founder and Senior Pastor (and prolific and consequential author), Xenos Christian Fellowship (now Dwell Community Church) in Columbus, Ohio, for inspiring this book and for allowing us to share his essay, "The Mystery Hidden for Eons Past."

To Josh Cales for his most helpful efforts in getting this book ready for publication and his deep encouragement.

To David Ochoa, Senior Pastor, Calvary Chapel Frederick of Frederick, Maryland, for his meaningful review and helpful feedback.

Introduction

Steganography

- A compound word constructed from the root Greek words,
  - o steganos ("concealed") and
  - o graphein ("writing")
- A means to conceal hidden messages in plain view.

MANY CHRISTIANS THINK that Jesus first appeared in the New Testament.

The Old Testament and the existence of Jesus are foundational to everything we see in the New Testament and to the Gospel itself. In fact, a central theme throughout the Old Testament is the story of Jesus for those who will see it. It is often said that the Old Testament is Jesus Christ concealed, and the New Testament is Jesus Christ (now) revealed. The Apostle Paul described this message as being "hidden for ages past and now revealed."

The Old Testament is filled with passages that point to both Jesus' first historical mission and His second coming. However, the fact that His mission would be split into two parts was not revealed until after His resurrection. The Jews, God's chosen people, and Christians, as His adopted people, both look forward to the Messiah's yet predicted coming. However, most contemporary Jews fail to recognize that this will be the Messiah's second arrival and are therefore missing significant information. How did this happen?

From our modern vantage point, Jesus is clearly visible in the Old Testament as both the suffering servant and warrior king. The Jews were known for their remarkable knowledge of

Scripture. That begs the question, why did so many fail to see Christ as the Messiah, then and now? Their doubts are reasonable on the surface. After all, why would the Messiah come to be crucified? And why didn't He take command of the governments of the earth as the Old Testament said He would?

Did God provide any proof to the Jews who were willing to see it, and is that proof still available to us? What if you would like to believe this story but consider yourself a skeptic? Perhaps it all just seems too fantastic to accept without irrefutable proof. The good news is this: God used steganography to place iron-clad answers to these questions within an encoded message, hidden in plain view for all to see. This message was spread throughout the pages of the Old Testament. However, the key to decoding this message, what Dennis McCallum calls "the light of Christianity," was not provided until after Christ had fulfilled all the prophecies regarding His first coming. These include the prophecies that ancient scholars believed referred to a mysterious character called "the suffering servant." The final key was provided when Jesus explained the promise of His second coming.

In the pages of this book, we intend to reveal the steganographic keys needed to help you see and decode this mystery. With it, we want you to confidently see and then communicate to others how God credentialed Christ's mission in advance, across centuries, through numerous disconnected authors, and in a manner that no other religious system can ever hope to reproduce. We also intend to share proof that Jesus Himself used the revelation of this divine credentialing to reinvigorate the early disciples. They were discouraged and disillusioned after His death on the cross. The apostles also used this information to instill confidence in early believers by showing supernatural evidence that the Gospel was trustworthy, unique, timeless, and eminently powerful.

We also desire to make the case that the true Church today should still be preparing individual Christians to wield this powerful story in much the same way that the early apostles did. We will also make the case that we should still teach this message from the pulpit as an evangelistic tool today. And finally, we want this book to serve as a reference for those who wish to study, teach, or otherwise share this amazing story with others.

Ephesians, Chapter 3: Verses 1-13 ESV

For this reason I, Paul, a prisoner of Christ Jesus on behalf of you Gentiles—assuming that you have heard of the stewardship of God's grace that was given to me for you, how the mystery was made known to me by revelation, as I have written briefly. When you read this, you can perceive my insight into the mystery of Christ, which was not made known to the sons of men in other generations as it has now been revealed to his holy apostles and prophets by the Spirit. This mystery is that the Gentiles are fellow heirs, members of the same body, and partakers of the promise in Christ Jesus through the gospel.

Of this gospel I was made a minister according to the gift of God's grace, which was given me by the working of his power. To me, though I am the very least of all the saints, this grace was given, to preach to the Gentiles the unsearchable riches of Christ, and to bring to light for everyone what is the plan of the mystery hidden for ages in God, who created all things, so that through the church the manifold wisdom of God might now be made known to the rulers and authorities in the heavenly places. This was according to the eternal purpose that he has realized in Christ Jesus our Lord, in whom we have boldness and access with confidence through our faith in him. So I ask you not to lose heart over what I am suffering for you, which is your glory.

I won't name the seminary my father attended so that I won't cause a stumbling block for anyone who might hold it in high regard. However, I'll say that after struggling financially to get through Johns Hopkins, as a very poor undergraduate whose father had passed away while he was quite young, my father was excited to obtain his master's in divinity from a very well-regarded seminary. Once he had come to truly know Christ, my father would refer to that school as a "theological cemetery." He said his idealistic young faith had gone there to die. My father was taught how to give twenty-five-minute messages on how people ought to live, supported by various scriptural passages which made the message sound more authoritative.

As I have come to know many pastors, I have observed that the average tenure for the American church leader is about three years. Sometimes this is because the job is harder than anyone expects. Often this lack of longevity is due to a death of passion. But far too often, the harsh reality is that after a pastor has recited his favorite topics, eloquently backed by his favorite passages, he finds himself running out of original content with which to inspire.

The Bible, however, is inexhaustible. One can study the same passages year after year and, with the aid of the Holy Spirit, continuously discover new and deeper meaning. But God's Word is still more profound than our discoveries. While it certainly won't do justice to the Word of God, using the properties of CDs vs. DVDs might be a helpful metaphor.

While a CD-ROM could store roughly 680 MB worth of information, a new medium called the DVD arrived in the marketplace a few years later that could hold 4 GB or more of data. However, to the untrained eye, their outward appearance looked the same. They were the same size, and a newer DVD reader could also read a CD-ROM. The significant difference between the two was how the information was recorded and read back. A CD stores information in grooves. The track's width and the laser's potential resolution to read the difference between pits and high points on the track limits the amount of data that can be stored on a CD. The amount of information available on the DVD drive is substantially higher because new technology created more facets on high and low points within each groove. This permitted multiple lasers to look at the same track and now pick up more information at the same time.

This metaphor does not suggest that two students of the Bible will get conflicting information. That is not possible. Those two may get different parts of the information, and when combined, those parts will become even more meaningful.

Consider these Scriptures that record Jesus speaking to both the crowd that was following Him and the teachers of the law. Those teachers were, at that time, espousing that one could follow all their rules and achieve holiness and thereby a relationship with God. While it was true that if a person could keep all of the Law, he could be in a relationship with God on that basis, they failed to teach God's more critical aspect that no man could actually do it. Jesus helped His audience see that the Law was not the end. Rather, the Law was a tutor designed to show men their need for a Savior on the spiritual level. On the natural level, the Law was also a set of yet insufficient standards that God established to maintain order until He provided a better way, the coming New Covenant.

> *Matthew 5:21,22,27,28,31-37, NASB*
>
> *You have heard that the ancients were told, "You shall not murder," and "Whoever commits murder shall be answerable to the court." But I say to you that everyone who is angry with his brother shall be answerable to the court; ...*
>
> *You have heard that it was said, "You shall not commit adultery"; but I say to you that everyone who looks at a woman with lust for her has already committed adultery with her in his heart. ...*
>
> *Now it was said, "Whoever sends his wife away is to give her a certificate of divorce"; but I say to you that everyone who divorces his wife, except for the reason of sexual immorality, makes her commit adultery; and whoever marries a divorced woman commits adultery. ...*
>
> *Again, you have heard that the ancients were told, "You shall not make false vows, but shall fulfill your vows to the Lord." But I say to you, take no oath at all, neither by heaven, for it is the throne of God, nor by the earth, for it is the footstool of His feet, nor by Jerusalem, for it is the city of the great King. Nor shall you take an oath by your head, for you cannot make a single hair white or black. But make sure your statement is, "Yes, yes" or "No, no"; anything beyond these is of evil origin.*

When we first read passages like this, our limited perspective as sinners who do not yet understand the Gospel can be simple conviction and perhaps a sense of hopelessness. After all, it would be reasonable if we were to think to ourselves, "If that's the bar, I'm never going to make it!" And that's the point of the Law. We can never measure up on our own, regardless of the number of rules we keep or our good works, which is what God wants us to see. It is critical that we understand the humble and insufficient standing we have before God. However, once we understand the full counsel of the Gospel and recognize that Christ has paid for all our sins (past, present, and future), we can return and read the same passage and think to ourselves, "I could never make it over that bar, *so thank God for Christ's death on the cross!*"

As you continue to make progressive trips through the Bible, much like the more advanced DVD reader, you will find that you can now pick up the deeper information. This is by God's design. At times your perspective will be different due to circum-stances. Sometimes your perspec-tive will be more profound because you have already absorbed the surface truth in a prior pass. Sometimes, new information is perceived because you finally see the  bigger picture. The Holy Spirit illuminates more and helps us grow as we dig deeper.

Some prophecies don't look like prophecies until you've looked at the story with that additional perspective. Consider the example many of us were playfully taught as children, the story of Daniel in the lion's den. Were you ever taught that this, too, was a foreshadowing of Christ and His relationship to the Father?

Daniel's Persian King had issued a decree that could not be reversed. Similarly, God the Father demands justice, and His righteous requirements cannot be negotiated away. The Persian King loved Daniel and saw him as a faithful servant, but the treachery of the King's other servants led him to have to sacrifice Daniel in order to fulfill his decree. Likewise, God loved His Son and those He created, but the treachery of His creation led God to have to sacrifice Jesus. Jesus' sacrifice was the only way to satisfy God's requirement for righteousness and fulfill His commitment to justice. When Daniel was thrown into the lion's den, a stone was rolled over the entrance. Likewise, when Jesus was crucified and laid in the tomb, a stone was also rolled over the entrance. Daniel spent the night in darkness with beasts that desired his flesh, but he survived. The king was over-joyed to release him in the morning when the requirements of the law had been fulfilled. Likewise, Jesus went to retrieve those held captive and preach the Good News in dark places but was surrounded by those who had desired His flesh. Jesus survived, and the Father was delighted to resurrect Him and raise Him to sit at His right hand once the requirements of the Law had been fulfilled. You may also notice that Daniel's accusers, who thought they had ensnared him, had now revealed their own character, ending up in the very trap they had laid for Daniel. This revealing of the evil intent and nature of the accusers is essential to note. We will be diving back into that concept later in the book in numerous ways.

Maybe you noticed the depth of prophetic imagery in this amazing story before, or perhaps you didn't. There is still more that can be extracted from this story about Daniel, but that is already more than you would typically pick up on a first pass. This is an example of the depth of God's incredible message. The Bible, at the surface, is a book filled with remarkable history. The Bible is sufficient to convict us, guide us, and renew us. And in time, as we continue to study it, the Bible can also show us, as no other book, movement, or religious system has ever been able to do, that it is from a supernatural being not bound by time as we know it.

Consider the story of Jonah and the great fish. Jonah spent three days in the belly of that fish, uniquely credentialing him to the Ninevites. Many churchgoing children have learned of this story, but few are taught how it also foreshadows Christ. There are many other examples, and we will expand upon some of them in this book. More of these credentialing forecasts will leap off the page as you make your way through the Scriptures in subsequent passes. This will confirm what you have already received by faith.

Many people reject Christianity for a perceived lack of proof. To be transparent, despite spending my childhood in the church and a Christian home, I was one of them. However, after finally seeing this "Mystery Hidden for Ages Past," I can no longer accept that the Bible lacks rational, philosophical, or intellectual proof. Nonetheless, I have significant empathy for the perspective of a skeptic. Christianity is often presented as a faith you should accept because "God said so." However, we have too often failed to show that it was God Himself that "said so" and that He has also proven it. This is not because of any weakness of the Bible but because, as a religious system, Christianity often fails to recognize the embarrassing treasure of authority and credentialing the Bible has made available. No human being has the power to convince another human being to yield control of their lives to a God they cannot see. Only God can do that. However, as His ambassadors of reconciliation, He has given us powerful tools of persuasion.

For the willing, He has given us the Holy Spirit who is able to speak quietly into the hearts of men who desire to know God, assuring them, "this is the truth." For the willing and the unwilling, He has given us the apocalyptic warnings of a cataclysmic end that we can all sense is coming. Even this is intended as a last means of bringing us to repentance. And for the skeptic, God has provided incredibly detailed, superiorly authoritative, and uniquely self-credentialing words in the form of the Bible.

While this topic of the Mystery Hidden for Ages Past and now revealed is independently sufficient for faith, it is not the only way God has credentialed Himself. Thus, this book is not meant to be a final authority on the topic of God's self-credentialing. Instead, the objective is to encourage the reader to take an in-depth look at this specific and extraordinary way that God has revealed and authenticated Himself.

The Singularity – The Written Work Superior to All Others

LET'S START WITH the examination of predictive prophecy.

Predictive prophecy, the credentialing signature of the Author behind the authors

IN THE OLD Testament, the office of a prophet was not a job for the fainthearted. It was not the plaything of people who had too much coffee on a Sunday morning. The law required that anyone who was proven to be a false prophet was to be stoned. It was the old-fashioned kind of "getting stoned" where people would gather and throw large rocks at someone until they were broken and dead.

> *Deuteronomy 13:5, NASB*
> *But that prophet or that dreamer of dreams shall be put to death, because he has spoken falsely against the Lord your God who brought you out of the land of Egypt and redeemed you from the house of slavery, to drive you from the way in which the Lord your God commanded you to walk. So you shall eliminate the evil from among you.*

Nobody wanted to be specifically responsible for the death of the person about to be stoned. Consequently, the crowd would continue throwing stones until the person could no longer hold up their arms to defend themselves, and their skull or some other vital area was eventually crushed. When the offender's body stopped moving, the work was done. Since most of the people in an area would be present when a stoning took place, or at the very least hear about it shortly thereafter, can you imagine how excited someone's mother might be when a rabbi came and said, "We would like to train your son to be a prophet"? This office was taken quite seriously. The person who held it was truly considered to be speaking for God. Therefore, if the things a prophet predicted were proven to be false, they were quickly dealt with and left for the birds.

Moses was careful to set this high bar for prophets:

Deuteronomy 18:22, NASB

When a prophet speaks in the name of the Lord, if the thing does not happen or come to pass, that is the thing which the Lord has not spoken; the prophet has spoken it presumptuously; you shall not be afraid of him.

Moses valued prophecy in this way because he knew that fulfilled prophecy was the unique evidence that God was indeed at work in both the words and heart of the prophet. Predictive prophecy credentialed the prophet as one who could offer others real insight into the heart of God. Though many have tried, not a single man alive or past has ever been able to reliably predict the future without God's help. And because they knew they would get stoned for trying, the odds of anyone taking a haphazard crack at it went down.

However, the Bible provides a wealth of specific prophecies and their exact fulfillment. The prophecies recorded in the Old Testament that have already been fulfilled are more than enough to demonstrate the accuracy and divine inspiration of the Bible and the truth of Christianity. Some predictive prophecy was intended for the contemporary hearer. For instance, "repent or be taken into captivity in Babylon" is not meant for us today. It was meant for the readers of that specific message, who were soon to be taken to Babylon for ignoring it. Other prophetic utterances were meant for later readers, such as Daniel's predictions about the kingdoms that would rise and fall between the end of his lifetime and the arrival of Jesus. Other prophecies are for the benefit of future readers, such as us, to interpret the times we are in according to special insight given to us by God. Only God can "declare the end from the beginning" and forecast to the very day "things that are not yet done" (Isaiah 46:10).

As an example of this, you can find specific prophetic writings in the book of Ezekiel where God provides prophecy in rich imagery, recorded for us by Ezekiel himself. Later in the same book, God also explains to Ezekiel exactly what those prophecies mean. Many of these prophecies were fulfilled long after Ezekiel was dead and gone, but God had described exactly what the prophecies meant. Then, across time, they were also fulfilled precisely as God had described.

Ezekiel 37:1-10, NASB
Vision of the Valley of Dry Bones
The hand of the Lord was upon me, and He brought me out by the Spirit of the Lord and set me down in the middle of the valley; and it was full of bones. He had me pass among them all around, and behold, there were very many on the surface of the valley; and behold, they were very dry. Then He said to me, "Son of man, can these bones live?" And I answered, "Lord God, You Yourself know." Again He said to me, "Prophesy over these bones and say

3

to them, 'You dry bones, hear the word of the Lord.' This is what the Lord God says to these bones: 'Behold, I am going to make breath enter you so that you may come to life. And I will attach tendons to you, make flesh grow back on you, cover you with skin, and put breath in you so that you may come to life; and you will know that I am the Lord.'"

So I prophesied as I was commanded; and as I prophesied, there was a loud noise, and behold, a rattling; and the bones came together, bone to its bone. And I looked, and behold, tendons were on them, and flesh grew, and skin covered them; but there was no breath in them. Then He said to me, "Prophesy to the breath, prophesy, son of man, and say to the breath, 'The Lord God says this: "Come from the four winds, breath, and breathe on these slain, so that they come to life."' So I prophesied as He commanded me, and the breath entered them, and they came to life and stood on their feet, an exceedingly great army.

Before we continue in this passage, let me quickly explain that most of Ezekiel's prophecies were quite visual and fantastic. Ezekiel's famous "wheel within a wheel" has led to many a '70s TV show wondering if Ezekiel had seen UFOs. His in-depth descriptions of the things he saw visually make his style so different. His visions were often of things that were impossible in the ordinary world and even more unimaginable in Ezekiel's time. But as fantastic as this prophecy is, with imagery of bones rattling together from around the desert and flesh growing on them, what is far more fantastic is to realize that God then explained to him exactly what the prophecy meant and that it has since come true in specificity. Ezekiel saw something that made no sense to him at the time and was completely impossible, yet he faithfully recorded it for our benefit and recorded how God took the time to explain these things to him. God did this to show that He was using it to credential Ezekiel in our eyes as a valid Prophet, and to credential Himself as the God who knows the end from the beginning.

Let's jump back in where we left off:

Ezekiel 37:11-14, NASB
The Vision Explained

Then He said to me, "Son of man, these bones are the entire house of Israel; behold, they say, 'Our bones are dried up and our hope has perished. We are completely cut off.' Therefore prophesy and say to them, 'This is what the Lord God says: "Behold, I am going to open your graves and cause you to come up out of your graves, My people; and I will bring you into the land of Israel. Then you will know that I am the Lord, when I have opened your graves and caused you to come up out of your graves, My people. And I will put My Spirit within you and you will come to life, and I will place you on your own land. Then you will know that I, the Lord, have spoken and done it," declares the Lord.'"

Isaiah also predicted this same remarkable event, unparalleled throughout human history. No displaced nation has ever retaken its homeland, ever, and certainly not in one day. How could such a thing ever happen? Yet God claimed, through Isaiah, that it would happen in precisely that way.

Isaiah 66:7, 8, NASB

> *Before she was in labor, she delivered;*
> *Before her pain came, she gave birth to a boy.*
> *Who has heard such a thing? Who has seen such things?*
> *Can a land be born in one day?*
> *Can a nation be given birth all at once?*
> *As soon as Zion was in labor, she also delivered her sons.*

On May 5, 1948, the United Nations saw the plight of the Zionists and the many displaced Jews now spread across the world looking for a home, and they sought to address their guilt. With a single vote, they recreated the modern nation of Israel. Modern Israel was *birthed in a single day*, just as Isaiah had foretold. What happened next reflected what Ezekiel foretold as the nation of Israel was regathered from around the world.

> *Since 1917, the portion of the Middle East called Palestine had been under the control of Britain, which became a holding place for refugee Jews and oppressed Arabs from the surrounding countries. Sympathy for the Jewish cause grew during the genocide of European Jews during the Holocaust. In 1946, the Palestine issue was brought before the newly created United Nations, which drafted a partition plan. The plan, which organized Palestine into three Jewish sections, four Arab sections and the internationally administered city of Jerusalem, had strong support in Western nations as well as the Soviet Union. It was opposed by Arab nations.*
>
> *On Nov. 29, 1947, the United Nations General Assembly passed a resolution calling for Palestine to be partitioned between Arabs and Jews, making way for the formation of the Jewish state of Israel. The General Assembly voted, 33-13, in favor of partition, with 10 members, including Britain, abstaining. The six Arab nations in the General Assembly*

staged a walkout in protest. The New York Times reported: "The walkout of the Arab delegates was taken as a clear indication that the Palestinian Arabs would have nothing to do with the Assembly's decision. The British have emphasized repeatedly that British troops could not be used to impose a settlement not acceptable to both Jews and Arabs, and the partition plan does not provide outside military force to keep order. Instead, it provides for the establishment of armed militia by the two nascent states to keep internal order."

It would be easy to offer the lazy argument that the Jews somehow orchestrated this to fulfill these prophecies. But logic would strike that down quickly. Wouldn't the American Indians quickly exercise the same technique if it were available? Why do we no longer hear of the Edomites? What about the Moabites? Why not the nation of Tyre? Why not the old kingdom of Babylon? What about the many kingdoms that rose and fell in Europe? For that matter, would not the ancient Greek or Roman empires also be glad to reconstruct themselves today if only they could? But they cannot. It has never occurred because nations cannot will themselves into the future, nor do their people retain their national identities once a nation falls. This event is unique across history, and God predicted it specifically, not only for the benefit of the Jewish people but also for us, so that we could see that God Himself is unique.

Throughout this work, we will reference many prophecies where God had provided specific details or allusions that show exactly what He had planned so that we can clearly see the divine nature once the prophecy has been fulfilled. There are also examples such as Cyrus, a well-documented historical figure predicted by name to be a future leader even though he was not yet born, nor born of nobility. We will cite examples where God predicts to the day that a particular thing will happen hundreds of years in advance. We will reference the passage in Ezekiel's prophetic writings where God took the time to explain exactly what the vision that He had just shown to Ezekiel meant. This is unique and noteworthy because it exemplifies how God has made an unwarranted effort to credential Himself to lowly creation.

Isaiah 46:10, NIV
"I make known the end from the beginning, from ancient times, what is still to come. I say, 'My purpose will stand, and I will do all that I please.'"

There is an erroneous perception among many that God is far off. Some view God as Wayne Dyer's "distant blue light of goodness, just waiting to lovingly accept all that we do," or as a distinctly judgmental being waiting to inventory our every error and hold us to account for them all. Many see God as planning our punishment without ever having given us a chance to be sure that He (the fuzzy blue light) was there. Nonsense! Not only is that not true, but God is, in fact, a personal being who quite directly understands our weakness. He has given us every opportunity to be convinced that He is who He says He is, that He does what He says He will do and that He is willing to go to great lengths to prove all of that to us.

God is the ultimate judge of all mankind, and on the day that He chooses, He will judge all of mankind based on the fruit of our lives. It may seem difficult to believe, but this same mighty God who will righteously judge the nations has also humbled Himself, presenting a mountain of evidence to us as if we are worthy to judge Him. Jesus came to show us God's nature. He is most certainly the King of kings, but He allowed Himself to be born in a stable. This was not out of character for God the Father who had sent Him. In fact, it was normatively reflective of His character. God has every right to measure us as coming up short for refusing to believe in Him without making any case for us to believe. However, even in the Old Testament, before our sins were dealt with through Christ, God was busy proving Himself to mankind with the same credentialing we have available today, namely predictive prophecy.

God's predictive prophecy is uniquely specific, making it a critical credentialing mechanism. Yet, it is also essential for us to consider because, within this book, we will delve into an area of prophecy where God was not as specific and did not explain the details in advance. This change in prophetic format stands out and makes it even more exciting when we see the ultimate revelation for the meaning of these passages was hidden within the text itself.

These prophetic areas were intentionally left as a mystery. Paul describes this mystery as "The Mystery Hidden for Ages Past and Now Revealed." These mysterious prophetic writings were interspersed throughout other topics, poetry, and predictive utterances across the entire Old Testament. The information was hidden in plain view until after the coming crucifixion and resurrection of Christ. With the benefit of hindsight, we now see these passages clearly. However, at the time, the details were obscured by a lack of perspective. Before Christ's first coming, readers of these passages detailing His first arrival and mission did not see them for what they were, not the religious leaders, Jesus' disciples, nor even the fallen angels who knew the Scriptures in great detail.

Colossians 1:25-27, NASB
I was made a minister of this church according to the commission from God granted to me for your benefit, so

that I might fully carry out the preaching of the word of God, that is, the mystery which had been hidden from the past ages and generations, but now has been revealed to His saints, to whom God willed to make known what the wealth of the glory of this mystery among the Gentiles is, the mystery that is Christ in you, the hope of glory.

Paul also describes this previously hidden mystery in his conclusion to the book of Romans.

Romans 16:25-27, ESV
Now to him who is able to strengthen you according to my gospel and the preaching of Jesus Christ, according to the revelation of the mystery that was kept secret for long ages but has now been disclosed and through the prophetic writings has been made known to all nations, according to the command of the eternal God, to bring about the obedience of faith—to the only wise God be glory forevermore through Jesus Christ! Amen.

The Uniqueness of the Bible: A Critical Building Block of our Faith

As we have already laid out, the Bible is unlike any other book. The revelation that it brings, when considered in total, inspires a one-to-one relationship with God unlike any other religion or spiritual system. I do not offer that as an opinion that I hope you will accept, but again as an authoritative fact that God Himself has credentialed through predictive prophecy. However, the authority and power of this predictive prophecy are under taught. The specificity and veracity of the Bible's foreknowledge are unique and worthy of study. This credentialing signature, issued by God Himself, is too often overlooked, leaving many to view the Bible as just a collection of stories. When we add that credentialing signature back in and see that we are beholding truth, things begin to change, and so do the people who see it.

In Paul's writings, in the sixth chapter of Ephesians, he describes the armor of God using the metaphor of the Roman praetorian guard. Just such a man would have been guarding Paul full-time at his home in Rome while he awaited trial. Paul discussed the soldier's equipment as a spiritual metaphor. A heavy breastplate. A shield. A helmet. Well-made leather sandals. A sword. And finally, a heavy and wide leather belt. This foundational item, which Paul called the Belt of Truth, was critical. The breastplate was fastened to it. The sword was suspended from it. The money pouch they would carry was connected to it. This thick leather belt also provided strength and protection in the warrior's weakest area. How shameful to send modern spiritual warriors into battle without this critical "belt of truth."

I have seen far too many students who are delighted to live the Christian life, congregate in Christian circles, attend many regular "Bible studies," and head off to college having never studied the Bible itself—at least to any level of depth. Having never been deeply convinced of its truthfulness in intellectually satisfying ways, they are like the proverbial lambs to the slaughter. Unable to defend their faith, they find themselves under attack and quickly lose confidence. Sadly, their entire belief system and their ability to function as an ambassador for Christ are quickly disassembled now that they have been isolated. Parents are saddened when they find out their child has taken to drugs or alcohol and wild parties at college. They ask other Christian parents for prayer when they hear that their previously perfect child's grades are now declining. Even worse, some parents overlook a more salient concern. Their children are walking away from their faith, but many parents are just happy to say, "Thank God, my child's grades are not declining, and they are *not* doing the party scene at college." In either case, we should be most concerned about the eternal state of these young souls. We never equipped them with the "full" armor of God before we sent them into a war zone.

It is not good enough to tell people that the Bible is unique because "it teaches you how to be good." Any zealous anti-Christian professor will quickly refer that ill-prepared student to other religious writings, especially the sections that *also* tell you "how to be good" without requiring Christ.

It is not good enough to tell people that the Bible is unique because it teaches us how to reach God. Someone from another faith will share the Koran or another religious writing that offers a path to god.

Perhaps our children (or the converts we failed to disciple) will believe that we were right and decide to follow our path... but then perhaps they will learn of another way and decide they believe that too. The result? Syncretism. Syncretism is the belief that all religions lead to God, an incredibly effective tool that the enemy uses to deceive untrained young Christians (regardless of their age). We never showed them that God credentialed His Word as unique among all religious works. Perhaps we didn't even know.

If we taught new believers the uniqueness of the Bible, as we ourselves may wish we had been taught, and if we also equipped them with the means to defend that thesis relentlessly, is it possible that they would be more difficult to lead astray? The

Apostle Peter advised us that we should be wise so that we are not led astray by unscrupulous people.

> *2 Peter 3:17, NASB*
> *You therefore, beloved, knowing this beforehand, be on your guard so that you are not carried away by the error of unscrupulous people and lose your own firm commitment.*

Paul also explicitly directed leaders to equip the people so that *we* would not be swayed by every wind of false doctrine.

> *Ephesians 4:11-14, ESV*
> *And he gave the apostles, the prophets, the evangelists, the shepherds and teachers, to equip the saints for the work of ministry, for building up the body of Christ, until we all attain to the unity of the faith and of the knowledge of the Son of God, to mature manhood, to the measure of the stature of the fullness of Christ, so that we may no longer be children, tossed to and fro by the waves and carried about by every wind of doctrine, by human cunning, by craftiness in deceitful schemes.*

And finally, Jesus told us to go into all the world and make disciples.

It seems there is a chasm between what Peter, Paul, and Jesus directed us to do and what we seem to have degraded to in the modern church. A wide chasm. Jesus did not say, "go into all the world and make converts." Rather, He told us to "go into all the world and make disciples."

The process of making disciples, defined as producing mature Christian workers, is something that the New Testament shows us is likely to take several years. Several New Testament authors referred to their readers as people "who by now ought to be ready to teach or should be mature and moving beyond basic spiritual matters" [para]. These letters (the epistles) can be historically verified to have been received just a few years after the recipients had first learned about the Gospel, often from the very same authors of those letters. However, on the other hand, there was no expectation that someone would hear the Gospel and then be immediately ready to serve. To the contrary, Paul, in 1 Timothy 3 and Titus 1, was particular in pointing out that new Christians should *not* be placed into *leadership* because of the risks it places on them and on those they would serve.

What we can ascertain here is the presence of an intentional process that led people from "new believer" to workers and leaders who were now ready to "go into all the world and make disciples." If we only teach our converts how to be "good Christians" or "good people" but never prepare them to answer tough questions or take on the most challenging arguments, we have not prepared them at all. It is not enough to ask them to just believe. Why on earth would we lower the bar when God, who knows unbelievers far better than we do and loves them far more than we do, went to so great an effort to convince us all that He is real and that He is who He says He is?

The case this book asks you to consider is that the formula has already been established and that all we need to do is imitate God. He has already presented the data necessary to convict and convince the heart of a man. That is what is so unique about the Bible. All we need to do is learn it well enough to recall the key points in meaningful ways and allow the Holy Spirit to draw open hearts into discipleship. By the time we have taken several people through the complete conversion process to becoming disciples, we will find that we ourselves also get better in each iteration at giving an answer for the hope that is within us. The uniqueness of the Bible is critical for us to understand and convey because its reliability provides us with the foundation for the full armor of God.

Why is God's credentialing so important?

Imagine someone you don't know knocks on your door and, when you answer, says, "Quick, I need your phone!" Would you hand them your expensive new mobile phone? You would probably not if you had just heard about a scam like this on the radio. But what if the person explains she is your new neighbor, who had moved in the day before, and you had seen the moving trucks, and she points to a man lying on the sidewalk and says, "That's my husband. He just passed out!" Would you hand her your phone then?

The truth is that both scenarios could be a scam, and both scenarios could be based in truth, but one gave you more information upon which to base your trust. What if she took it further and simply asked you to call 911? Would you refuse?

God credentialed Himself because He knows we have reasons to fear deception. Legitimate reasons! In fact, He was present when we were first deceived. He knows that the enemy of our souls, who has always accused God of being a liar intent on holding us back, still roams the streets today like a lion "seeking whom he may devour" with brand new versions of his same old lies and distortions. If we are willing to hear God, He gently assures us, "I can be trusted." In much the same way as a police officer's badge helps us ensure that we are talking to the right person, God's credentialing of Himself is an even more irrefutable way to ensure we are talking to our Creator.

Many of us come to the Bible already knowing there is a God. Some come hoping to find Him. Some, such as Lee Stroebel, who wrote the book *The Case for Christ*, come as skeptics hoping to disprove His existence.

To each of these, the Bible responds consistently, showing us that God exists. Consider these passages that show us that we can see that God exists through what He created.

Psalm 19:1-4, ESV
The heavens declare the glory of God,
and the sky above proclaims his handiwork.
Day to day pours out speech,
and night to night reveals knowledge.
There is no speech, nor are there words,
whose voice is not heard.
Their voice goes out through all the earth,
and their words to the end of the world.

Romans 1:19-21, ESV
For what can be known about God is plain to them, because God has shown it to them. For his invisible attributes, namely, his eternal power and divine nature, have been clearly perceived, ever since the creation of the world, in the things that have been made. So they are without excuse. For although they knew God, they did not honor him as God or give thanks to him, but they became futile in their thinking, and their foolish hearts were darkened.

This is an example of an argument the Bible makes in defense of the Creator. This is referred to as a teleological argument for the existence of God. It is rooted in the understanding that there must be a purposeful intelligence that created the world because the world shows both purpose and intelligence. In the view of many (including the authors of this book), this argument from purpose and design remains effectively unanswered by the atheist and the agnostic.

These arguments are made for the benefit of noble skeptics who seek to find and verify the truth.

2

Skeptics Are Welcome!

MANY PEOPLE GROWING up in a religious home hear that to doubt God is a sin. However, so is just about everything else most of us have ever managed to do outside of the influence of the Holy Spirit. But how do we escape the sin of doubt if we don't yet know enough to accept what we are being asked to believe? God Himself is eager to engage our doubt as the first step in our rescue. God must overlook many sins to affect our rescue, so why do we then imagine He would reject us for expressing the sin of doubting Him?

We need to learn to see doubt as God does. It is a reasonable response for those who lack the needed information. Therefore, the correct response to doubt is to provide compelling and verifiable information, and it is the responsibility of the hearer to verify it and to act accordingly.

Consider this historical account of a remarkable group of skeptics, relayed in Acts 17.

Acts 17:10, NKJV, "Then the brethren immediately sent Paul and Silas away by night to Berea. When they arrived, they went into the synagogue of the Jews."

The Bereans that Luke refers to here were a group of Jews from Berea who demonstrated a critical discipline by studying the Scriptures daily as a basis to verify what they were taught by

Paul. They were a people whose ultimate standard for authority and truth was the Word of God.

Acts 17:11, NKJV, "These were more fair-minded than those in Thessalonica, in that they received the word with all readiness, and searched the Scriptures daily to find out whether these things were so."

Unlike others who had rejected this new information about the Messiah, the Bereans were quick to receive the message that Paul and Silas brought them, yet they did not receive it naïvely. They didn't just take Paul's word but *"searched the Scriptures daily to find out whether these things were so."* Because they gauged what they heard against the Word of God that they already knew and trusted, they could see and verify the credentialed truth of Paul's message about the Lord Jesus Christ, and they believed:

Acts 17:12, NKJV, "Therefore many of them believed, and also not a few of the Greeks, prominent women as well as men."

Here is what we can learn from how the Bereans handled the new revelation brought to them by Paul.

1) They were skeptical.
2) They remained open-minded enough to listen to the details.
3) They put those details to the test and asked, "Could this supposed good news be overlaid onto other trust-worthy information we already had access to, and would

it then reveal this new information to be consistent and trustworthy?"

4) As a group of people who knew the Old Testament well enough to gauge this new information against it, they deemed the Good News to be true.

5) We can see that their knowledge of the Bible was an asset to them, even before they were believers in Jesus Christ.

6) Their story makes the argument that *we* should be able to do the same research when also presented with the truth of the New Testament (i.e., validating it through the predictive prophecy and fulfillment of the Old Testament).

7) Their story proves that neither Paul nor God, who sent him, was offended by skepticism. In fact, the text of verse 11 commended their diligence.

When our skepticism is addressed, it calls us to make a decision

We live in a time marked by an embarrassing wealth of evidence. This ever-growing mountain of evidence credentials both the Old and New Testaments by proving both the pre-existence of detailed predictive prophecies in the Old Testament and their subsequent fulfillment within the historically and archeologically supported writings of the New Testament. Some of these prophecies have even been fulfilled, to exact detail, within the last 100 years. In the face of this prolific body of evidence, we find ourselves challenged to either accept the evidence and render a verdict on the truthfulness of the Bible's claims or to admit that we are willing to ignore them. The boldest claim in all of history is Jesus' own, namely that He is the Son of God and the only way to reach God.

The question at hand is this: Who do you say Jesus is?

Consider some of the common and insufficient efforts to wish this topic away:

It isn't enough to say that **Jesus was a "good person."** If we do not believe that He came as the Son of God to die in the place of guilty men, we need to be honest with ourselves. We are saying that He was no more than a famous madman. After all, if He were not who He says He is, who short of a madman would orchestrate a movement where He claims to be God only to end up crucified?

It isn't enough to say that **Jesus was a "nice teacher."** If we stop there, it is equivalent to saying that although He lied about significantly important things and deceived the whole world for generations, He was otherwise a nice man, and we should follow His teachings. Well, other than the fact that He was crazy and a liar. This argument doesn't make sense. Yet when we want to resist the call to examine the facts, this is an easy if not a lazy way out so long as we are willing to overlook the fact that we just said something ridiculous.

It isn't enough to say that **Jesus was a "great prophet."** Remember, in those days, a false prophet was stoned, and all record of him was wiped away. Jesus predicted He would rule the earth. That will be completed in His second coming, but if He is not the Son of God, and is not returning to rule, then He is just another false prophet. If we believe that Jesus was simultaneously a false prophet and a great prophet, we find ourselves in a logical paradox.

It isn't enough to say that **Jesus was a "great rabbi."** The Jews who lived while He walked the earth had Him killed for blasphemy. I'm pretty sure that wouldn't be a great credential for getting into the local temple, even in modern times. Just imagine the introduction at the local temple, "He's a pretty good Rabbi, other than that one time we had to crucify Him for blasphemy."

If you examine the evidence for yourself and see that God has credentialed the supernatural uniqueness of Jesus' visit to the earth, you only have a handful of options. In the words of the '80s rock band, Rush, "If you choose not to decide, you still have made a choice." God has presented a steganographic message throughout the Old Testament that uniquely credentials Jesus as the Messiah, and it deserves a response. If we choose to respond, we are down to just two choices. We can either decide to ignore it and wish away what we have seen or to dig in and pursue the truth.

To give an answer for the hope that is within us

Let's assume for the moment that you have helped a friend get past their skepticism. Maybe you have led them through some of God's remarkable credentialing that we are detailing in this book. Now, they have decided to trust that God is real. Is that it? Do we high-five each other and move on to our next convert? Well, sure, but let's not make the error of calling this first convert a disciple.

Discipleship is not conversion, and conversion is not discipleship. We will go into that in greater detail later in the book, so if you are skeptical of that statement, good! You should be. But here's the highest-level argument we will offer you: if your new convert is not ready to give an answer for the hope that is within them, they may be a new believer, but they are not prepared to lead other skeptics to conversion. They may also be easily led astray. They have crossed the first precipice and said, "Okay, I believe this is real," and they have grabbed onto the proverbial life ring. However, this is not the end of the journey. It is the beginning.

From here, your new convert may be delighted about having come to faith, but their natural skepticism will return when someone questions their new faith in a way for which they were unprepared. Friends and family may call them a "Jesus Freak" and accuse them of being weak-minded. Will this credentialing they have learned about be enough for them, or might they wonder if they have been hoodwinked or drawn into a cult? Their new beliefs need to get rooted deeply, or they will not survive the secondary onslaught of doubt they are about to face. After all, haven't you ever bought into a new fad only to later look back at that period and say, "How did we ever fall for that?" The difference between a new convert and a mature Christian is roots, and those roots take cultivation, and they are also the needed basis for future and further growth. Those roots come from knowledge, and knowledge comes from the Word of God.

Romans 10:17, ESV, "So faith comes from hearing, and hearing through the word of Christ."

I used to think that just going to church was getting discipled. Make no mistake, it helps, and God's Word directs it.

Hebrews 10:24, 25, ESV, "And let us consider how to stir up one another to love and good works, not neglecting to meet together, as is the habit of some, but encouraging one another, and all the more as you see the Day drawing near.

Fellowship in the body of Christ is necessary. That is where we will develop the relationships we need for growth and accountability. We are hard-wired to be social, even introverts like me. As we develop close relationships in the Body of Christ, we are more likely to reveal (whether by design or by error) who we really are. That is also where we will begin to *work* on who we actually are. That is a good thing—ordained by God Himself. **We are made in His image. He is one God yet also three distinct persons who are close, personal, and deeply relational with each other, just as He designed us to be.** But this is only a tiny part of discipleship. The critical part, the most crucial part of all, is to gain an understanding of who God truly is so that we cannot be easily led astray by every wind of false doctrine.

Ephesians 4:11-16, ESV

And He gave the apostles, the prophets, the evangelists, the shepherds and teachers, to equip the saints for the work of ministry, for building up the body of Christ, until we all attain to the unity of the faith and of the knowledge of the Son of God, to mature manhood, to the measure of the stature of the fullness of Christ, so that we may no longer be children, tossed to and fro by the waves and carried about by every wind of doctrine, by human cunning, by craftiness in deceitful schemes. Rather, speaking the truth in love, we are to grow up in every way into him who is the head, into Christ, from whom the whole body, joined and held together by every joint with which it is equipped, when each part is working properly, makes the body grow so that it builds itself up in love.

If, as a body joined together under Christ, we are called to change the world around us through ministry, how will we fulfill this if:

-   We have no idea what we are called to do?
-   We are unable to defend what we claim as truth?
-   We neither recognize nor find ourselves prepared to refute false teaching?

Effective discipleship can be defined as people being trained to give an authentic and complete answer for the hope that is within them.

One of the most striking examples of effective discipleship I have ever seen looked almost nothing like what I expected. I led a small group Bible study in our home for several years. It was growing, and so were many of the people who attended. I can't quite remember whether I volunteered or was asked, but the next step was that I took on leading and supporting the other home group leaders in the same church. I wanted to inspire them to follow this recipe that I saw work well. We were taking people who had not spent a lot of time in the Bible and going through it book by book, chapter by chapter, and verse by verse. I had never been exposed to this form of study. I simply did it because I didn't know what else to do, yet it worked wonders. I found myself moved and changed as I prepared for our studies. I saw the same effect on others as we dug in.

Nonetheless, as I tried to share this discovery with others, I found that many of these leaders were uncomfortable with this approach. They did not feel like they had the skills or knowledge necessary to teach directly from the Bible. Several even outright argued that this is the realm of professionals, and we are likely to end up in error. That is why they felt it would be better if we continued "studying books *about* the Bible instead of the books *of* the Bible." However, as I dug into some of the books these small groups were studying, I felt concerned that the "professional Christians" they were leaning on seemed more prone to error than my cadre of leaders, but my cadre of leaders couldn't see that. This was a discouraging state of affairs. It led me to look around for working examples of effective discipleship in other churches or small groups.

Let me provide some context. Several years earlier, I had been leading a Bible study on the book of Romans at the same church. This exercise was the beginning of my falling in love with studying the Bible sequentially. I wasn't sure how to lead the study, and I certainly wasn't qualified. I didn't have anyone telling me what to do, and I didn't have an outline or syllabus provided to me either. I was on my own, and at the start, I was also not very excited about that! Leading this study was hard work and way over my head!

I was quite pleased when I found a British seminary where one of the professors was publishing one or two PowerPoint presentations online for each chapter of the book of Romans. I went through the first few chapters of his study material and found it to be excellent! Problem solved! I would simply borrow his materials (while giving him credit) and would now have meaty studies. Imagine my surprise when halfway through Chapter 12, I discovered that he had passed away before finishing the course!

Looking for another source, I happened upon a website full of expository teaching (the style of going chapter by chapter, verse by verse through one book at a time, and exposing the whole contextual meaning of the covered material). That was the website of a church in Columbus, Ohio, called "Xenos" (a Greek word meaning stranger or alien) and now known as "Dwell."

The name Xenos seemed strange to me, but I needed another place to lift more teachings from, so I had to dig in. The second teaching I got into, on Romans 13, challenged my "conservative Christian" thinking. That made me uncomfortable, and I felt like I'd better get back into the Berean mode myself. Before I would use any more of their material, I decided to listen to the rest of their teachings from the entire book of Romans. I compared it to what I found through other scholars and studied the underlying passages.

I felt even more uncomfortable as I continued to run into parts of their teachings that I disagreed with but could not refute as I searched the Scriptures. Their positions were well researched and consistently well-articulated. Their principles were also deeply rooted and grounded in the whole context of the Bible itself. The teaching on each passage was well supported by referring to numerous other passages, and in the end, I not only found a source for the rest of my class, but I also began a journey in being Berean.

The pastor whose material I was now leaning on for my Bible study will be coming up again. Still, for now, the point that I want to make is that I returned to this website to see what information they might have available regarding small group studies and discipleship. I found that they had a wealth of information that was helpful to me as I tried to facilitate or "equip" the other leaders in our shared mission of equipping the saints they supported. In fact, I was so moved by the hard-to-believe claims they made about the results they were getting I decided to travel to Columbus and see it for myself. The pastor of the church I attended at the time decided to travel out there with me.

In Chapter 9, *The way that we should teach*, we will discuss some of the shocking findings of this trip. For now, suffice to say that a critical element was a cascading study of God's Word that led relatively new believers to see themselves not just as recipients of the Gospel. Instead, they were active students who could also help mentor more junior students along their road.

This was discipleship. The people we encountered at Xenos intentionally met together in small groups and one-on-one settings. The Bible was at the center of it all. God's Word helps us see God and understand more of how He views things. It shows us how He designed us and teaches us to confidently believe that He knows best how we should live within this grand system that He has created. His Word also helps us avoid being negatively impacted by the subsystem that the enemy of our souls has temporarily created within it.

God welcomed skepticism from the very beginning. Luke commended the Bereans for being noble skeptics who carefully examined what they heard and put it to the test. Christ's disciples are not scorned for doubt. They are encouraged to share their doubts and press them against the Word of God. His Word can withstand all of the arguments made against it, and with the aid of His Holy Spirit, so can we.

3

The Incredible Hidden Story

IN THE 1987 movie Predator, there was a scene where a key character, Blain, played by Jesse Ventura, had just been killed by the predator. Another character, known as Mac, played by Bill Duke, rushed into the scene looking to help his friend. It was the first scene where we could see or partially perceive the movie's nemesis. It was a striking scene because Mac saw the partially visible predator standing over his dead friend as he ran into the clearing. To be clear, Mac could not see the predator. Instead, he was only seeing light that was being imperfectly bent around the predator's cloaking technology, a chameleon-like pattern making him blend in with the scenery around him. It was an intense moment as Mac began to shoot into the jungle in terror, and the rest of the men joined him, irrationally responding out of a fear of the unknown.

The premise of the movie was about an alien creature, "the Predator," that would come to hunt human beings in the jungle during the hottest summers. It was humanoid in form but superior in size, technology, and advanced weaponry. Its most impressive capability was an exterior suit that could make it nearly invisible. It bent light around itself, making it difficult to see anything other than a moving outline of the creature as it would easily travel from tree to tree or run across the ground.

What struck me, watching this scene, after having studied the story of the Mystery of the Gospel, was the metaphor of limited visibility of something that was in plain sight. To reiterate, Mac saw nothing in the jungle but leaves and branches, as he would have expected to see. But a distortion in the patterns of the leaves revealed something worthy of squinting to see, especially in light of what had just happened. Likewise, throughout the passages of the Old Testament, we see an overlay of additional information above the stories that show us something worthy of greater focus, especially in the light of the story of our crucified Savior. God had masterfully orchestrated and led men to record information relevant to Old Testament times. Yet with a mastery of steganography only possible to the supernatural mind of God, these texts also delivered a light-bending overlay stitched across numerous Scriptures. After Jesus' first coming, these hidden references allow us to see the pattern of the suffering servant with a previously impossible clarity.

In no way would I want to associate Jesus Christ with the nemesis of the movie Predator. Instead, I simply want to focus on the metaphor of being able to see extra information when one story is overlaid above another in plain sight. As one who has already seen the movie, the second time through, you can see the light-bending image of the predator and now perceive what it is. Likewise, we are quite privileged in our time to know the whole truth of the Mystery Hidden for Ages Past. We now understand what we see when we view the Old Testament's forecasts of Christ's first coming. Our rich blessing is being alive when the Mystery is "Now Revealed."

At a high level, that "mystery," hidden within the pages of the Old Testament, was that Christ would come twice. He would come once to be a sacrifice (the part not made clear until after it had occurred) and a second time to harvest the souls He bought through that sacrifice, bringing them into the presence of the Father and taking His rightful place as King of kings.

The unwitting list of contributors

Next, let's consider the story of the people who, unaware of their divinely inspired contributions or collaborations, recorded the hidden details of the Messiah's first coming in advance.

The most pressing question we face as humans is what are we going to do with Jesus?

- Suppose Jesus is who He says He is and has opened the pathway back to relationship with God, and the now understood foretelling of His second coming is also true. Doesn't this reality-altering news deserve a critical response?
- Wouldn't so much of what we trouble ourselves with be little more than a distraction in the face of this good news?
- Given the perplexing story of self-sacrifice and the devoted following of Jesus that persists across thousands of years, even today. Shouldn't we at least attempt to ascertain whether this is some elaborate hoax or not?

However, if the premise of these questions is true, it demands a verdict. Again, hoping to wish this compelling demand away, many attempt to reconcile the unreconcilable by stating that Jesus is at once a good teacher and a suicidal maniac. This argument posits that this "good teacher" crafted his own course to crucifixion, thereby fostering a devoted movement that has led and continues to lead many to martyrdom. This dissonant solution is insufficient, and as humans, we instinctively know it, which is why these questions still plague us if we leave them unanswered.

God Himself, understanding our plight, knew that a claim this large deserved an equally large body of evidence to credential it. God commissioned an unwitting list of contributors to build an iron-clad case across multiple formats, including specific and detailed prophecies, unmistakable shadow pictures, and powerful allusions. He also orchestrated that this work should be spread across the millennia through numerous disconnected authors and characters, unaware they were collaborating on the effort. Let's take it further. These steganographically encoded messages were hidden within plain view by these contributors despite being fully indiscernible until after Jesus Christ's redemptive work on the cross was completed.

This unwitting list of contributors was by no means the craftwork of a group of men huddling together to create a messianic story. In fact, their work often amounts to a tragedy deemed not to be messianic at all before Christ first helped his disciples connect the dots. The contributors themselves did not see what they were building, nor would they have seen it as messianic. At the time of Jesus' life, none of the Jewish scholars recognized what was in plain sight. Nor did Jesus' disciples see it until He explained it to them after His resurrection.

And as we will demonstrate later in the book, the celestial scholar and expert distorter of God's Word himself, Satan, also seems to have failed to see it. The message was undoubtedly visible, and the quandary it created was certainly discussed frequently by Jewish scholars. However, an enormous chasm existed between passages that described the Messiah as coming to rule with an iron scepter and those representing what seemed like a tragic figure. These vague passages told of a coming servant who would shut the mouths of kings but who would also be disfigured and marred beyond recognition. They led to a well-documented and generally accepted theory that these writings about "the servant of the Lord" referred to a non-messianic character who also became known as "the Suffering Servant." Yet Jesus quietly fulfilled more than 300 of these prophecies during His first coming, many of which were previously connected to that same "Suffering Servant."

Statistical Improbability

J. Barton Payne identified 574 verses in the Old Testament that point to the Messiah. Alfred Edersheim identified 456 Old Testament references to the Messiah or His times. Most scholars agree there are more than 300 prophecies in the Old Testament that Jesus Christ fulfilled. These prophecies, relating to His birthplace, lineage, and the details of His execution, could not have been accidentally or deliberately fulfilled. It is a mathematical improbability.

In the book *Science Speaks*, Peter Stoner and Robert Newman discuss the statistical improbability of one man, whether accidentally or deliberately, fulfilling *just eight* of the prophecies Jesus fulfilled. The chance of this happening, they say, is 1 in 10^{17} power. Stoner presents a scenario that illustrates the magnitude of such odds. Take 10^{17} silver dollars and lay them on the State of Texas. They will cover all the state two feet deep. Now mark one of these silver dollars and stir the whole mass thoroughly, all over the State. Blindfold a man and tell him that he can travel as far as he wishes, but he must pick up one silver dollar that was marked. What chance would he have of getting the right one? Just the same chance that the prophets would have had of writing just eight prophecies and having them all come true in any one man, from their day to the present time, provided they wrote using their own wisdom.

Critics have often made a charge of conspiracy. They claim that a theoretical group of bronze-aged men (the prophets) conspired together to fabricate a story hoping that some future person would be willing to sacrifice himself to make their manufactured religion more credible. Straining the credulity of this charge is the inconvenient fact that the authors of these passages, those foretelling the suffering servant or the first visit of the Messiah, were significantly divided by time and distance. These authors were also often the subjects of non-Jewish kingdoms that culturally and geographically separated them from the heart of their Jewish faith. In other words, they had no practical way to collude at all.

Reading the following passages will also show that those authors frequently failed to perceive that they had predicted anything related to the Messiah. Contrast the picture of the suffering servant with Isaiah's Messiah, who will "rule with an iron scepter."

Dennis McCallum writes in his essay, "*The Mystery Hidden for Aeons Past*":

Any careful reader of Old Testament messianic prophecy quickly becomes aware of the two portraits of Messiah. On the one hand, we have the picture of the reigning Messiah, who banishes his enemies and lives forever. On the other hand, we have the portrait of the suffering servant. This one "has no stately form or majesty," lives in obscurity, is rejected by the people, and dies badly. But his death is redemptive like a guilt offering, and he is raised from the dead to lead many to God and to glory.

I became convinced that the predictions of Jesus' first coming were not mistaken readings. They are amazing confirmations of the authenticity of Christ. Passages like the servant songs in Isaiah must refer to Jesus, and to no one else. And while some predictions could be read in more than one way, they certainly can be seen in the Christian light without distortion."

Old Testament Prophecies of Jesus

The books of the Old Testament contain many passages about the Messiah and His first coming—all prophecies that Jesus Christ fulfilled. For instance, the crucifixion of Jesus was foretold in first-person form throughout Psalm 22, approximately 1,000 years before Christ was born and long before crucifixion, the most horrible of death sentences had appeared.

It was not until Christ's resurrection that the New Testament church began to declare that Jesus was the Messiah officially:

Acts 2:36, ESV
"Let all the house of Israel therefore know for certain that God has made him both Lord and Christ, this Jesus whom you crucified."

The following chart references Scriptures showing Jesus Christ's first visit as forecasted in the Old Testament and at least one reference to where it is also fulfilled in the New Testament. While we are providing this as a summary reference, we encourage you to take a deep dive into the specific passages on your own. Please explore the passages and make your own discoveries of how Christ was systemically cloaked throughout the entire Old Testament and then systematically revealed across the Gospels.

Then, you can return and re-read those Old Testament passages, and you will see Christ as clear as day.

A Sample List of Prophecies of Jesus as the Suffering Servant in the Old Testament

Century of Authorship	Author of Record	Prophecy/ Type & Shadow	Old Testament	New Testament
14-13th BC	Moses	Would be born of a woman and to crush evil	Genesis 3:15	Galatians 4:4 1 John 3:8
		Would come from the tribe of Judah	Genesis 49:10	Luke 3:33 Hebrews 7:14
		Would be a prophet	Deuteronomy 18:15	Acts 3:20-22
11th BC	David	Would be called King	Psalm 2:4-12	Matthew 27:37
		Would be declared the Son of God	Psalm 2:7	Matthew 3:16-17
		Would be praised by little children	Psalm 8:2	Matthew 21:16
		Would be resurrected from the dead	Psalm 16:10-11	Matthew 28:1-7 Acts 2:22-32
		Would be forsaken by the Father	Psalm 22:1	Matthew 27:46
		Would be mocked and ridiculed	Psalm 22:7-8	Luke 23:35-37
		Would have hands and feet pierced	Psalm 22:16	John 20:25-27 Revelation 1:7
		Would have soldiers gamble for garments	Psalm 22:18	Luke 23:34
		Would ascend to heaven	Psalm 68:18-20	Luke 24:51 Ephesians 4:7-10

Century of Authorship	Author of Record	Prophecy/ Type & Shadow	Old Testament	New Testament
		Would be given vinegar to drink	Psalm 69:21	John 19:28-30
	Asaph	Would speak in parables	Psalm 78:2-4	Matthew 13:10-15 Matthew 13:34-35
	David	Would be a priest in the order of Melchizedek	Psalm 110:4	Hebrews 5:5-6
8th BC	Hosea	Would spend time in Egypt	Hosea 11:1	Matthew 2:14-15
8th BC	Isaiah	Would speak in parables	Isaiah 6:9-10	Matt 13:34-35
		Would be born to a virgin and called Emmanuel	Isaiah 7:14	Matt 1:22-23
		Would bring light to Galilee	Isaiah 9:1-2	Matt 4:12-16
		Would be preceded by a messenger	Isaiah 40:3-5	Luke 3:2-6
		Would be spat upon and struck	Isaiah 50:6	Matthew 26:67
		Would be rejected by His own people	Isaiah 53:3	John 1:11
		Would be a sacrifice for sin	Isaiah 53:5-12	Romans 5:6-8
		Would be silent before His accusers	Isaiah 53:7	Mark 15:4-5
		Would be buried in the grave of a rich man	Isaiah 53:9	Matt 27:57-60
		Would bring good news for the brokenhearted	Isaiah 61:1-2	Luke 4:16-19
7th BC	Micah	Would be born in Bethlehem	Micah 5:2	Matthew 2:1
6th BC	Zechariah	Would be pierced	Zechariah 12:10	John 19:34 John 20:25-27

Century of Authorship	Author of Record	Prophecy/ Type & Shadow	Old Testament	New Testament
		Would be called King	Zechariah 9:9	Mark 11:7-11
		Would enter Jerusalem on a donkey	Zechariah 9:9	Matthew 21:1-9
		Would be betrayed	Zechariah 11:12-13	Luke 22:47-48
		Would be betrayed by one who used the money to buy a potter's field	Zechariah 11:12-13	Matthew 27:9-10
6th BC	Jeremiah	A massacre of children at His birth	Jeremiah 31:15	Matthew 2:16-18
5th BC	Malachi	Would be preceded by a forerunner	Malachi 3:1	Matthew 11:7-10
		Would be preceded by Elijah *	Malachi 4:5-6	Luke 1:13-17 Matthew 11:13-14

*This specific reference from Malachi was, by design, a type. The passage could be seen as explicitly referring to the coming of Elijah in the end times, ahead of the traditionally recognized "great and terrible day of the Lord" described in Revelation. However, Jesus' quote, "if you will accept it," could also be rightly seen as predicting John as a Type of Elijah. John's arrival (as a type of Elijah) foreshadowed another "great and terrible day," wherein mankind was both being saved and participating in the murder of the Son of God.

A careful review of the Old Testament will reveal numerous previews of the coming Christ. Many of these were not traditional prophecies. Instead, they were stories lived out by real people that had no idea their stories foreshadowed Jesus. We also find Jesus in types and shadows, Christophanies/Theophanies, miracles, the seven feasts of Israel, the sacrificial system, the Tabernacle, etc. Let's review a few of these categories.

Types and Shadows

God uses types and shadows as standard symbols to foretell biblical truth. Let's define a type as a prophetic symbol: We are seeing something in the Old Testament that foreshadows something in the New Testament.

Types are as much a part of the general scope of prophecy as the more specific event-based predictions are. Along with these more clearly spelled out forecasts, types bind the Old Testament to the New Testament and lead us to see or understand the person, life, and mission of Jesus Christ.

A brief survey of the examples of types:

- **Persons** such as:
    - Adam as a type of forefather:

        Romans 5:14, NKJV
        *"Nevertheless, death reigned from Adam to Moses, even over those who had not sinned according to the likeness of the transgression of **Adam, who is a type of Him who was to come.**"*

    - Abraham sacrificing his son, a picture of God sacrificing His Son:

        Hebrews 11:17-19, NIV
        *"Abraham... offered Isaac as a sacrifice... his one and only son... he reasoned that **God could even raise him from the dead.**"*

o   Jonah.

When the crowds asked Jesus for a sign, He related His coming death, burial, and resurrection to the story of this prophet.

o   Joseph.

Joseph suffered before being lifted to the authority needed to rescue all of Israel from starvation.

o   Daniel.

Daniel was placed into a pit full of beasts, and a stone was rolled over the entrance. Daniel emerged unscathed. His enemies were then thrown into the very trap they thought they had set for him. This is both a type and shadow of Christ. Jesus was placed in the tomb, resurrected, and defeated death and sin.

Even Satan has a type and shadow. Haman set a trap for the Jews but ended up being hung on his own gallows for false accusations, just as Satan believed he was defeating the Son of God but was instead defeated on a celestial level in his very moment of planned success.

• **Events** such as the preservation of Noah, the redemption of the Israelites from Egypt, or the lifting up of the brazen serpent, which Jesus Himself referred to in the following passage.

John 3:14, ESV
And as Moses lifted up the serpent in the wilderness, so must the Son of Man be lifted up.

- **Things or Symbols**
    - o The veil in the Temple,

        Hebrews 10:19-20, NIV
        Therefore, brothers and sisters, since we have confidence to enter the Most Holy Place by the blood of Jesus, by a new and living way opened for us through the curtain, that is, his body.

    - o The Passover lamb, having been "prepared" as a sacrifice for the passing over, is placed into the clay oven, a stone rolled in front of it, and is partaken as a means of escaping judgment.

        1 Corinthians 5:7, ESV
        Cleanse out the old leaven that you may be a new lump, as you really are unleavened. For Christ, our Passover lamb, has been sacrificed.

- **Institutions** such as the Sabbath, Melchizedek's priesthood, David's kingdom, or the entire sacrificial system itself.

    Hebrews 9:11-12, NKJV
    But Christ came as High Priest of the good things to come, with the greater and more perfect tabernacle not made with hands, that is, not of this creation. Not with the blood of goats and calves, but with His own blood He entered the Most Holy Place once for all, having obtained eternal redemption.

- **Practices**
  o Circumcision has its fulfillment in Christ.

    Colossians 2:11, ESV
    In him also you were circumcised with a circumcision made without hands, by putting off the body of the flesh, by the circumcision of Christ.

- **The law** commanded sacrifices for sins, and each sacrifice showed the need for and foreshadowed Jesus—the true and greater Sacrifice for sins.

    Hebrews 10:1, ESV
    The law [was only] a shadow of the good things to come instead of the true form of these realities.

- **Miracles** in the Old Testament often prefigured miracles that Jesus would perform.
  - o "The Man of God" healed King Jeroboam's withered hand in 1 Kings 13:4-6, just as Jesus would heal the man with the withered hand in Luke 6:10.
  - o Elisha fed one hundred men with twenty loaves in 2 Kings 4:42–44, and Jesus fed 5,000 and later 4,000 men with just a handful of loaves as seen in Matthew 14:13–21 and 15:32–39.
  - o Elisha's death gave one person temporary life in 2 Kings 13:21, but Jesus' death provides eternal life for all who will receive it, as clarified in Romans 5:18.

- **Christophanies/Theophanies**

  Christophanies: a visible appearance of Christ before His human incarnation.

  Theophanies: a tangible manifestation or appearance of God, often in human form.
  - o In Genesis 16:7-13, Jesus is identified as the "Angel of the LORD." Jesus is very distinct from other angels or "messengers" that appear in the Bible in this form. In verse 13, Hagar "called the name of the LORD who spoke to her, You-Are-the-God-Who-Sees"; for she said, "Have I also seen Him who sees me?" Since "God is a Spirit," and "no man has seen God at any time," this manifestation must be none other than the pre-incarnate Jesus, "the image of the invisible God" (Colossians 1:15).
  - o Jacob wrestles with a man all night in Genesis 32:22-32, and that man was God. He said to Jacob, "*Your name shall no longer be called Jacob, but Israel for*

you have striven with God, and with men, and have prevailed." Afterward, Jacob named the place Peniel and said, "For I have seen God face to face, and yet my life has been delivered."

Conclusions

Atheists make the case that the prophetic writings that Jesus fulfilled are collusion among ancient authors and Jesus Himself. Common sense calls us to question the difficulty of coordinating all of this. There are numerous prophetic authors and writings to sort out. Consider the problem of influencing or altering historical accounts to combine them into a sophisticated steganographic message that spans centuries. Even more absurd is the idea that some future character might willingly conclude such an undertaking (who, by the atheist's argument, lacks supernatural means). This character would also have to possess both the intellect required to decode this steganographic message and a willingness to fulfill it by orchestrating His own martyrdom. And finally, this terrible final act would have to be delivered through a prophetically articulated means (crucifixion) that did not yet exist when those unwitting contributors described it in great detail. This argument would even require the cooperation of secular nations to develop such a specific means of punishment by the time this future character arrives.

If the conspiracy seems far-fetched, imagine how difficult it would be to live out the story itself without anyone noticing that you've been doing it, across thirty-three years of life, until the moment you explain it to them… after you've been crucified. Consider for a moment how few people have ever explained anything to anyone after they've been crucified, and you may begin to understand the further improbability of this argument for some grand religious collusion creating such a Messianic spectacle.

Consider the famous quote from Chuck Colson, one of President Nixon's inner circle who fell during Nixon's Watergate scandal. After going to prison as a man indifferent to faith, Colson confidently believed that Jesus Christ was who He said He was. Colson's unique perspective as a man who had tried to help conceal a coordinated scandal is quite revealing.

"I know the resurrection is a fact, and Watergate proved it to me. How? Because 12 men testified they had seen Jesus raised from the dead, then they proclaimed that truth for 40 years, never once denying it. Every one was beaten, tortured, stoned and put in prison. They would not have endured that if it weren't true. Watergate embroiled 12 of the most powerful men in the world—and they couldn't keep a lie for three weeks. You're telling me 12 apostles could keep a lie for 40 years? Absolutely impossible."
—Chuck Colson

I would add to what Colson said that many of these early disciples' followers were also martyred. Consider the story of Polycarp, the bishop of Smyrna. Many say that he was discipled and appointed directly by the Apostle John and was a peer to Ignatius. At well over eighty years old, Polycarp was taken into a Roman marketplace and burned at the stake for his faith, which he refused to recant even under the threat of this horrible and certain death.

From Foxe's Book of Martyrs:

> *The proconsul then urged him, saying, "Swear, and I will release thee;—reproach Christ."*
>
> *Polycarp answered, "Eighty and six years have I served him, and he never once wronged me; how then shall I blaspheme my King, Who hath saved me?" At the stake to which he was only tied, but not nailed as usual, as he assured them he should stand immovable, the flames, on their kindling the fagots, encircled his body, like an arch, without touching him; and the executioner, on seeing this, was ordered to pierce him with a sword, when so great a quantity of blood flowed out as extinguished the fire...*

It is difficult to reconcile, as Colson alluded to, the idea that a fraudulent story would be protected at so great a price. In fact, it is doubtful and, from a human or legal perspective, not worthy of a response. However, God Himself does respond to the skeptic's questions. He goes to the ends of the earth looking for those who are willing to believe and accept His free gift of reconciliation.

Romans 8:32, ESV
> *He who did not spare his own Son but gave him up for us all, how will he not also with him graciously give us all things?*

Considering the extravagance of what God has already done, should we be surprised that He worked through countless men, stories, and events to foreshadow that His rescue plan was credible, sufficient, and worthy of a response? Of course not. The only reasonable question that remains is why those alive at the time when Jesus walked the earth didn't understand what was happening. In the next chapter, we'll look into that very question.

4

The Confusion

WHY NOBODY SAW it coming and the part that John the Baptist played.

God deceives no one, including His enemies. That is not in His nature. However, we are not entitled to the entirety of His plans, which is the realm of mystery. Nonetheless, God provided enough detail within the Old Testament to assure we could see that Christ's first mission fulfilled the Father's plans. God had sufficiently encoded the details of the true purpose of Christ's first mission to ensure that no created being would see what God had planned until that plan had already come to pass.

How and why Satan missed it

God's great moment of reconciliation included Satan, a free-will being, who walked straight into a truth-revealing snare that God had set for him as a key part of His masterful plan. In a single moment, God revealed numerous truths to all of His created beings. He put Satan's true character as both a liar and murderer on full display. God demonstrated His own character as our truthful and faithful rescuer. By Christ's selfless act of sacrifice, necessary to pay the price for our part in this great rebellion, He put to rest the enemy's most significant charge.

One perhaps obvious alternative available to an all-powerful God upon being accused was to decimate His opposition. However, that would have played into the narrative already proffered by Satan. God had been falsely accused, by the tireless and brilliant liar, with the charge that God was self-serving, not to be trusted, and secretly intended to hold us all back through forced compliance. Predictably, Satan was accusing God of his own behaviors and malintent. Satan wanted to be worshiped instead of God and was willing to lead the gullible into destruction to get it, yet he claimed to be leading a rebellion of the free. Also predictable, Satan underestimated God on a cosmic scale. Satan foolishly believed he could ensnare God by crafting a charge to box God in. Instead, God exercised His patience quietly, laying out a far more sophisticated trap for Satan. That reversal would both reveal the baselessness of Satan's charges and save God's beloved creation despite them having joined the rebellion of the deceived.

Dennis McCallum explains this anomaly brilliantly in his essay, which we have attached in its entirety, with the author's permission, as Appendix 2. The following unedited excerpt focuses on the anomaly of Satan's role in this pinnacle moment.

Satan's Strange Role

Nobody behaved more strangely during this time than God's enemy, Satan. We read in John 13:2 that at the last supper, "devil had already put into the heart of Judas Iscariot, the son of Simon, to betray Him." What an odd thing for Satan to do! If Jesus had come to die for human sin, why would Satan actively cooperate in his death? Hadn't Jesus just warned that the cross would be the undoing of Satan? (John 12:31,32) Wasn't it the cross that made it possible for Paul to say, "When He had disarmed the rulers and authorities, He made a public display of them, having triumphed over them through Him" (Col. 2:15)?

This part of the story is like a poorly written novel where people's motivations don't line up with the action. Why would a creature as brilliant as Satan, not just acquiesce, but actually assist in doing the very thing that would be most destructive to himself?

Several answers have been advanced.

One suggestion is that Satan was compelled to do what he did, because God sovereignly made him. Since the cross was God's plan, Satan was made to play his part in that plan. This suggestion is certainly possible, although it is speculative. The Bible never claims Satan was acting under compulsion, only that the cross was part of the "predetermined plan and foreknowledge of God." (Acts 2:23) Certainly God knew Satan would do what he did, as he also knew the other players, like Pilate and Herod would do what they did. But unlike the human players, Satan had everything to lose from the cross.

Others have argued that Satan was so arrogant that he thought he could hold Jesus in death after the cross. Again, this is possible, although speculative. Certainly, Satan is arrogant, but would he be this stupid? He certainly knew who Jesus was. And we see him backing down from God's power in cases like that involving Job.

Others argue that Satan knew the cross would destroy him, but he couldn't resist the sadistic pleasure of watching Jesus suffer. Again, we can imagine this, and we do know that Satan is irrationally hateful at times. But it seems to me like quite a stretch to see the anointed cherub behaving in such a self-destructive way.

Maybe Paul offers us another explanation in 1 Cor. 2:6,8:

"Yet we do speak wisdom among those who are mature; a wisdom, however, not of this age, nor of the rulers of this age, who are passing away; but we speak God's wisdom in a mystery, the hidden wisdom, which God predestined before the ages to our glory; the wisdom which none of the rulers of this age has understood; for if they had understood it, they would not have crucified the Lord of glory."

Could it be that Satan, the great adversary, didn't know that Jesus actually wanted to die? If so, it would perfectly explain why he helped orchestrate his death.

Many feel this passage is not referring to Satan, but to the human rulers who put Jesus to death. That's possible, although Paul uses the term "God of this world" to refer to Satan. (2 Cor. 4:4) Also, the "world rulers of this darkness" refers to demons (Eph. 6:12 the term here is kosmos, rather than aeon, but the sense is similar). Also, if he was referring to Pilate, Herod, and Caiaphas, why would he use the present tense "who are passing away" when all of them were now dead or at least no longer in power?

I will argue, based on this and other passages in the New Testament that this is exactly what happened: The brilliant, bitter, and arrogant enemy of God acted freely, thinking he was disrupting God's plan to take over and rule the world through Jesus. But instead he played directly into Jesus' hands, doing exactly what Jesus wanted him to do, and proving in the process, his own character as hate as well as God's character as true, self-giving love.

Did Satan Know Jesus Planned to Die?

Some readers find it difficult to believe that Satan would have made such a colossal blunder when all the information was right there in front of him for hundreds of years. But let's think about it. How would he have known what Jesus was doing? He would have had the same information everyone else had—the predictive Scriptures. But we have seen that God crafted those in such a way that a reader before the time of Christ could not have discovered the plan for two comings. The missing information made it impossible to reach this conclusion. Why would Satan be any different than anyone else?

Again, if we accept the premise that God was intentionally veiling his intentions in the first coming, the hanging question remains: Why would he do so? Here, we may have an answer. Perhaps in God's eternal plan of salvation, he was also putting the permanent smackdown on Satan and his accusations.

We know that the devil (diabolos = slanderer) gets much of his power from his ability to create suspicion about God. His accusations are not just directed to us and about us, but about God. From his first appearance in Genesis we see him implying that God can't be trusted—that he is self-serving and oppressive. This fallen angel was so persuasive that not only the first humans, but much of the angelic host followed him into rebellion in spite of the fact that these creatures must have actually seen God.

This accusing of God is interesting to consider in light of the dilemma it creates for God. Each part of this carefully crafted lie contains self-validating implications that would seem to prevent God from opposing the lie effectively.

For instance, Satan claims that God is self-serving when he calls on his creatures to follow him. We know God's counter claim that he calls on the creation to follow him for their own good. But to fallen creatures, a God who enforces a rule to follow his will may indeed seem self-serving. Satan's picture of a God duping his creatures into thinking that he is self-giving, when he is actually self-serving has been very persuasive in the history of the universe. Millions have bought into this suspicion.

Secondly, Satan postures God as mean, oppressive, and unfair. We see this claim implied when he told Eve that the real reason God didn't want her to eat the forbidden fruit was because it would result in her gaining wisdom and becoming like God. This pictures God as willing to oppress people in order to keep them from attaining to all they could be. God declares that he is love, that he is compassionate, and that he is always perfectly fair. But how can he punish rebellious creatures (which is fair) without seeming to confirm the suspicion that he is mean? How can he spare any rebellious creature from punishment without becoming unfair?

Satan continually tries to play off God's love against his justice. Any God who would judge cannot be loving, he argues. A judging God is vindictive and hateful, according to Satan. Satan must advance a form of permissiveness as love. Again, if God destroyed Satan, wouldn't that suggest that Satan was right after all, and that God is vindictive and hateful?

This cosmic dilemma is the background for the Bible. Satan is a careful student of Scripture (Luke 4) and was well-aware that God was developing a plan of salvation. He has opposed that plan at every point, as he still does today.

Suppose, for the sake of argument, that when Jesus came, Satan, like everyone else, concluded that he had come, not as a suffering servant, but as reigning king. King Messiah is said to destroy his enemies, and rule the world with a "rod of iron." This picture of dominance fits all too well with Satan's concept of God as the mean, vindictive destroyer of freedom. Aside from anything in prophecy, Satan would be inclined to see Messiah this way because of his prejudice against God.

I will argue that Satan did, in fact, make this mistake. He thought Jesus had come to rule, not to suffer. Jesus' self-effacing behavior must have been confusing, but most people thought he was going to unveil his power any day. Satan may have thought this as well. In one instance, some demons cried out to Jesus, "have you come to torment us before the time?" They were apparently surprised to see him there earlier than expected, but saw his mission only as one of torment. How typical this is of demonic thinking.

If Satan was mistaken about Jesus' intentions, he would naturally conclude that arranging to kill him would short-circuit the planned kingdom. Suddenly, his actions with Judas make sense. But what was the outcome? Too late, he would realize that he had actually facilitated not the destruction of the kingdom, but the salvation of humankind. At the same time, his greatest weapon, his accusations of God, were now useless. The cross demonstrated in an undeniable way the loving and sacrificial nature of God. Instead of God being vindictive and cruel, it was Satan who was unmasked as utterly vindictive and cruel.

Perhaps this is what Paul alludes to when he says in Colossians 2:15, "When He had disarmed the rulers and authorities, He made a public display of them, having triumphed over them through Him." The cross forever disarmed Satan by striking down his main contention: that God is self-serving, mean, and unfair.

This would account for Jesus' declaration that "now is the judgment of this world, now is the prince of this world cast out." (John 12:32) Paul seems to echo this explanation in several places:

Now to Him who is able to establish you according to my gospel and the preaching of Jesus Christ, according to the revelation of the mystery which has been kept secret for long ages past, but now is manifested, and by the Scriptures of the prophets, according to the commandment of the eternal God, has been made known to all the nations... (Rom. 16:25,26)

In this remarkable passage, Paul reveals that God was, indeed, keeping something secret for aeons—something that had recently been revealed. This "mystery" or secret is tied up with Paul's gospel. I believe the cross and God's whole redemptive intent in the first coming of Messiah, are the mystery to which he refers. It was secret because, although predicted, it was predicted in a way that was undecipherable until too late, as we have seen. Only after Satan had made his violent and hateful move against Christ did the truth emerge.

As McCallum has laid out, Satan willingly played his part in this remarkable story because he failed to discern God's more excellent plan to have the Messiah come twice. In God's wisdom, the Messiah would come once to be a sacrifice for His loved ones and again to return as ruler and conqueror. A trap always becomes clear to the one trapped the moment after it has sprung. Later in this book, we will expand upon the moment that Satan would most likely have seen what had just happened and how he had unintentionally revealed his own murderous character while Christ still hung upon the cross.

This component of Jesus' work (that His sacrifice would reveal the true thoughts of many—implying the presence of a falsehood) was prophesied over Jesus while He was still an infant in Jerusalem by a man named Simeon.

Luke 2:25-35, ESV
Now there was a man in Jerusalem, whose name was Simeon, and this man was righteous and devout, waiting for the consolation of Israel, and the Holy Spirit was upon him. And it had been revealed to him by the Holy Spirit that he would not see death before he had seen the Lord's Christ. And he came in the Spirit into the temple, and when the parents brought in the child Jesus, to do for him according to the custom of the Law, he took him up in his arms and blessed God and said,

"Lord, now you are letting your servant depart in peace,

according to your word;
for my eyes have seen your salvation
that you have prepared in the presence of all peoples,
a light for revelation to the Gentiles,
and for glory to your people Israel."

And his father and his mother marveled at what was said about him. And Simeon blessed them and said to Mary his mother, "Behold, this child is appointed for the fall and rising of many in Israel, and for a sign that is opposed (and a sword will pierce through your own soul also), **so that thoughts from many hearts may be revealed."**

As revealed through Christ's work on the cross, the stark contrasts between God's and Satan's intentions remain the most profound and meaningful for those willing to see.

How and why the Jews and Jesus' disciples missed it

The Jews recognized the predictions of the Messiah and a character they called "The Suffering Servant," but they did not see that these two characters would be the same person.

The New Testament makes it clear that Jesus has a two-fold objective. We, as Christians, can plainly see that with the advantage of hindsight. However, during Old Testament times, the Messiah was seen as a coming liberator, not a suffering servant. Even when Jesus walked the earth with His chosen Hebrew disciples, they did not see what was to come. In fact, practicing non-messianic Jews today still expect the Messiah to come and fulfill this role. The Jews of Jesus' day did not recognize Jesus as the Messiah, nor do those of the traditional Hebrew faith today.

This point is well articulated in another excerpt from McCallum's essay.

In Jesus' preaching and discussion, we see many comments that seem to perpetuate the confusion. For instance, when he appeared, Mark says:

And after John had been taken into custody, Jesus came into Galilee, preaching the gospel of God, and saying, "The time is fulfilled, and the kingdom of God is at hand; repent and believe in the gospel." (Mark 1:14,15)

Anyone familiar with Jewish theology of the time sees that this could mean only one thing to his audience. They would see this as Jesus proclaiming himself King Messiah, and the kingdom would be the one promised in messianic prophecies of the second coming. Although Jesus later qualified his proclamation of the kingdom as being different than the Old Testament picture of a world-wide compulsory rule of God, he did so in a veiled way.

The best known discussion on this is in Mat. 13. There, Jesus gave the parables of the kingdom—each one stressing the difference between what they were expecting, based on Old Testament prophecy, and what he was there to start. Instead of a sudden takeover, there would be gradual growth from obscure beginnings (parable of the mustard seed, and the leaven). Instead of "ruling the nations with a rod of iron" and banishing all sinners, believers and non-believers would live side by side (parable of the soils, dragnet, wheat and tares, etc.).

In his comments to the disciples on these parables, Jesus made it clear that he didn't expect his audience to understand them. In fact he indicates that he was deliberately speaking in a way that they could not understand:

And the disciples came and said to Him, "Why do You speak to them in parables?" And He answered and said to them, "To you it has been granted to know the mysteries of the kingdom of heaven, but to them it has not been granted… Therefore I speak to them in parables; because while seeing they do not see, and while hearing they do not hear, nor do they understand." (Mat. 13:10,11,13)

We see here an ongoing effort to keep the nature of his mission veiled to the public. In other places, it seems like he wanted the disciples to understand the nature of his mission as the suffering servant:

Jesus took the Twelve aside and told them, "We are going up to Jerusalem, and everything that is written by the prophets about the Son of Man will be fulfilled. He will be handed over to the Gentiles. They will mock him, insult him, spit on him, flog him and kill him. On the third day he will rise again." (Luke 18:31-33)

This was clear enough. However, we also read in verse 34,

The disciples did not understand any of this. Its meaning was hidden from them, and they did not know what he was talking about.

Why didn't the disciples understand? Was it because they couldn't break out of the paradigm of the eternal Messiah who cannot die? Or was it God himself who "hid" the meaning from them? We don't know. But if we study all of the similar disclosures Jesus made, we see sixteen passages where Christ told his disciples what he was going to do (although some are referring to the same discussion). The list is as follows: Mark 8:31*; 10:45*; 9:9,10,12*; 10:32-34; 9:31-32; Matthew 20:17-19*; 17:22,23; 16:21; Luke 9:22*; 9:44,45; 18:31-34; John 3:14*; 10:15-18,20; 12:32-34; 16:17-18,25. In each of the starred passages, it records the disciples' reaction, and makes it plain that they did not understand what he was saying.

It seems they never did understand. Right up to the end of his ministry they were asking him, "So is this the time when you will reveal your kingdom?" Even the question they asked at the Mount of Olives, "What will be the sign of your coming?" may be misleading to modern readers. It sounds to us like they now knew he would leave and come back. But the term "coming" may have meant a triumphal entry, or presentation of himself as king. It's entirely possible that they were still thinking that the coming might happen any day.

Notice the paradigmatic thinking of the crowd in John 12:34. After Jesus mentioned being "lifted up" on the cross, "The multitude therefore answered Him, 'We have heard out of the Law that the Christ is to remain forever; and how can You say, "The Son of Man must be lifted up"? Who is this Son of Man?'" Since they couldn't conceive of a Messiah that would die, they tended to shift the identity of the Son of Man in order to compensate. This must have been the norm throughout Jesus' life.

At the last supper, Jesus makes a series of significant statements. After dinner Jesus said, "Little children, I am with you a little while longer. You shall seek Me; and as

I said to the Jews, I now say to you also, 'Where I am going, you cannot come.'" (John 13:33)

Then we read, "Simon Peter said to Him, 'Lord, where are You going?'" (36) Clearly, Peter still didn't know what was about to happen. This confusion is echoed by Thomas as well. (14:5) Then, when Jesus promises that those who receive the Spirit after his departure will receive revelation of Christ, Judas Alpheus asks, "Lord, what then has happened that You are going to disclose Yourself to us, and not to the world?" (14:22) Clearly, they were incredulous that he was not going to reveal his true identity to the world. Remember, this conversation occurred the night before the cross. Even at this late date, none of his disciples realized that he intended to die, rise, leave, and come again.

Later in that same conversation, Jesus said, "These things I have spoken to you, that you may be kept from stumbling." 16:1 Later, he expanded, "But these things I have spoken to you, that when their hour comes, you may remember that I told you of them. And these things I did not say to you at the beginning, because I was with you." (4) and, "A little while, and you will no longer behold Me; and again a little while, and you will see Me." (16)

Again, dismay and confusion reigned: "Some of His disciples therefore said to one another, 'What is this thing He is telling us, "A little while, and you will not behold Me; and again a little while, and you will see Me"; and, "because I go to the Father"?' And so they were saying, 'What is this that He says, "A little while"? We do not know what He is talking about.'" (17,18)

Jesus' only response was "These things I have spoken to you in figurative language; an hour is coming when I will speak no more to you in figurative language, but will tell you plainly of the Father." (25)

As we read this exchange, we get the strong sense that Jesus was pursuing a course identical to what God earlier did in the Old Testament. He was telling them things they did not understand, but which they would remember after the events occurred. How similar to God's apparent strategy of predicting the first coming in a way people would miss until after it happened! Once the cross and the resurrection occurred, these statements all made perfect sense, but beforehand, Jesus himself acknowledges that they couldn't grasp what he was saying.

Before contemplating all of this, I viewed the disciples with confusion. They had walked with Jesus for multiple years. How could they not see what Jesus seemed to be so plainly telling them was going on? But once we recognize the pattern of the Mystery Hidden for Ages Past, how God the Father so exquisitely hid all of this forecasting throughout the Old Testament, it becomes easier to see that Jesus was doing the same thing, as MacCallum has explained above. The disciples were not dunces with a myopic or selfish view of the Messiah as their liberator. Rather, that was what God had promised and still promises to all of us. It would not have mattered if they had the intellect and training of the most prestigious scholars of their time, as none of them could perceive the truth of what was going on either. This dilemma beautifully credentials the work that God did. He laid His plan out in great detail, in plain sight, so that everyone could see it in clarity, but only after the plan had been fulfilled and not a moment sooner.

Aren't there still portions of the Bible that we view in this same way today? Consider the significant division between parts of the body of Christ on various topics. For example, eschatological passages (passages about the end times) still invoke dogmatic stances. You can easily walk into serious Bible-believing churches today and encounter radically different perceptions, even scripturally based arguments, about if and when specifically the church will be removed from the period known to most as the tribulation. I am equally confident that once those final events have unfolded, those raised in the air and those who remain behind will be able to look rearwards at the passages and suddenly have remarkable clarity. As we stated at the beginning of this chapter, God deceives no one, but we are not entitled to *understand* all the details of His plans. It is a kindness to allow us these details in a way that becomes self-evident once the events forecasted have come to pass. These self-credentialing events assure us that God is and remains involved in human history. They assure us that He is just, even when His patience or mercy delays His justice. They assure us that He is who He says He is and does what He says He will do.

Again, in the case of Christ's first coming, God decided not to make His full plan clear to anyone until after it occurred. This steganographic concealment not only credentialed what God was doing but also provided a basis for confident belief. God was operating on a significantly higher level than those who opposed Him. He not only laid out a plan that outsmarted Satan but revealed it to and through His people, putting it in plain view yet without exposing it to His enemies in any way. I believe we would be hard-pressed to find any such event in all of history.

Not even the most genius of leaders has ever telegraphed the specifics of a wartime plan in this way. Imagine a leader communicating a plan that required his enemies to willingly participate in it, concluding with their own destruction. This is the realm of God alone.

We should not look down on the Jews or the disciples for failing to see what was coming. In their shoes and in their time, we would not have seen it either. We would very likely have stood in the crowds chanting "crucify Him," and if we think we are above that, we are failing to contemplate how our life of sin and failure to acknowledge Christ as our Savior has already done precisely that. Until we see this truth, we are in league with the deceived. Peter first challenged the masses on this topic from Solomon's portico (or porch) in the Jewish Temple.

Acts 3:11-26, ESV

Now as the lame man who was healed held on to Peter and John, all the people ran together to them in the porch which is called Solomon's, greatly amazed. So when Peter saw it, he responded to the people: "Men of Israel, why do you marvel at this? Or why look so intently at us, as though by our own power or godliness we had made this man walk? The God of Abraham, Isaac, and Jacob, the God of our fathers, glorified His Servant Jesus, whom you delivered up and denied in the presence of Pilate, when he was determined to let Him go. But you denied the Holy One and the Just, and asked for a murderer to be granted to you, and killed the Prince of life, whom God raised from the dead, of which we are witnesses. And His name, through faith in His name, has made this man strong, whom you see and know. Yes, the faith which comes through Him has given him this perfect soundness in the presence of you all.

*"**Yet now, brethren, I know that you did it in ignorance, as did also your rulers.** But those things which God foretold by the mouth of all His prophets, that the Christ would suffer, He has thus fulfilled. **Repent therefore and be converted, that your sins may be blotted out,** so that times of refreshing may come from the presence of the Lord, and that He may send Jesus Christ, who was preached to you before, **whom heaven must receive until the times of restoration of all things, which God has spoken by the mouth of all His holy prophets since the world began.** For Moses truly said to the fathers, 'The Lord your God will raise up for you a Prophet like me from your brethren. Him you shall hear in all things, whatever He says to you. And it shall be that every soul who will not hear that Prophet shall be utterly destroyed from among the people.' Yes, and all the prophets, from Samuel and those who follow, as many as have spoken, have also foretold these days. You are sons of the prophets, and of the covenant which God made with our fathers, saying to Abraham, 'And in your seed all the families of the earth shall be blessed.' To you first, God, having raised up His Servant Jesus, sent Him to bless you, in turning away every one of you from your iniquities."*

Acts 4:4, ESV

However, many of those who heard the word believed; and the number of the men came to be about five thousand.

We today have the very same opportunity they did. We can repent, accept the Gospel, grab hold of the feet of our Savior, and begin to live a new life as ambassadors of His reconciliation. As ambassadors, we spread the Good News while shedding the bondage of our former lives once lived in league with the enemy of our souls.

The part that John the Baptist played

John the Baptist played a critical role during Christ's first coming. His position and timing as "a voice in the wilderness" helped bring many to believe in Christ as the promised Messiah, yet not even John himself was expecting Jesus to fulfill the role of "suffering servant."

Matthew 3:3-6, NIV
In those days John the Baptist came, preaching in the wilderness of Judea and saying, "Repent, for the kingdom of heaven has come near." This is he who was spoken of through the prophet Isaiah:
"A voice of one calling in the wilderness,
'Prepare the way for the Lord,
make straight paths for him.'"
John's clothes were made of camel's hair, and he had a leather belt around his waist. His food was locusts and wild honey. People went out to him from Jerusalem and all Judea and the whole region of the Jordan. Confessing their sins, they were baptized by him in the Jordan River.

In a previous chapter, we discussed "types." John the Baptist was a "type" of Elijah the prophet. However, while John dressed the part and came in the spirit of Elijah, he was NOT Elijah. Consider this description of Elijah, the wilderness prophet from 2 Kings:

> *2 Kings 1:7-8, ESV*
> *He said to them, "What kind of man was he who came to meet you and told you these things?" They answered him, "He wore a garment of hair, with a belt of leather about his waist." And he said, "It is Elijah the Tishbite."*

We can see in Luke 1 that the Angel Gabriel told Zacharias, John the Baptist's father, that John would come "in the spirit of Elijah," just as Malachi had predicted.

> *Malachi 4:5-6, ESV*
> *"Behold, I will send you Elijah the prophet before the great and awesome day of the Lord comes. And he will turn the hearts of fathers to their children and the hearts of children to their fathers, lest I come and strike the land with a decree of utter destruction."*

The forecast of this coming of Elijah is intriguing. It was first fulfilled through John the Baptist, as a *type* of Elijah. Yet most scholars believe this will also be fulfilled just before Jesus' second coming as Elijah himself returns to the earth in a spectacle that Revelation predicts all the world will be able to see. Additionally, we see that the angel, Gabriel, expressly referred back to the prediction of Malachi 4:6, the very last words of the Old Testament. Here, after 400 years known as the silent period, the silence is broken with a prediction that John will come in the spirit of Elijah to turn the hearts of the fathers back to their children.

Luke 1:17, ESV
And he will go before him in the spirit and power of Elijah, to turn the hearts of the fathers to the children, and the disobedient to the wisdom of the just, to make ready for the Lord a people prepared.

Neither God nor His angel said that John the Baptist *was* Elijah. Likewise, Jesus only said, "If you will, he is Elijah **to come**" [para].

Matthew 11:13-14, ESV
For all the Prophets and the Law prophesied until John, and if you are willing to accept it, he is Elijah who is to come.

God used John the Baptist to both fulfill Malachi's prophecy ("I will send my messenger, who will prepare the way before me") and Isaiah's prophecy ("a voice of one calling in the wilderness"). Jesus' careful choice of words here lays out that John is a type of Elijah without claiming he *is* Elijah. Notice that Jesus said of John, "If you will accept it, is Elijah **to come**." His statement was neither present nor past tense. This careful play on words allowed Satan to hear what he wanted to hear and the Jews to remain unable to see Jesus' plan. Like a perfectly executed basketball move, this head-fake of John, appearing to be Elijah, facilitated Jesus' enemies (both mortal and supernatural) to believe that Jesus was, in fact, here to fulfill the entire mission of the Messiah. God was allowing them to believe this to make a spectacle of His enemies while also doing the unthinkable, delivering His Son as the willing sacrifice for all mankind.

We can also see that John the Baptist himself was unaware of the vital part he was playing. Let's go back and look at the bigger picture of Matthew 11. We will see that Jesus' discussion of John the Baptist in this passage was within the context of John's own disciples being sent to ask Jesus, on John's behalf, "are you the one?" What a tremendous spectacle for us to see that John, about whom Jesus said, "*among those born of women there has arisen no one greater,*" is now struggling with doubt and having to ask this difficult question. He sent his messengers from a prison where he was soon to be beheaded for preaching the message that he believed Jesus had come to fulfill. It is unlikely that John foresaw this or would have thought he was "preparing the way" for the suffering servant. He believed he was preparing the way for the Messiah King, who would rule with an iron scepter.

Matthew 11:2-15, ESV

Now when John heard in prison about the deeds of the Christ, he sent word by his disciples and said to him, "Are you the one who is to come, or shall we look for another?" And Jesus answered them, "Go and tell John what you hear and see: the blind receive their sight and the lame walk, lepers are cleansed and the deaf hear, and the dead are raised up, and the poor have good news preached to them. And blessed is the one who is not offended by me."

As they went away, Jesus began to speak to the crowds concerning John: "What did you go out into the wilderness to see? A reed shaken by the wind? What then did you go out to see? A man dressed in soft clothing? Behold, those who wear soft clothing are in kings' houses. What then did you go out to see? A prophet? Yes, I tell you, and more than a prophet. This is he of whom it is written,

"'Behold, I send my messenger before your face, who will prepare your way before you.'

"Truly, I say to you, among those born of women there has arisen no one greater than John the Baptist. Yet the one who is least in the kingdom of heaven is greater than he. From the days of John the Baptist until now the kingdom of heaven has suffered violence, and the violent take it by force. For all the Prophets and the Law prophesied until John, and if you are willing to accept it, he is Elijah who is to come. He who has ears to hear, let him hear.

It is unlikely that John ever understood his part in this story until explained to him in heaven, yet he played it masterfully. The moment when God would show His hand to the rest of us was coming soon. That moment would unveil what Paul later described as "the mystery hidden for ages past and now revealed," the mystery that explains all things, fulfills all things, and credentials all things. The things that Christ has done, which can be hard to believe without understanding this powerful credentialing, were all part of God's plan to pay the price for our sin and fully reveal the depths of His love and commitment.

This was a mystery, a mystery that is now revealed.

5

The Big Reveal – Part 1

AT THE CROSS, God created a universal-grade spectacle. He orchestrated and led natural and supernatural forces and agents into playing their parts and irrefutably disclosing their true natures. This was a moment of revelation on a scale the universe has never witnessed before nor since. This revelation unfolded in real-time through Christ and subsequent analysis of the Old Testament Scriptures. We can ascertain how certain actors in this grandest of moments may have come to see God's plan through careful study. These characters, present at the time of Christ's sacrifice, would come to see that this revelation had far more facets than previously considered. In the following two chapters, we will contemplate these moments of revelation from several essential viewpoints and examine what we can learn from each of them.

For those with enough years to understand my reference, this was the Colombo moment! It was the moment when Satan and his army of rebels, fallen angels, and religious leaders who suppressed the truth all discovered together that they were now in a trap they helped build. The most base and evil intentions of God's enemies were laid bare, while His own true nature was revealed.

In this chapter, we will first consider the moment that Satan realized Christ had defeated him. We will also review how this incredible hidden story was revealed to Jesus' closest disciples. In the following chapter, we will look at how and when the Jews were brought into this new inner circle and, finally, how this mystery, hidden for ages past, was also shared with the Gentiles.

Satan's Aha moment

Job 5:13, ESV
He catches the wise in their own craftiness, and the schemes of the wily are brought to a quick end.

Satan was a participant who did not see what God was doing. We can ascertain that from his actions and God's word. Satan thought he was springing a trap on the Son of God but was, in fact, ensnared in his own craftiness. The most likely moment that Satan became aware of how he had been walked into this trap likely occurred when Jesus spoke this line, "My God, my God, why have you forsaken me?", taken verbatim from Psalm 22.

Psalm 22:1, ESV
My God, my God, why have you forsaken me?
Why are you so far from saving me, from the words of my groaning?

We know that Satan knows the Scriptures. He attempted to wield them against Jesus in the desert. His demons asked Jesus, "Have you come before your time, to torment us?" Can you imagine being a created being who vehemently hates the rest of God's creation, discovering a book purporting to show how and when you will be defeated and ultimately destroyed? Wouldn't you be keenly interested in studying every detail of that plan with hopes of avoiding or defeating it? Satan, regardless of how carefully he may have studied the Scriptures, had no more insight into the two-part mission of Jesus Christ than anyone else. Imagine his glee as he saw Jesus heading to the cross. Can it be? Have I truly defeated God's plan?

When Christ spoke those words, imagine the thoughts racing through the mind of the one the Bible tells us was once called the anointed guardian cherub. Imagine as he contemplates the familiarity of that exact phrase… Why yes! It is a Psalm of suffering written by David hundreds of years earlier! This is the same David from whose bloodline God had promised the Messiah would come. Imagine, with Christ in agony on the cross before Him, how Satan must have been marveling with wonder at how he seemed to be defeating the Son of God through manipulating the very people that Jesus intended to save. But that delight would be short-lived as Satan also considered the rest of that very same passage:

Psalm 22:6-18, ESV
But I am a worm and not a man,
scorned by mankind and despised by the people.
All who see me mock me;
they make mouths at me; they wag their heads;
"He trusts in the Lord; let him deliver him;
let him rescue him, for he delights in him!"
Yet you are he who took me from the womb;
you made me trust you at my mother's breasts.
On you was I cast from my birth,
and from my mother's womb you have been my God.
Be not far from me,
for trouble is near,
and there is none to help.

Many bulls encompass me;
strong bulls of Bashan surround me;
they open wide their mouths at me,
like a ravening and roaring lion.

I am poured out like water,
and all my bones are out of joint;
my heart is like wax;
it is melted within my breast;
my strength is dried up like a potsherd,
and my tongue sticks to my jaws;
you lay me in the dust of death.

For dogs encompass me;
a company of evildoers encircles me;
they have pierced my hands and feet—
I can count all my bones—
they stare and gloat over me;
they divide my garments among them,
and for my clothing they cast lots.

Remember, the enemy of our souls, the enemy of our Savior, is a master of the Scripture. The fallen one is an ancient being, created with superior abilities and intellect. Ezekiel tells us that he was in the Garden of Eden. We know that Satan walked with God, saw God, served God, and enjoyed the delight of God before his fall.

Ezekiel 28:13-19, ESV

> *You were in Eden, the garden of God;*
>> *every precious stone was your covering,*
>> *sardius, topaz, and diamond,*
> *beryl, onyx, and jasper,*
> *sapphire, emerald, and carbuncle;*
>> *and crafted in gold were your settings*
>> *and your engravings.*
> *On the day that you were created*
>> *they were prepared.*
> *You were an anointed guardian cherub.*
>> *I placed you; you were on the holy mountain of*
>> *God;*
>> *in the midst of the stones of fire you walked.*
> *You were blameless in your ways*
>> *from the day you were created,*
>> *till unrighteousness was found in you.*
> *In the abundance of your trade*
>> *you were filled with violence in your midst, and*
>> *you sinned;*
> *so I cast you as a profane thing from the mountain of*
> *God,*
>> *and I destroyed you, O guardian cherub,*
>> *from the midst of the stones of fire.*
> *Your heart was proud because of your beauty;*
>> *you corrupted your wisdom for the sake of your*
>> *splendor.*
> *I cast you to the ground;*
>> *I exposed you before kings,*
>> *to feast their eyes on you.*

By the multitude of your iniquities,
*   in the unrighteousness of your trade*
*   you profaned your sanctuaries;*
so I brought fire out from your midst;
*   it consumed you,*
and I turned you to ashes on the earth
*   in the sight of all who saw you.*
All who know you among the peoples
*   are appalled at you;*
you have come to a dreadful end
*   and shall be no more forever."*

The end of that passage describes events that have partially happened and are partially yet to come. This unique passage speaks to the *Prince* of Tyre yet clearly seems to reference Tyre's wealthy *king*, whose great kingdom would eventually fall to Alexander the Great, precisely as predicted by Ezekiel. The second half of Ezekiel 28, which we have included above, describes the *king* of Tyre, yet this *king* is clearly not a man, as no man alive at the time of Ezekiel would have walked in the Garden of Eden nor been called an "anointed guardian cherub." This spectacular being, described as once being spiritually adorned with great beauty, is enraged by being cast down. As Revelation reveals, Satan deceived one third of the angels into joining him in his rebellion against God. Yet this passage predicts his ultimate and spectacular demise. This malevolent crime boss, murderer, deceiver, and fiend now believed he was defeating the Son of God, the very one through whom Ezekiel had predicted Satan would one day be "no more."

Considering the motivations and means of God's enemy, let's go back through Psalm 22, often called "The view from the cross," and contemplate David's poetic description of his own time of trouble. This poetic lament turned out to be prophetic forecasting with remarkable specificity regarding a real-time event playing out before the eyes of the world and before the eyes of that ancient enemy, the devil himself.

Psalm 22:6-8, ESV
But I am a worm and not a man,
scorned by mankind and despised by the people.
All who see me mock me;
they make mouths at me; they wag their heads;
"He trusts in the Lord; let him deliver him;
let him rescue him, for he delights in him!"

Let's compare this to the Gospel account of what Christ was experiencing when He was on the cross, the same spectacle that Satan himself would've been observing at the very moment when Christ cried out, "My God, my God, why have you forsaken me?"

Matthew 27:37-46, ESV
And over his head they put the charge against him, which read, "This is Jesus, the King of the Jews." Then two robbers were crucified with him, one on the right and one on the left. ***And those who passed by derided him, wagging their heads*** *and saying, "You who would destroy the temple and rebuild it in three days, save yourself! If you are the Son of God, come down from the cross." So also the chief priests, with the scribes and elders, mocked him, saying, "He saved others; he cannot save himself. He is the King of Israel; let him come down now from the cross, and we will believe in him.* ***He trusts in God; let***

God deliver him now, *if he desires him. For he said, 'I am the Son of God.'" And the robbers who were crucified with him also reviled him in the same way.*

The Death of Jesus

Now from the sixth hour there was darkness over all the land until the ninth hour. And about the ninth hour Jesus cried out with a loud voice, saying, "Eli, Eli, lema sabachthani?" that is, "My God, my God, why have you forsaken me?"

Can you see how the glee that Satan was feeling a moment earlier, at defeating God's Son and His plan and perhaps imagining there might be a way to escape his predicted fate, might now be turning to a cold sweat? Did God already see this coming? What a moment earlier seemed to be Satan's derailing of God's plan was now being revealed as a part of God's plan. Satan would have begun to recognize that he was little more than a willing pawn.

Psalm 22:9-11, ESV
> *Yet you are he who took me from the womb;*
>> *you made me trust you at my mother's breasts.*
> *On you was I cast from my birth,*
>> *and from my mother's womb you have been my God.*
> *Be not far from me,*
>> *for trouble is near,*
>> *and there is none to help.*

Even the thief on the cross next to Jesus recognized His innocence. This same passage that Satan was all too well aware of shows us that David's poetic lament again provides a remarkable clarity as it identifies Jesus Himself. While David may have intended the phrase "you are He who took me from the womb" to show his recognition that God had always been his Lord, at this moment, Satan (and we) could rightly also read it as a remarkable reference to the virgin birth. The Bible tells us that the Spirit of God came upon Mary and she was with child. After hearing Jesus utter the opening phrase from this passage of Scripture, the connection would have at least been unsettling from Satan's perspective.

> *Psalm 22:12-13, ESV*
> *Many bulls encompass me;*
> *strong bulls of Bashan surround me;*
> *they open wide their mouths at me,*
> *like a ravening and roaring lion.*

When the Roman Empire expanded through conquest, it was known for providing the strongest men in a conquered society the opportunity to gain Roman citizenship through service in the Roman army. The Roman uniform included the breastplate, specifically designed to make even normally built men that wore it look strong. Picture Roman soldiers at the foot of the cross, whom the Scriptures also tell us tormented Jesus with their words and actions and consider that they would have looked like the most plentiful recipients of testosterone in the crowd below Him. The region of Bashan was also the northernmost region of the divided Palestine. It was an area known for its beautiful geography and lush pastures. The men from this region were known to be strong and good warriors. When the Romans conquered this region on their way to Judea, they became a good reservoir of soldiers to draw from as they continuously expanded their efforts at conquest.

> *Psalm 22:14, ESV*
> *I am poured out like water,*
>   *and all my bones are out of joint;*
> *my heart is like wax;*
>   *it is melted within my breast;*

As we continue the analysis of this remarkable passage, consider that modern science has taught us that victims of crucifixion typically died by way of a heart attack or suffocation. While most of us have contemplated the apparent physical pain of crucifixion, few have considered the reason it caused death. As was well-represented in the movie, The Passion of the Christ, the person being crucified was often stretched to the point where ligaments were torn and joints separated. This assured that the person was tightly suspended on the cross, inducing great difficulty in breathing because of few muscular movements available to lift the person to reduce the pressure on vital organs necessary to breathe and for the heart to pump oxygen around the body. Forensic medical experts who have contemplated this horrific means of execution have shown that the lungs would fill up with fluid as this excruciating effort to fight for breath extended, sometimes across multiple days. We know that Jesus was already experiencing this because when He gave up His Spirit, the Roman guard put a spear through His chest, releasing water from Jesus' lungs. If Jesus were not already dead, this assured He would be within moments. However, we can be sure that Jesus was dead because otherwise, His still-beating heart and the many blood vessels in His lungs would have also begun to pour out a massive amount of fresh red blood.

Psalm 22:15, ESV
My strength is dried up like a potsherd,
and my tongue sticks to my jaws;
you lay me in the dust of death.

David's metaphor for his suffering, in Psalm 22, again describes the experience of crucifixion and echoes what the Scriptures tell us about Jesus' experience. The medical experts explain why breathing becomes difficult as the muscles are stretched across the chest, compressing the lungs and the heart. This same compression, and the filling of the lungs with fluid, make it increasingly difficult for the body to provide moisture to the mouth and esophagus as it normally does. In addition, the weight of holding one's head up while in excruciating pain would make it increasingly difficult to breathe through the nostrils, and so breath, in the arid Israeli climate, would have been coming in and out through the open mouth. We know that during His agony, Jesus told those around Him, "I thirst."

Psalm 22:16, ESV
For dogs encompass me;
a company of evildoers encircles me;
they have pierced my hands and feet—

Perhaps by this time, we might wonder whether or not this poetic illustration of David's mental suffering genuinely identifies the future suffering of Jesus Christ. But it is hard for even the most determined skeptics to overlook David's claim that "they have pierced my hands and feet," when David's metaphor was verifiably written long before the Roman Empire existed and before crucifixion had even been invented.

There are atheist arguments against the validity of this passage. Motivated militant anti-Christians will claim that a careful study of the original Hebrew for Psalm 22 is less clear about the claim of piercing my hands and feet, rather stating that David alludes to his hands and the word "Lions." There is enough of a case that could be made for that point to make it worth mentioning here so as not to leave the reader vulnerable to having this truth, this powerful truth, stolen from them later. I do not think one associates their hands with lions and expects it to turn out well. However, this passage by no means requires this specific claim to have already made a circumstantial case that would stand up in any reasonable court.

David has undeniably and uniquely described the crucifixion of Jesus Christ. But for the record, it is worth noting that the non-messianic Jews, i.e., those who do not recognize Jesus as the Messiah, have long interpreted this passage the same way we have presented it to you here. Additionally, the Hebrew translation of this passage, the Masoretic text, seems to be missing a verb. In other words, it reads awkwardly like "lions my hands and feet." The Greek Septuagint, however, is based on older text also aligning with a fragment of the Dead Sea Scrolls. That text includes the missing verb "to dig"; in other words, it would read, "Lions 'dig at' my hands and feet."

Psalm 22:17, ESV
  I can count all my bones—
  they stare and gloat over me;

As we continue through the passage, we see a claim that would not have made sense for David. David was known to be extremely strong for his size. It is unlikely that one would've been able to "count all of his bones." But consider Jesus, who began His ministry during a period without food in the desert. This crash diet was followed by a three-and-a-half-year ministry that included travel by foot around the extended region of Israel. Additionally, as previously described, the stretching of an individual and the medical effects of the process of crucifixion would've exposed the appearance of their bones. Even more so, we know that Christ had recently been flogged in the Roman tradition, which typically involved whips with nails and sharp stones connected to the end, which may have literally revealed the bones of the individual receiving the scourge.

Psalm 22:18, ESV
> *They divide my garments among them,*
> *and for my clothing they cast lots.*

This remarkable and astounding reference from David's Psalm talks specifically about those who divided Christ's garments, as we see fulfilled in multiple Gospel accounts, including the following passage:

Matthew 27:35, ESV
> *And when they had crucified him, they divided his garments among them by casting lots.*

And, if you will, consider how the Psalm ends:

Psalm 22:29-31, ESV

All the prosperous of the earth eat and worship;
before him shall bow all who go down to the dust,
even the one who could not keep himself alive.
Posterity shall serve him;
it shall be told of the Lord to the coming
generation;
they shall come and proclaim his righteousness to a
people yet unborn,
that he has done it.

If Satan, as we and many before us propose, were able to recall Psalm 22, this moment when Christ uttered the phrase "My God, My God, why have you forsaken me?" would have been at least the start of the dark-hearted one's big reveal. As his mind raced to the end of the passage, he would have realized "the one who could not keep Himself alive" is also the one before whom "all who go down to the dust" will bow.

There was no need to keep Satan uninformed about God's plan any longer. He had already played his part. This was when his ancient accusations against God were finally and permanently exhausted before a watching universe. It was also the moment Satan's fury expanded and the moment that Peter tells us that "even the angels longed to look into."

1 Peter 1:10-12, ESV

Concerning this salvation, the prophets who prophe-
sied about the grace that was to be yours searched and
inquired carefully, inquiring what person or time the
Spirit of Christ in them was indicating when he predicted
the sufferings of Christ and the subsequent glories. It was
revealed to them that they were serving not themselves

but you, in the things that have now been announced to you through those who preached the good news to you by the Holy Spirit sent from heaven, things into which angels long to look.

Jesus enlightens the disciples

Though they had walked with Jesus and been personally mentored by Him, the disciples were also unable to see what was about to unfold. We know that they didn't see the unveiled mystery until Jesus Himself finally "opened the Scriptures" for them as He taught them along the road to Emmaus. We see this recorded in Luke 24. First, we'll read of the resurrection account and then move into the story that unfolded as Jesus first personally disclosed "the mystery hidden for ages past and now revealed" to the disciples.

Luke 24:1-12, ESV

The Resurrection

*But on the first day of the week, at early dawn, they went to the tomb, taking the spices they had prepared. And they found the stone rolled away from the tomb, but when they went in they did not find the body of the Lord Jesus. While they were perplexed about this, behold, two men stood by them in dazzling apparel. And as they were frightened and bowed their faces to the ground, the men said to them, "Why do you seek the living among the dead? He is not here, but has risen. **Remember how he told you, while he was still in Galilee, that the Son of Man must be delivered into the hands of sinful men and be crucified and on the third day rise." And they remembered his words,** and returning from the tomb they told all these* *things to the eleven and to all the rest. Now it was Mary Magdalene and Joanna and Mary the mother of James and the other women with them who told these things to the apostles, but these words seemed to them an idle tale, and they did not believe them. But Peter rose and ran to the tomb; stooping and looking in, he saw the linen cloths by themselves; and he went home marveling at what had happened.*

Jesus had forecasted for them exactly what was coming. They heard Him, but they did not yet understand. Even the night before Jesus' crucifixion, His disciples were still asking Him when He would come into His kingdom. Only days before He was to be lifted on a cross with a thief on His left and His right, the mother of two of His disciples asked Jesus if her sons could be placed on Jesus' left and right. Jesus' response to this request is easier to understand in the light of His crucifixion that soon occurred. However, at the time, expecting Jesus to imminently grab hold of the iron scepter and displace the Roman system of government, it made sense for her to ask that her sons, both close and loyal to Jesus, be allowed to serve next to Him. But now, only three days after His crucifixion, the disciples were shocked, dismayed, disheartened, and struggling to believe the news that Jesus had been resurrected.

We see from Luke's account that Peter went and saw the linen cloths and marveled. It is not clear to us whether Peter now believed that Christ had been resurrected, but Peter still didn't understand the bigger picture of what had just happened. Here's the Good News from the Gospel itself: from the beginning of time, God had already orchestrated a plan for the Messiah to first come as the perfect sacrifice creating a perfect atonement "once for all," as Hebrews explains. This exquisite plan was beyond the understanding or perception of any natural man at the time. It was also intentionally crafted only to be clear once the events were unfolded and revealed.

Let's return to the same passage where Jesus Christ Himself steps into the role of the first teacher ever to reveal the Mystery Hidden for Ages Past to men, and first among them His disciples.

Luke 24:13-35, ESV
On the Road to Emmaus

*That very day two of them were going to a village named Emmaus, about seven miles from Jerusalem, and they were talking with each other about all these things that had happened. While they were talking and discussing together, Jesus himself drew near and went with them. But their eyes were kept from recognizing him. And he said to them, "What is this conversation that you are holding with each other as you walk?" And they stood still, looking sad. Then one of them, named Cleopas, answered him, "Are you the only visitor to Jerusalem who does not know the things that have happened there in these days?" And he said to them, "What things?" And they said to him, "**Concerning Jesus of Nazareth, a man** who was a prophet mighty in deed and word before God and all the people, and how our chief priests and rulers delivered him up to be condemned to death, and crucified him. But **we had hoped that he was the one to redeem Israel**. Yes, and besides all this, it is now the third day since these things happened. Moreover, some women of our company amazed us. They were at the tomb early in the morning, and when they did not find his body, they came back saying that they had even seen a* vision of angels, who said that he was alive. Some of those who were with us went to the tomb and found it just as the women had said, but him they did not see." And he said to them, "O foolish ones, and slow of heart to believe all that the prophets have spoken! Was it not necessary that the Christ should suffer these things and enter into his glory?" **And beginning with Moses and all the Prophets, he interpreted to them in all the Scriptures the things concerning himself.**

So they drew near to the village to which they were going. He acted as if he were going farther, but they urged him strongly, saying, "Stay with us, for it is toward evening and the day is now far spent." So he went in to stay with them. When he was at table with them, he took the bread and blessed and broke it and gave it to them. And their eyes were opened, and they recognized him. And he vanished from their sight. **They said to each other, "Did not our hearts burn within us while he talked to us on the road, while he opened to us the Scriptures?"** And they rose that same hour and returned to Jerusalem. And they found the eleven and those who were with them gathered together, saying, **"The Lord has risen indeed, and has appeared to Simon!"** Then they told what had happened on the road, and how he was known to them in the breaking of the bread.

Later in the same chapter, we see that Jesus met with the disciples again, and His continued teaching was described as having "opened their minds to understand the Scriptures."

Luke 24:45-47

Then he opened their minds to understand the Scriptures, and He said to them, "Thus it is written, that the Christ should suffer and rise again from the dead the third day; and that repentance for forgiveness of sins should be proclaimed in His name to all the nations, beginning from Jerusalem."

We can only imagine how remarkable it must've been to have Jesus Himself, the single most authoritative expert on biblical prophecy ever to walk the earth, explain the Mystery of the Gospel. I've experienced this myself in several ways. The first time was when I listened to a detailed teaching that Dennis McCallum had posted on his church's website. The hairs on my arm literally stood up. I can still remember driving down the road and beginning to realize for the first time that God had not only laid out and perfectly executed a plan to save all mankind but that He had also hidden it in plain view for us to see.

As I realized how many different individuals had contributed to the story without realizing they were doing it, I felt overwhelmed by God's majesty. I had always been impressed with God as the creator. I had always considered Him to be a genius beyond all imagination. But being someone who has always struggled with understanding, and even more so with managing and motivating sentient free-willed beings, I found myself astounded by God's ability to accurately predict the response that people would have thousands of years in advance. Predicting any of these events so far in advance is worthy of honor. Still, anticipating all of them, in combination, is worthy of the praise due to the only true God, who planned to save us from before the foundations of the earth and even recorded it as something we could perfectly see once these events had occurred. All of this was steganographically hidden, then cataclysmically revealed, to assure us of the truthfulness and reliability of His love for us.

A handful of weeks later, I was doing my best to roughly share this same topic with a group of men at the local rescue mission. It was my turn to lead a weekly Bible study. We came to the passage in Colossians Chapter 1 where Paul refers to "the mystery hidden for ages past and now revealed." I took about fifteen minutes to explain the idea that God put this mystery within plain sight and how no one saw it until after Christ had fulfilled the Father's plan. At the time, I wasn't sure this teaching was having the same impact on this group of men that it had on me. Nonetheless, I pressed through the rest of the passage we were studying that night, wrapped up with prayer, and headed out to my wife's van to drive home.

I will never forget what happened next for as long as I live. The rescue mission is housed in an old jail donated by our city many years ago. It was a dark and rainy night, and the rain was very heavy. I had just pulled the van out of a parking space and into the rough, dimly lit gravel parking lot. I was ready to back out of the lot when I saw the door that I had just come out of on the side of the old jail burst open. One of the men going through a recovery program, who had sat through the study that night, came running out of the open door yelling my name. I wasn't sure if he had noticed something I left behind or if he was perhaps upset with me. He yelled my name five or six times because it was dark, and he couldn't tell if I'd realized yet that he was coming. I put the van in park, and he ran through the pouring rain, jumped up on the running board, and stuck his head into the window I had just lowered. I didn't realize his face was covered with tears at first because of the heavy rain. He struggled through the words as he both cried and spoke simultaneously. He said, "He knew it! Didn't He?"

His name was Nicky, and I asked him, "He knew what?" Nicky responded, and I saw for the first time that the epiphany I had experienced was not specific to me. Nicky said, "God knew it all along! He had a plan all along! He knew that Satan would show his true character! He knew that Satan would fall into His trap, didn't he?" My heart was warmed. Now I was beginning to tear up. I responded, "Yes, and not only did He know, but He also hid it all in plain sight so that we could see, after the fact, that He had always planned this. He had always planned to sacrifice Himself for us." Nicky got it! It may have taken a few minutes of processing for him to connect the dots, but when he got it, it broke his heart, and seeing that broke mine.

A year later, my wife and I were walking through a large open park in the city we lived in when the sound of a nearby street preacher caught my attention. A group of men was cooking hotdogs on an open grill and serving them to the homeless. They could eat all they wanted so long as they were willing to stay and listen to the teaching that was going on. There he was! It was Nicky standing at the makeshift lectern teaching about the Mystery of the Gospel. He was delivering it with all his heart and the fervor of an angry Southern preacher. Nicky saw me, ran over, hugged me, and immediately reminded me of that night when he came running out in the rain. He had never forgotten the time that the Mystery of the Gospel had been revealed to him, and it had changed everything.

That was more than ten years ago, as of the time this is being written. I am pleased to tell you that Nicky went from being a serial addict in a recovery program to being a business owner, a husband, an employer, a father, an occasional volunteer preacher, and a genuinely goodhearted man of God. This is the power of what Jesus taught on the road to Emmaus. It opens our minds to understand the Scriptures, and if we are willing, it opens our hearts to the hope of salvation and the New Life that Paul describes to us in the book of Ephesians; the new life that Nicky was now living.

6

The Big Reveal – Part 2

The Jews and the Mystery Hidden for Ages Past

THE JEWS BEGAN to understand what had just happened when the Pentecost (and thereby the Holy Spirit) revealed the truth about the Messiah to them in uniquely unmistakable ways. Jesus had already meticulously fulfilled the elements of the Passover feast. For ages, the Jewish people had practiced Pentecost as "The Feast of Weeks." Now, that was also being fulfilled before their eyes. Their choice, as Acts shows us, was to accept or reject the Gospel that Peter was unapologetically presenting.

In the last section, we laid out how Jesus had revealed the Mystery of the Gospel to the disciples while they were on the road to Emmaus. While some observant Jews may have begun to see patterns, the greatest clarity was still concealed until this first post-resurrection Pentecost. In the book of Acts, Jesus told the disciples, just before His ascension, to go into Jerusalem and wait for the arrival of the Holy Spirit. From that point, in Acts 1:8, he said that they would go out into "Jerusalem, Judea, Samaria, and to the ends of the earth."

Acts 1:4-9, NIV

On one occasion, while he was eating with them, he gave them this command: "Do not leave Jerusalem, but wait for the gift my Father promised, which you have heard me speak about. For John baptized with water, but in a few days you will be baptized with the Holy Spirit."

Then they gathered around him and asked him, "Lord, are you at this time going to restore the kingdom to Israel?"

He said to them: "It is not for you to know the times or dates the Father has set by his own authority. But you will receive power when the Holy Spirit comes on you; and you will be my witnesses in Jerusalem, and in all Judea and Samaria, and to the ends of the earth."

After he said this, he was taken up before their very eyes, and a cloud hid him from their sight.

Note in verse 6 above the disciples were still in the dark regarding Jesus' two-part mission. This underscores the point that the revelation of the Mystery of the Gospel was still unfolding.

Some describe Acts 1:8 as the thesis verse for the entire book of Acts, as here Jesus lays out all that was about to take place as the Good News would soon begin to spread around the known world.

Having heard these instructions from Jesus, the disciples nervously waited in Jerusalem. Keep in mind that they had every reason to believe they were being hunted. Jerusalem was probably the last place they felt comfortable. However, they waited for over forty days, which must have felt like years. They were huddled together without clarity about what was coming next except for the basic predictions shared with them by Jesus, whom they obviously trusted. When the Holy Spirit came, the evidence was quite dramatic and at least partially intended to be for the benefit of the watching Jewish community. Many of the Jews there had made a trek from around the world to be in

Jerusalem during this holy period. Those still there would have been there awaiting the feast of Shavuot. The remarkable events of that day are described in Acts 2.

Acts 2:1-13, NIV

When the day of Pentecost came, they were all together in one place. Suddenly a sound like the blowing of a violent wind came from heaven and filled the whole house where they were sitting. They saw what seemed to be tongues of fire that separated and came to rest on each of them. All of them were filled with the Holy Spirit and began to speak in other tongues as the Spirit enabled them.

Now there were staying in Jerusalem God-fearing Jews from every nation under heaven. When they heard this sound, a crowd came together in bewilderment, because each one heard their own language being spoken. Utterly amazed, they asked: "Aren't all these who are speaking Galileans? Then how is it that each of us hears them in our native language? Parthians, Medes and Elamites; residents of Mesopotamia, Judea and Cappadocia, Pontus and Asia, Phrygia and Pamphylia, Egypt and the parts of Libya near Cyrene; visitors from Rome (both Jews and converts to Judaism); Cretans and Arabs—we hear them declaring the wonders of God in our own tongues!" Amazed and perplexed, they asked one another, "What does this mean?"

Some, however, made fun of them and said, "They have had too much wine."

Keep in mind that vinyl windows had not yet been invented. In fact, windows, as we know them, had not really been invented at all. Instead, windows were just lengthy portholes on the side of a wall, typically using curved surfaces to assure that rain would run to the outside of the wall versus the inside. They were otherwise wide-open unless shuttered. However, at this time of the year, these windows would have been open to benefit airflow and cooling. When it says that the house filled up with a sound like a violent wind, this is not something that would be heard only by people inside the home. We know that people in the area heard the sound of the wind and the disciples speaking in tongues because the text tells us that this was why they came to explore what they were hearing. Astounded, they found people not from their regions speaking their native tongues.

Imagine taking a modern-day trip to Beijing, China, perhaps to visit the Olympics. Imagine a group of Chinese nationals coming out onto a field with flames of fire above their head while some of them spoke "Texan," others spoke perfect French, yet others spoke flawless Bengali with all of them articulating the message of the Gospel. Now, to put it into context, take away whatever you've imagined about them being college graduated business sophisticates and instead imagine this is a group of poor peasants from the farmlands on the outskirts of China. If a sudden rushing wind drew your attention to this spectacle, and you hear these peasants speaking in your local tongue or dialect at the same time as hearing others speaking other languages, would you not be surprised?

Suppose you are one of those peasants realizing you are drawing the ire of the crowd around you and the Chinese government (in our metaphor having already crucified your leader). Might you not feel inclined to run for the hills, having now delivered your message? Instead, Peter (who recently denied Christ under pressure) stood up, speaking authoritatively with challenging words directed at the gathering crowd. Through the influence of the promised Holy Spirit, the convicting power of truth, and a previously unseen gift of public speaking, Peter now sees the church begin to grow. The Holy Spirit's first harvest was the hearts of thousands accepting Jesus Christ as their Messiah.

Please read the text, place yourself into the story, and imagine being there on that day. Perhaps imagine yourself a devout Jew who has traveled from far away because of your deep love and devotion to the Jewish faith. Now, after seeing something extraordinary, you see a strange man stand up and accuse you of being part of a movement that killed the Son of God.

Acts 2:14-41, NIV
Peter Addresses the Crowd

Then Peter stood up with the Eleven, raised his voice and addressed the crowd: "Fellow Jews and all of you who live in Jerusalem, let me explain this to you; listen carefully to what I say. These people are not drunk, as you suppose. It's only nine in the morning! No, this is what was spoken by the prophet Joel:

"'In the last days, God says,
I will pour out my Spirit on all people.
Your sons and daughters will prophesy,
your young men will see visions,
your old men will dream dreams.
Even on my servants, both men and women,
I will pour out my Spirit in those days,
and they will prophesy.
I will show wonders in the heavens above
and signs on the earth below,
blood and fire and billows of smoke.

The sun will be turned to darkness
and the moon to blood
before the coming of the great and glorious day of
the Lord.
And everyone who calls
on the name of the Lord will be saved.'

"*Fellow Israelites, listen to this: Jesus of Nazareth was a man accredited by God to you by miracles, wonders and signs, which God did among you through him, as you yourselves know. This man was handed over to you by God's deliberate plan and foreknowledge; and you, with the help of wicked men, put him to death by nailing him to the cross. But God raised him from the dead, freeing him from the agony of death, because it was impossible for death to keep its hold on him. David said about him:*

"*'I saw the Lord always before me.*
Because he is at my right hand,
I will not be shaken.
Therefore my heart is glad and my tongue rejoices;
my body also will rest in hope,
because you will not abandon me to the realm of the dead,
you will not let your holy one see decay.
You have made known to me the paths of life;
you will fill me with joy in your presence.'

"*Fellow Israelites, I can tell you confidently that the patriarch David died and was buried, and his tomb is here to this day. But he was a prophet and knew that God had promised him on oath that he would place one of his descendants on his throne. Seeing what was to come, he spoke of the resurrection of the Messiah, that he was not abandoned to the realm of the dead, nor did his body see decay. God has raised this Jesus to life, and we are all witnesses of it. Exalted to the right hand of God, he has received from the Father the promised Holy Spirit and has poured out what you now see and hear. For David did not ascend to heaven, and yet he said,*

"'The Lord said to my Lord:
"Sit at my right hand
until I make your enemies
a footstool for your feet."'

"Therefore let all Israel be assured of this: God has made this Jesus, whom you crucified, both Lord and Messiah."

When the people heard this, they were cut to the heart and said to Peter and the other apostles, "Brothers, what shall we do?"

Peter replied, "Repent and be baptized, every one of you, in the name of Jesus Christ for the forgiveness of your sins. And you will receive the gift of the Holy Spirit. The promise is for you and your children and for all who are far off—for all whom the Lord our God will call."

With many other words he warned them; and he pleaded with them, "Save yourselves from this corrupt generation." Those who accepted his message were baptized, and about three thousand were added to their number that day.

This passage conveys an astounding story! Let's drill into the outcome here. A group of people who quickly gathered to ridicule the disciples, accusing them of being drunk in the early hours, soon offered up the first group of early converts. The truth can be difficult to hear. It can also be difficult to speak. It is natural for us to feel a great deal of trepidation once we understand that God's Word reveals that men are rebels against His Kingdom and are, therefore, now in great danger. Sharing that truth can be especially fearsome when those rebels have surrounded us or become the majority in our society or community. Likewise, fear will increase if we are convinced that they will not want to hear our message and stand ready to persecute us if we speak it. Nevertheless, in this passage, God has also shown us that the church flourishes most in these very times. Accordingly, we are called to have confidence in the truth regardless of what it may cost us. And at times, with the aid of the Holy Spirit, the truth, no matter how uncomfortable to share, brings rapid and massive change.

Peter specifically showed his audience how the Old Testament had pre-authenticated what they knew had just happened regarding Jesus Christ. Surely the Jewish population who had come to Jerusalem would have heard of the events of Jesus Christ. He was a character of notoriety. His trial and crucifixion were the talk of the town. We know this because when Jesus walked along the road to Emmaus with the disciples, they asked Him surprisedly, "Are you the only visitor to Jerusalem who does not know the things that have happened there in these days?" Similarly, Christianity's detractors today have certainly heard of Jesus Christ. He is no longer concealed. God has revealed him to the world.

Muslims believe Jesus was a great prophet. They believe His mother is the greatest woman in history, but they do not believe that Jesus is the Son of God. Atheists believe He existed but try to dismiss Him as a good teacher or a great man of peace. Agnostics recognize Him as a remarkable historical character but refuse to respond to His call, and the ambivalent prefer not to think about Him at all.

As we have discussed earlier, the question of Jesus is always a challenging one. How can we say that Jesus was a great teacher yet claim His teachings were false? How can we say He was a man of peace yet claim that His teachings have led to nothing but war? If Jesus claimed to be the Son of God yet was willing to die instead of denying the claim, how can we say that He is anything other than one of these two conclusions: Jesus was either who He said He was or a madman. The valid question regarding Jesus is this, which one was He?

Throughout this book, we will continue to dig into how the Old Testament underscores the Gospel. Our focus will be on using the Old Testament to credential Jesus Christ and the specifics of His first visit, just as Peter did when he first shared the Mystery of the Gospel with the Jews on Pentecost. We will focus on the power of that message and how it is unique among all world religions. Next, we will dig into how Jesus Himself and the early church teachers delivered that message to various audiences with significant effect. But what we can see most clearly here in Peter's spontaneous dissertation was a gut punch to the whimsical dismissal of Jesus as anything other than the Messiah.

As we traverse further through the book of Acts, we will find that Peter and others began to challenge the Jewish culture with the very Scriptures they already knew and loved, showing they authoritatively credentialed Jesus as the Messiah. This revelation was powerful and effective, and it demanded a response. That response always came, just as Jesus had predicted. It either brought about repentance, willful disregard, or outright rage.

Consider Saul, across chapters 6, 7, and 8 of Acts, who participated in the effort to seize and ultimately kill Stephen, one of the first Gentile converts to Christianity. We enter chapter 8 with the Scripture telling us that Saul approved of what had just happened, but there is more there if we care to see it. The passage tells us that those who stoned Stephen laid their outer garments at the feet of Saul. Though the Jews lacked the authority to put someone to death, Saul (both a Roman citizen and a Jew) guarded the outer garments of those about to put Stephen to death, though he had not received the due process he was entitled to under Roman law.

Saul was one of those who were unable to collectively refute Stephen's rebuttal offered at the temple of the freedmen. They so hated him for this that they collectively orchestrated His death.

Saul was no lightweight. We know that he had studied at the feet of Gamaliel. This school he attended, known as the school of Hillel, was reserved for the elite of the elite. Being from Tarsus and not Jerusalem, Saul's parents would have leveraged significant political capital and financial resources to get Saul into the school and keep him there. Entrance into that school required a Jewish boy to be able to recite the Torah (the first five books of the Old Testament) from memory without a single error. The school was expensive because of its reputation for producing people who would rise high up into the Jewish system of religious government. After his conversion, Saul (later called Paul) tells us in his writings that he was more zealous than his peers.

Across the book of Acts, we can see that God orchestrated the affairs of Saul so that he was required to take the place of the eloquent Stephen, whom he had helped remove from God's service. This service eventually cost Paul his life, but it was a price he was glad to pay because he had come to know the truth.

It is easy for us to fear the reaction we will get from men and women dangerously convicted by the truth we possess. Just as

Jesus' message divided people between acceptance and rejection, Stephen's message brought the same, and so it was with Saul. When he shared the truth with others, it was as difficult to refute as Stephen's teachings had been for Saul himself and similarly led to either repentance or significant anger, as we will see in Acts Chapter 9.

Acts 9:1-31, NIV
Saul's Conversion

Meanwhile, Saul was still breathing out murderous threats against the Lord's disciples. He went to the high priest and asked him for letters to the synagogues in Damascus, so that if he found any there who belonged to the Way, whether men or women, he might take them as prisoners to Jerusalem. As he neared Damascus on his journey, suddenly a light from heaven flashed around him. He fell to the ground and heard a voice say to him, "Saul, Saul, why do you persecute me?"

"Who are you, Lord?" Saul asked.

"I am Jesus, whom you are persecuting," he replied. "Now get up and go into the city, and you will be told what you must do."

The men traveling with Saul stood there speechless; they heard the sound but did not see anyone. Saul got up from the ground, but when he opened his eyes he could see nothing. So they led him by the hand into Damascus. For three days he was blind, and did not eat or drink anything.

In Damascus there was a disciple named Ananias. The Lord called to him in a vision, "Ananias!"

"Yes, Lord," he answered.

The Lord told him, "Go to the house of Judas on Straight Street and ask for a man from Tarsus named Saul, for he is praying. In a vision he has seen a man named Ananias come and place his hands on him to restore his sight."

"Lord," Ananias answered, "I have heard many reports about this man and all the harm he has done to your holy people in Jerusalem. And he has come here with authority from the chief priests to arrest all who call on your name."

But the Lord said to Ananias, "Go! This man is my chosen instrument to proclaim my name to the Gentiles and their kings and to the people of Israel. I will show him how much he must suffer for my name."

Then Ananias went to the house and entered it. Placing his hands on Saul, he said, "Brother Saul, the Lord—Jesus, who appeared to you on the road as you were coming here—has sent me so that you may see again and be filled with the Holy Spirit." Immediately, something like scales fell from Saul's eyes, and he could see again. He got up and was baptized, and after taking some food, he regained his strength.

Saul in Damascus and Jerusalem

Saul spent several days with the disciples in Damascus. At once he began to preach in the synagogues that Jesus is the Son of God. All those who heard him were astonished and asked, "Isn't he the man who raised havoc in Jerusalem among those who call on this name? And hasn't he come here to take them as prisoners to the chief priests?" Yet Saul grew more and more powerful and baffled the Jews living in Damascus by proving that Jesus is the Messiah.

After many days had gone by, there was a conspiracy among the Jews to kill him, but Saul learned of their plan. Day and night they kept close watch on the city gates in order to kill him. But his followers took him by night and lowered him in a basket through an opening in the wall.

When he came to Jerusalem, he tried to join the disciples, but they were all afraid of him, not believing that he really was a disciple. But Barnabas took him and brought him to the apostles. He told them how Saul on his journey had seen the Lord and that the Lord had spoken to him, and how in Damascus he had preached fearlessly in the name of Jesus. So Saul stayed with them and moved about freely in Jerusalem, speaking boldly in the name of the Lord. He talked and debated with the Hellenistic Jews, but they tried to kill him. When the believers learned of this, they took him down to Caesarea and sent him off to Tarsus.

Then the church throughout Judea, Galilee and Samaria enjoyed a time of peace and was strengthened. Living in the fear of the Lord and encouraged by the Holy Spirit, it increased in numbers.

While we are not given much detail about the potential positive impacts of Paul's teaching in these areas, shortly after his conversion, we are given insight into its power in the text above. Do we not still see the same reactions today? When people have decided to place their faith in something untrue, and the truth is irrefutably presented to them, they are forced to either accept that truth or do everything they can to ostracize, diminish, or censor it. This is what we also see in response to Paul's early teaching. But take heart, as Paul continued making his compelling arguments, leveraging his extraordinary knowledge of the Old Testament, God used him in mighty ways. Paul was used to lead tens of thousands to faith within his lifetime. His writings have also helped billions come to faith across the ages.

The truth that Jesus was the Messiah was revealed to the Jews through extraordinary events in the life of Jesus, signs brought through the early disciples (such as their speaking in other tongues on the day of Pentecost), and later by way of the extraordinarily effective historical, philosophical, and logical arguments of an expert in their treasured Scriptures. The Jews had a front-row seat to the mission of the suffering servant and Christ's completion of that divine calling. As Dennis McCallum describes it, the post-facto "light of Christianity" allows the details of that mission to be put together in an obvious way. That clarity still demands a response. All we need to do is share it.

The Gentiles receive the light

Paul was assigned to replace Stephen, and it took three days of blindness for him to finally see the message he was commissioned to take to the Gentiles (as he said in his own words in Colossians 1:24-26 and Ephesians 3:1-13).

When Saul interacted with the risen Jesus Christ on the way to Damascus, he was headed there to persecute Christians. We can ascertain a lot from this brief but extraordinary interaction. When Jesus said, "Saul, Saul why do you persecute me?" Paul responded with a most interesting question, "who are you, Lord"? This allows us to see that Saul knew he was in the presence of a supernatural being, as he referred to the person speaking to him as "Lord." For the next several days, Jesus' carefully chosen response surely echoed through Paul's head, "I am Jesus, whom *you* are persecuting," He replied.

Paul later wrote a great deal about the Mystical Union, another facet of the Mystery Now Revealed. Through the Holy Spirit, Christ now indwells His saints personally and persistently. It is not a stretch to say that Paul could have developed his understanding of this critical theological point simply by replaying this short conversation with Jesus in his mind. Jesus had already been crucified and ascended into heaven and confronted Saul in His spiritual form. But Saul was not persecuting Jesus directly. Rather, he was on his way to persecute Christians. Yet Jesus described Saul's persecution in the first person. When Saul arrived in Damascus, he did not eat or drink anything as he sat blinded for three days, providing a great deal of time to contemplate the idea that he had been persecuting Jesus by persecuting Christians.

I recently met with a friend for a conversation over a breakfast we had planned a few weeks earlier. However, when we met, he could not eat. I asked him why and he shared painful details of a recently discovered affair that his wife had been having. He was wrestling with the internal pain of having placed great faith in something untrue. Similarly, Paul must have wrestled in every sense as he processed the original intention of his mission to Damascus and how Jesus Himself had derailed it. We don't usually feel like eating when we are processing something as profound as the question: "Has my whole life been built upon a lie?"

Paul had just three days to reconcile the extraordinary Old Testament knowledge he possessed with the now life-altering events that had just occurred on his trip to Damascus. He had convincingly experienced the presence of the risen Lord firsthand, but this experience countermanded everything that he had previously believed. It wasn't that he didn't know the

Scriptures; he had read them and memorized them but had been unable to ascertain the correct conclusion. I believe this is why Paul wrote and spoke so personally and passionately about the Mystery of The Gospel, as being something that we are blessed to have revealed to us now, in this last age. It was a truth that Paul believed he must teach about boldly, even asking others to pray that he would do just that.

When Paul, many years later, began his missionary journeys, he would first enter the Jewish synagogue in each of the towns he visited. Only upon completing his work there, gaining converts or angering enemies, would he move on to the Gentiles. However, his approach toward these two groups differed slightly before converging onto the same track.

Acts 17:16-34, NIV

While Paul was waiting for them in Athens, he was greatly distressed to see that the city was full of idols. So he reasoned in the synagogue with both Jews and God-fearing Greeks, as well as in the marketplace day by day with those who happened to be there. A group of Epicurean and Stoic philosophers began to debate with him. Some of them asked, "What is this babbler trying to say?" Others remarked, "He seems to be advocating foreign gods." They said this because Paul was preaching the good news about Jesus and the resurrection. Then they took him and brought him to a meeting of the Areopagus, where they said to him, "May we know what this new teaching is that you are presenting? You are bringing some strange ideas to our ears, and we would like to know what they mean." (All the Athenians and the foreigners who lived there spent their time doing nothing but talking about and listening to the latest ideas.)

Paul then stood up in the meeting of the Areopagus and said: "People of Athens! I see that in every way you are very religious. For as I walked around and looked carefully at your objects of worship, I even found an altar with this inscription: to an unknown god. So you are ignorant of the very thing you worship—and this is what I am going to proclaim to you.

"The God who made the world and everything in it is the Lord of heaven and earth and does not live in temples built by human hands. And he is not served by human hands, as if he needed anything. Rather, he himself gives everyone life and breath and everything else. From one man he made all the nations, that they should inhabit the whole earth; and he marked out their appointed times in history and the boundaries of their lands. God did this so that they would seek him and perhaps reach out for him and find him, though he is not far from any one of us. 'For in him we live and move and have our being.' As some of your own poets have said, 'We are his offspring.'

"Therefore since we are God's offspring, we should not think that the divine being is like gold or silver or stone— an image made by human design and skill. In the past God overlooked such ignorance, but now he commands all people everywhere to repent. For he has set a day when he will judge the world with justice by the man he has appointed. He has given proof of this to everyone by raising him from the dead."

When they heard about the resurrection of the dead, some of them sneered, but others said, "We want to hear you again on this subject." At that, Paul left the Council. Some of the people became followers of Paul and believed. Among them was Dionysius, a member of the Areopagus, also a woman named Damaris, and a number of others.

Even in Athens, Paul first visited the synagogue seeking to reason with the Jews and God-fearing Gentiles. We can take the word "reason" at its most straightforward meaning, i.e., he gave them reasons to believe. Or, we can take it to its loftier meaning, whereby he was calling out their own ability to reason through the presented information. There is little cause to think that Paul would have tried to convince Jewish believers that Jesus was the Messiah by using anything other than the Scripture. He would not have been able to entertain their attention for any length of time were he to claim that his own opinions or experiences were some kind of new authoritative source that should lead them to abandon their confidence in the Scriptures. Instead, Paul was using his extraordinary knowledge and training *of* the Scriptures to press in and show them that Jesus was well-credentialed as the Messiah throughout the Old Testament.

This is the same approach that Paul would take with the Gentiles, but not until (as we see above) he had first captured their attention by using philosophy, logic, and reason to confront their own inferior beliefs. Unless he could show a flaw in their worldview, why bother trying to convince the Gentiles that the Old Testament would credential his new message when they may not even have known what the Old Testament was? Paul did not confront their view from a pious absence of familiarity. In other words, he was not afraid to be around the idolatrous Athenians and their corrupt ways. He never resorted to meme-level platitudes like, "Athenian bad. Jewish good". Rather, Paul had made himself familiar with the practices of the Athenians. As seen in the passage above, we can extrapolate that from his response. Paul had explored their worship and was so familiar with their culture that he could apply his intellect in concert with the Holy Spirit to find the opening.

The Athenians already doubted whether or not their religious views were complete. They had expressed this doubt through the Statue of the Unknown God. Paul leveraged this familiarity as he came in to explain to them that he was there to introduce them to their unknown God. He then ardently defined the true God, Yahweh, as superior to their whole class of lesser man-made gods. As you might expect, this was not universally successful, but that is no different from Paul's experience with the Jews or God-fearing Gentiles. The truth requires a response, but it does not always get the response we desire.

By engaging the culture and reasoning into man's natural desire for greater truth, Paul was able to engage the hearts and minds of the Athenian people. He counseled them to consider the general revelation of creation that shows us the invisible qualities of our designer. He also argued that those creative capabilities were beyond the reach of manufactured gods. From the starting line of natural revelation, Paul would lead his audience into the story of how this unknown God used detailed predictive prophecy to both pre-credential Christ and His astounding mission to save mankind. This was starkly different from the man-made idols and myths that predominated this culture before Paul arrived with the truth.

Likewise, this same powerful truth is still available to be revealed today. We can plainly see the emptiness and incompleteness of the alternatives. Consider modern spirituality, where people declare themselves spiritual beings but don't want to admit that there is a God. Atheism posits that all living things and the systems that support them have emerged from a complex series of physical and chemical accidents. And the spiritually indifferent find themselves wholly unable to answer the most important questions of all, why are we here, and where are we going?

God calls on us to engage the deleterious ways and beliefs of the neighbors, communities, and nations around us. We are not called to join the practices we find but to analyze them with empathy and the power of the Holy Spirit, to find and expose the insufficiencies of those ways, just as Paul did in Athens. We are called to gently correct and lift the thinking of those with whom God has given us influence. This opens the door, and we must be prepared to provide that better answer for "the hope that is within us."

7

The Way That the Resurrected Jesus Taught

JESUS TAUGHT THROUGH parables and metaphors that were often difficult to understand, and He did this for three and a half years. Christ's veiling of his message did not diminish the desire of the people to hear Him in the least. Though discerning the meaning behind Jesus' teachings may have been difficult, they could still tell that they were being taught by one with authority. We see just that in one of Mark's earliest references to Jesus' teaching.

Mark 1:22, ESV
And they were astonished at his teaching, for he taught them as one who had authority, and not as the scribes.

His disciples did not understand what happened to Jesus at first either. Still, after Jesus came into His glory, they began to remember these things spoken by or written about Him and that they had also happened as predicted. Consider this passage where Jesus' message confused His audience as He began to forecast the way that His first mission to earth would soon conclude:

John 16:17-19, ESV
At this, some of his disciples said to one another, "What does he mean by saying, 'In a little while you will see me no more, and then after a little while you will see

me,' and 'Because I am going to the Father'?" They kept asking, "What does he mean by 'a little while'? We don't understand what he is saying."

Jesus saw that they wanted to ask him about this, so he said to them, "Are you asking one another what I meant when I said, 'In a little while you will see me no more, and then after a little while you will see me'?

John 12:20-50, ESV
Some Greeks Seek Jesus

Now among those who went up to worship at the feast were some Greeks. So these came to Philip, who was from Bethsaida in Galilee, and asked him, "Sir, we wish to see Jesus." Philip went and told Andrew; Andrew and Philip went and told Jesus. And Jesus answered them, "The hour has come for the Son of Man to be glorified. Truly, truly, I say to you, unless a grain of wheat falls into the earth and dies, it remains alone; but if it dies, it bears much fruit. Whoever loves his life loses it, and whoever hates his life in this world will keep it for eternal life. If anyone serves me, he must follow me; and where I am, there will my servant be also. If anyone serves me, the Father will honor him.

The Son of Man Must Be Lifted Up

"Now is my soul troubled. And what shall I say? 'Father, save me from this hour'? But for this purpose I have come to this hour. Father, glorify your name." Then a voice came from heaven: "I have glorified it, and I will glorify it again." The crowd that stood there and heard it said that it had thundered. Others said, "An angel has spoken to him." Jesus answered, "This voice has come for *your sake, not mine. Now is the judgment of this world; now will the ruler of this world be cast out. And I, when I am lifted up from the earth, will draw all people to myself." He said this to show by what kind of death he was going to die. So the crowd answered him, "We have heard from the Law that the Christ remains forever. How can you say that the Son of Man must be lifted up? Who is this Son of Man?" So Jesus said to them, "The light is among you for a little while longer. Walk while you have the light, lest darkness overtake you. The one who walks in the darkness does not know where he is going. While you have the light, believe in the light, that you may become sons of light."*

The Unbelief of the People

When Jesus had said these things, he departed and hid himself from them. Though he had done so many signs before them, they still did not believe in him, so that the word spoken by the prophet Isaiah might be fulfilled:

"Lord, who has believed what he heard from us,
and to whom has the arm of the Lord been
revealed?"

Therefore they could not believe. For again Isaiah said,

"He has blinded their eyes
and hardened their heart,
lest they see with their eyes,
and understand with their heart, and turn,
and I would heal them."

Isaiah said these things because he saw his glory and spoke of him. Nevertheless, many even of the authorities believed in him, but for fear of the Pharisees they did not confess it, so that they would not be put out of the synagogue; for they loved the glory that comes from man more than the glory that comes from God.

Jesus Came to Save the World

And Jesus cried out and said, "Whoever believes in me, believes not in me but in him who sent me. And whoever sees me sees him who sent me. I have come into the world as light, so that whoever believes in me may not remain in darkness. If anyone hears my words and does not keep them, I do not judge him; for I did not come to judge the world but to save the world. The one who rejects me and does not receive my words has a judge; the word that I have spoken will judge him on the last day. For I have not spoken on my own authority, but the Father who sent me has himself given me a commandment—what to say and what to speak. And I know that his commandment is eternal life. What I say, therefore, I say as the Father has told me."

Jesus often explained His parables to the disciples privately but never made it fully clear that He was here to sacrifice Himself for mankind, at least not before it occurred. We can verify their lack of perception in this area by observing that they were still asking Him questions even in the final days before His crucifixion. They asked questions like, "when you come into your [earthly – implied] kingdom... ?" often troubling over what position they might hold in His coming earthly government, showing they were still not perceiving His true intentions. Yet Jesus had also told them that there was a time coming when He would be able to speak to them more clearly.

John 16:25, ESV

Jesus' only response was "These things I have spoken to you in figurative language; an hour is coming when I will speak no more to you in figurative language but will tell you plainly of the Father."

Consider the plight of the disciples. Just days after they were arguing over who would serve in what position within Jesus' coming government, Jesus was arrested, tried, and executed just before Passover. We know that they did not understand that Jesus had come to sacrifice Himself. This was privileged information that had not yet been revealed to them. From their perspective, this all-powerful miracle-wielding yet simple-living prophet, teacher, and to some, the Messiah Himself was about to take the iron scepter and reestablish the rightful kingdom of King David. And why shouldn't they think that? Though Jesus lived simply, the miracles and authority He wielded were anything but simple and anything but ordinary. So, when this soon-to-be king breathed His last upon the cross, imagine the disillusionment the disciples experienced.

Certainly, we can relate. Whether it be a promotion we are confident is coming, a Christmas present we were sure would be under the tree, or our expectations upon God Himself, have we not all been astounded at times with the contrast between the way we believed a thing should go and the way it went? The disciples experienced all of this at one time. While the Romans certainly brought peace and safety of travel to the Middle East, it came at a heavy price. The burden of their taxes was onerous. Unless you were politically connected, you were likely to spend the rest of your life simply getting by. At the same time, the fruits of your labor became the discretionary resources of the Roman government, and it was not at all voluntary. The disciples lived in a genuinely oppressed society. Slavery was not only common, but you could fall into it simply by missing a scheduled payment. The religious leaders had turned Judaism into a heavy burden making people feel separated from God and hopeless. As hope in Christ as the Messiah grew, it was not only His disciples who had come to expect that the conclusion of His ministry would be the reestablishment of the throne of David. The disciples were not only disillusioned, but they were also now the outcast faces of a failed coup.

But this is not the end of the story. God resurrected Jesus from the dead on the morning of the third day.

On the road to Emmaus

By the time we find several of the disciples walking along the road to Emmaus, it is not difficult for us to understand the significant despair and disillusionment they would be feeling. Jesus had not initiated the hoped for rebellion against the Romans. The religious leaders have conspired with the Romans to crucify their teacher. Several, if not all, of Jesus' inner circle, had become convinced that He was the Messiah. Peter outright called Him the Christ. Now, even these true believers were wondering if it was true. They asked if they had misunderstood. They wondered if they had wasted their years. Now, with the turning of the tide against Christ, all who had followed Him also wondered if they would survive.

It is in this context that we see a most remarkable story. The resurrected Jesus appears and walks along the road to Emmaus with several of His disciples, though they do not recognize Him. This lack of recognition is important at this moment. It allows Jesus to speak to them as a stranger and for them to focus on the information that He is about to share. Otherwise, their natural excitement to see Him again would have distracted them. Jesus inquires of them regarding their despair and then responds with His first post-resurrected teaching, unveiling the Mystery of The Gospel for the first time. Let's review this remarkable passage in Luke again, and then dig even deeper into the details of the interaction between Jesus and his disciples.

Luke 24:13-35, ESV
On the Road to Emmaus

That very day two of them were going to a village named Emmaus, about seven miles from Jerusalem, and they were talking with each other about all these things that had happened. While they were talking and discussing together, Jesus himself drew near and went with them. But their eyes were kept from recognizing him. And he said to them, "What is this conversation that you are holding with each other as you walk?" And they stood still, looking sad. Then one of them, named Cleopas, answered him, "Are you the only visitor to Jerusalem who does not know the things that have happened there in these days?" And he said to them, "What things?" And they said to him, "Concerning Jesus of Nazareth, a man who was a prophet mighty in deed and word before God and all the people, and how our chief priests and rulers delivered him up to be condemned to death, and crucified him. But we had hoped that he was the one to redeem Israel. Yes, and besides all this, it is now the third day since these things happened. Moreover, some women of our company amazed us. They were at the tomb early in the morning, and when they did not find his body, they came back saying that they had even seen a vision of angels, who said that he was alive. Some of those who were with us went to the tomb and found it just as the women had said, but him they did not see." And he said to them, "O foolish ones, and slow of heart to believe all that the prophets have spoken! Was it not necessary that the Christ should suffer these things and enter into his glory?" And beginning with Moses and all the Prophets, he interpreted to them in all the Scriptures the things concerning himself.

So they drew near to the village to which they were going. He acted as if he were going farther, but they urged him strongly, saying, "Stay with us, for it is toward evening and the day is now far spent." So he went in to stay with them. When he was at table with them, he took the bread and blessed and broke it and gave it to them. And their eyes were opened, and they recognized him. And he vanished from their sight. They said to each other, "Did not our hearts burn within us while he talked to us on the road, while he opened to us the Scriptures?" And they rose that same hour and returned to Jerusalem. And they found the eleven and those who were with them gathered together, saying, "The Lord has risen indeed, and has appeared to Simon!" Then they told what had happened on the road, and how he was known to them in the breaking of the bread.

Let's disassemble this passage a bit to gain context and insight regarding what exactly Jesus said to His disciples and the impact it had on them. First, at the end of verse 17, we are given an insight into the perspective and demeanor of the disciples. In response to the stranger's question, the text tells us that they stood still, looking sad.

There are several kinds of "being lost." One type of "lost" is when our proverbial fathers convinced themselves that they did not need to ask anyone for directions. For the younger reader, there was once a time before the advent of GPS when people had to use archaic things like paper maps and their memories to find infrequently visited places. That first kind of "lost" is knowing where you want to go but not being sure of the specifics of how to get there. Another "lost" type is a child losing track of their parents at a state fair. As the thick crowd goes by in all directions and they realize they have lost sight, the overwhelming sense comes upon them, "I am lost, and I don't know how to find my people!" These types are both alarming, but they don't measure up to the kind of "lost" the disciples would have felt at this critical moment. I'm sure you have experienced this at some point. Perhaps it was in the death of a loved one. Maybe it came upon reading a letter to find out that the college you hoped to attend did not accept you, or perhaps you didn't get the job you were sure was yours. "Everything I have based my future plans upon has just changed, and I don't know what to do next." This kind of "lost" was the unenviable state the disciples were experiencing. They had hitched their wagons to the one they had come to have faith in, but now they were disillusioned, disheartened, and deeply lost. They stood still and looked sad.

Luke 24:18, ESV
   Then one of them, named Cleopas, answered him, "Are you the only visitor to Jerusalem who does not know the things that have happened there in these days?"

In verse 18, we get a clear sense that the events that have just unfolded are not an obscure story that no one has heard.

Cleopas may be emotionally charged, but the question wouldn't make sense if no one were talking about what had just happened with Jesus. Some were probably glad that the rebel from Galilee had finally been put down. Some probably felt that it was righteous that this false teacher had finally met justice. Some who had heard Him teach were probably saddened and confused. Many who had been healed or had their lives radically changed by Him were having their faith shaken deeply. Jesus was (and is) the talk of the town. What His death on the cross meant is still the most important question of all time.

> *Luke 24:19-21, ESV*
>
> *And he said to them, "What things?" And they said to him, "Concerning Jesus of Nazareth, a man who was a prophet mighty in deed and word before God and all the people, and how our chief priests and rulers delivered him up to be condemned to death, and crucified him. But we had hoped that he was the one to redeem Israel. Yes, and besides all this, it is now the third day since these things happened.*

In verses 19 through 21, we can see how deep the disheartenment of the disciples really was. Several statements jump out to the attentive reader: first, the statement "a man who was a prophet." In their choice of words, Jesus had been demoted to the role of a prophet by His disillusioned disciples. In verse 20, we see their shock at His death and the manner by which it was delivered, and in verse 21, we see the impact that it has had. The phrase "but we had hoped" can be reasonably interpreted to convey the past tense. They describe this hope as one that has now been lost or blotted out. "But we had hoped that

He was the one to redeem Israel" shows us that they still did not understand that Jesus had come to save mankind. Though they followed Him, admired Him, valued His teachings, and loved Him personally, like many of us today, they were still so focused on the redemption they hoped He would bring to their personal situations that they struggled to see the bigger picture. They were hoping for things that were lower than God's plan, and they were reeling in despair just like we do when God lays down His lofty plans, but they don't include the specific parts we assumed would be "in it for us." We cannot condemn the disciples but rather underscore their relatable humanity and highlight their complete lack of understanding, at that point, regarding the true purpose of Jesus' first coming.

Luke 24:22-24, ESV
Moreover, some women of our company amazed us. They were at the tomb early in the morning, and when they did not find his body, they came back saying that they had even seen a vision of angels, who said that he was alive. Some of those who were with us went to the tomb and found it just as the women had said, but him they did not see."

The disciples are aware of the empty tomb, the vision of the angels, and the testimony of the women who went to the tomb before them. However, in the following few verses, we will see that they do not yet believe what they have heard because they went to the tomb themselves and did not find Jesus.

Luke 24:25-27, ESV

And he said to them, "O foolish ones, and slow of heart to believe all that the prophets have spoken! Was it not necessary that the Christ should suffer these things and enter into his glory?" And beginning with Moses and all the Prophets, he interpreted to them in all the Scriptures the things concerning himself.

Jesus' response is quick and serious. He stops them in their tracks by calling them "foolish ones, and slow of heart" and then lays out a thesis for what He is about to expound upon. Jesus says to them, "Was it not necessary that the Christ should suffer these things and enter into His glory?" This modifies the end of verse 25, where He challenges them for being slow to believe all that the prophets have spoken. And it lays out what verse 27 tells us. He is about to use the Old Testament Scriptures to credential His first coming.

But when the text tells us that Jesus opened the Scriptures to us, we can rest assured that Jesus is not talking about the writings of Paul. Paul is our modern "Greek" name for the Pharisee then called Saul, and he had not yet written any biblical text. Jesus is not going to "open" the books of Matthew, Mark, Luke, or John. These men themselves are Jesus' disciples and have not yet written any of the Gospels. No, Jesus is going to interpret the Old Testament for them, that ancient set of writings we far too often overlook.

We are explicitly told that "He interpreted to them in all the Scriptures the things concerning Himself." This reinforces the idea that the Old Testament is "Jesus Christ concealed" and that the New Testament is "Jesus Christ revealed." We have already explained how Jesus is seen throughout the Old Testament in various forms. There were direct appearances as the Angel of the Lord, types and shadows, stories that foreshadowed His coming, and traditions and specific prophecies that foretold the details of His first and second coming.

The restoration of hope

What a remarkable teaching this must have been! I find the writings of Paul, with his great knowledge of the Old Testament, to be quite inspiring when he illuminates the promise of the coming Jesus through the pages of the Old Testament. However, as impressive as Paul's theology and teaching may be, it cannot hold a candle to what the disciples must've experienced along the road to Emmaus. The risen Christ, understanding every reference to Himself throughout the Old Testament and having fulfilled all of those references regarding His first coming, was personally teaching the disciples. He was no longer explaining these things in parables or "figurative language." As promised, He was now explaining them plainly. Do you wonder what it must have felt like to receive and process this information along that road? Let's go back to the passage and examine its impact in the disciple's own words.

> *Luke 24:32, ESV*
> *They said to each other, "Did not our hearts burn within us while he talked to us on the road, while he opened to us the Scriptures?"*

The disciples gave us an unmistakable description of impassioned enlightenment. When you feel lost, as we described above (that sense of having no idea where to go or what to do next), is it reasonable to expect you to respond passionately about much of anything? Having recently suffered a serious bout of fever, weakness, and multiple weeks of trouble breathing due to the virus known as Covid, I remember one of the most challenging parts of the recovery was the feeling of having no interest in any of the things that I usually did. I was terrified, wondering whether or not that interest would return. The fever had passed, and the symptoms had cleared (as others could see them), but internally I felt lost. I had no interest in returning to work, but I also had no interest in returning to my hobbies or other activities I might consider fun. If someone had come along and told me about something I would typically get very excited about, I might have been able to feign the same expressions on my face for their benefit, but let me be honest, I wouldn't have cared in the slightest.

I was simply dealing with an illness. For the disciples, their whole world had been shaken from the foundation up. Is it normal that a conversation with a stranger along a road would shake you out of such despair and cause you to describe your response to their words as "did not our hearts burn within us?" No. That is not a standard response. The only way you could elicit a reaction like that would be to solve the malady currently depressing the mind of the hearer.

Consider our previous metaphor of someone who just received a letter informing them that they were not accepted to the college they had hoped to attend. It is unlikely to get them excited about an invitation from a friend to play miniature golf. However, if you told them you had just found a second letter showing there was a mistake at the college and that they had not only been accepted but given a full scholarship, it would be quite normal for them to get excited again.

Jesus had not only explained the truth to them, but in doing so, even in the voice of a stranger, He had reignited in them "the hope of things unseen." This is the extraordinary power of the Mystery of the Gospel! When we understand this story, we can also clearly perceive that God's ways are far higher than ours and that He was playing a game of 3D chess and winning.

It is impossible to live in the world we live in without experiencing despair. The depths of our despair can often be found in circumstances where we think the world has gone out of control, justifying our loss of hope. Yet, in many ways, our loss of hope reflects our lack of faith in God and His plan. This is what the disciples were experiencing at this moment. Christ's frustration toward them, expressed by referring to them as "foolish ones and slow of heart," is not so much directed toward them personally but rather toward their lack of understanding and the impact of that lack on their thinking.

Not unlike the disciples, we can also find ourselves in the middle of a masterful moment where God's plan is coming together for us, yet also find ourselves filled with despair because we cannot yet see His bigger picture. The Bible does not promise us that we will always see the bigger picture. Instead, it references God's track record that we can use to train up our hope.

God may allow evil, but He is not its author. He may allow us to experience despair, but He has never lost control. He may allow circumstances that fall short of our expectations, but God has never failed to hear our cries, has never forgotten our plight, and has never abandoned us. His ways are higher than ours, His rescues more spectacular and complete, and He is still at work in the world around us, unfolding the fullness of His trustworthy plan before our eyes.

We can either shudder in fear because we don't see how things will work out, or we can have hope in the future because of what we see He has already done in the past. Our ability to comprehend our current circumstances should no longer limit our hope because we, like the disciples, cannot ascertain all that He is doing at the time that He is doing it. We should confidently trust that all that He is doing is for our good and that in the end, when we finally get to open the second letter (from the college), and all is clarified, we too will know the restoration of hope as *our hearts burn within us.*

Jesus' excellent example

By decoding God's credentialing predictive prophecies from the Old Testament, Jesus was able to get at the core issue causing His disciples to despair. The loss of their hope stemmed from their uncertainty as to whether Jesus was who He said He was. Jesus helped them see that the Scriptures had already laid out that God was entirely in control, that everything was on schedule, and that their hope had been correctly placed in Him.

When we see the bigger picture, our hearts also burn within us, our hope is restored, and we naturally become ambassadors for the message of the hope of Christ. We are still called to share that same message of hope and reconciliation with others today. Doing this well requires that we invest time into studying the Old Testament. As Jesus established, it serves as a uniquely powerful credentialing tool underscoring the trustworthiness of God, demonstrating the superiority of His intellect, actions, and faithfulness.

At the end of this story, Jesus returned and revealed Himself to the disciples and shared a meal with them. We know that He returned to the same message, sharing it with more of the disciples and expanding upon it further. It is, after all, a message worthy of repeating. He wrapped this up with their call to the new Ambassadorship and a promise of the coming helper, the Holy Spirit, and a directive to wait in Jerusalem until that promise was fulfilled.

Luke 24:44-49, ESV

Then he said to them, "These are my words that I spoke to you while I was still with you, that everything written about me in the Law of Moses and the Prophets and the Psalms must be fulfilled." Then he opened their minds to understand the Scriptures, and said to them, "Thus it is written, that the Christ should suffer and on the third day rise from the dead, and that repentance for the forgiveness of sins should be proclaimed in his name to all nations, beginning from Jerusalem. You are witnesses of these things. And behold, I am sending the promise of my Father upon you. But stay in the city until you are clothed with power from on high."

When the power of the Holy Spirit arrived, an amazing new era began. The disciples were under pressure, but their results were inspired. They passionately shared what they had seen and heard, and their message changed the world.

"I know the resurrection is a fact, and Watergate proved it to me. How? Because 12 men testified they had seen Jesus raised from the dead, then they proclaimed that truth for 40 years, never once denying it. Every one was beaten, tortured, stoned and put in prison. They would not have endured that if it weren't

true. Watergate embroiled 12 of the most powerful men in the world-and they couldn't keep a lie for three weeks. You're telling me 12 apostles could keep a lie for 40 years? Absolutely impossible."

—Charles Colson

8

The Way the Disciples Taught

PAUL USED HIS extensive knowledge of the Old Testament to reveal the Mystery of the Gospel to others as proof to convince learned Jews, curious seekers, and total skeptics alike. Paul used Old Testament prophecies to authenticate the supernatural uniqueness and reliability of Jesus' (and thereby Paul's) message of hope.

While we could examine the teachings of the other disciples at length and find similar patterns, we will spend most of our time looking at the way Paul taught. The significant number of examples in the book of Acts and Paul's numerous letters to the churches give us solid context. Paul was the most prolific direct and indirect contributor to the New Testament. Paul's direct contributions were through his various letters (i.e., the Epistles) to the churches, such as in the books of Romans, Ephesians, Philippians, etc. Luke also recorded Paul's conversion and mission trips for us in the book of Acts.

1 Corinthians 4:1-2, ESV
This is how one should regard us, as servants of Christ and stewards of the mysteries of God. Moreover, it is required of stewards that they be found faithful.

Before we get started on the specifics of how Paul taught, it is worth spending a minute considering or reconsidering the depth Paul could deliver on this topic. As a young child, Saul, who would later become known to us as Paul, would have had to study the Scriptures at a level few of us can imagine. We know this not only because he was a practicing Jew whose parents were willing to invest in him becoming a Pharisee but also because he gives us specific insights into his training. For instance, Paul tells us that he studied at the feet of Gamaliel.

> *Acts 21: 1-3, ESV*
>
> *"Brothers and fathers, hear the defense that I now make before you."*
>
> *And when they heard that he was addressing them in the Hebrew language, they became even more quiet. And he said:*
>
> *"I am a Jew, born in Tarsus in Cilicia, but brought up in this city, educated at the feet of Gamaliel according to the strict manner of the law of our fathers, being zealous for God as all of you are this day.*

Earlier in Acts, we see Gamaliel as a member of the Council of the Sanhedrin when Peter and John were brought before them on the charge of preaching the name and message of Jesus Christ.

> *Acts 5:27-42, ESV*
>
> *And when they had brought them, they set them before the council. And the high priest questioned them, saying, "We strictly charged you not to teach in this name, yet here you have filled Jerusalem with your teaching, and you intend to bring this man's blood upon us." But Peter and the apostles answered, "We must obey God rather than men. The God of our fathers raised Jesus, whom you killed by hanging him on a tree. God exalted him at his right*

hand as Leader and Savior, to give repentance to Israel and forgiveness of sins. And we are witnesses to these things, and so is the Holy Spirit, whom God has given to those who obey him."

When they heard this, they were enraged and wanted to kill them. But a Pharisee in the council named Gamaliel, a teacher of the law held in honor by all the people, stood up and gave orders to put the men outside for a little while. And he said to them, "Men of Israel, take care what you are about to do with these men. For before these days Theudas rose up, claiming to be somebody, and a number of men, about four hundred, joined him. He was killed, and all who followed him were dispersed and came to nothing. After him Judas the Galilean rose up in the days of the census and drew away some of the people after him. He too perished, and all who followed him were scattered. So in the present case I tell you, keep away from these men and let them alone, for if this plan or this undertaking is of man, it will fail; but if it is of God, you will not be able to overthrow them. You might even be found opposing God!" So, they took his advice, and when they had called in the apostles, they beat them and charged them not to speak in the name of Jesus and let them go. Then they left the presence of the council, rejoicing that they were counted worthy to suffer dishonor for the name. And every day, in the temple and from house to house, they did not cease teaching and preaching that the Christ is Jesus.

We know from extra-biblical writings that Gamaliel was much more than a politically connected figure. He also ran the school of Hillel. The school of Hillel, initially founded by

Gamaliel's grandfather, was an expensive boarding school that boys would enter when they were twelve years old. In modern times, Harvard has often been held in high regard by parents who hope their children will become well-connected leaders in the business world. In their minds, this justifies Harvard's extraordinary tuition. In Paul's day, the school of Hillel held out the same promise for generating the future leaders of religious governance. And likewise, the tuition would've been extraordinary there as well.

Entry into the school of Hillel was reserved for only those students who could recite the first five books of the Bible, which was then referred to as the Torah. These are the books commonly agreed to have been written by Moses. But reciting these first five books from memory was not the only requirement. The recitation needed to be completely error free. This not only required massive amounts of work and dedication but a significant intellect capable of completing the task in the first place. While a ten- or eleven-year-old boy contemporary to that time may have benefited from a lack of TV, video games, or handheld screens, it should still not be assumed that the average child could have accomplished all of this. Yet, this was still not enough to get in.

The waiting list for the school of Hillel was quite long. Leveraged relationships were often required to gain access while the unconnected remained on the waiting list.

We can ascertain from the things we know about Paul: he was extraordinarily bright and capable of remembering significant amounts of information without error. His parents sent him to the best school money could buy, and they sent him from very far away. We also know that Paul's parents were politically connected. It would typically take a well-connected referral from a well-regarded Jewish leader or Rabbi to push one from the waiting list to the classroom. We also know that Paul undertook one of the hardest curricula a child could engage in, focused on what we now call the Old Testament. Finally, we know that Paul was intrinsically motivated to be an authority on the Scriptures, or he would not have made it through this superior schooling.

We know from Paul's writings that he came from Tarsus. We know that after he was converted to Christianity and rejected by the Jews, he returned to Tarsus after a period of exile in Arabia. That region is where Barnabas later found Paul when they drafted him to come and help with the massively growing church then developing in Antioch. This tells us that Paul's family was able to send him a great distance and leverage connections across that same distance when these areas were many days apart, even by the fastest means of travel available at the time.

We will quickly explore how Paul would rely upon three specific assets to help him communicate the Mystery of the Gospel.

1) His extensive knowledge gained through his training.
2) Direct revelation (which we can see both in the story of his conversion in the early part of Acts and also as he relays it during his defense in Acts 21).
3) The illumination and inspiration of the Holy Spirit.

As we examine the way that Paul taught, we will see that each of these aspects will provide specific empowerment for Paul's message and will reinforce an important point regarding how God also interacts with us today:

1) Primarily, God uses our life experience and training (even gained before serving Him).

2) God reveals greater truth to us as we are ready to accept it.

3) After appointing us as God's ambassadors on earth, the Holy Spirit gives us insight on how and when to communicate to the people we are called to serve.

To the Jews

Paul taught from the Old Testament that Christ had fulfilled all the requirements of the law and the prophetic writings previously believed to have been about the mysterious suffering servant. By fulfilling the call of "the suffering servant," Christ completely fulfilled the righteous and just but previously unsatisfied requirements of the sacrificial system and Abraham's prophetic promise to his son that "God would provide the sacrifice." Once Paul had used "the light of Christianity" to reveal this previously hidden information, he could now show that Christ had fulfilled God's requirement for justice, providing a means to offer salvation to all who would receive the gift. With this foundation laid, Paul could expound upon Christ's two-part mission and how His second coming would fulfill the remaining messianic prophecies.

As Paul traveled on his missionary journeys, we can see passages that show he would start at the temple in each town he visited.

Acts 14:1, ESV
Now at Iconium they entered together into the Jewish synagogue and spoke in such a way that a great number of both Jews and Greeks believed.

Paul made it clear that his love for the Jews was deep. In fact, it was deep enough that he stated in Romans 9 that he would exchange his standing with God if it allowed the Jews to come to the knowledge of truth. Jesus said He came to share the Gospel's message "first to the Jews and then to the Gentiles." Paul practiced the same order as he advanced the Gospel into the Gentile world. In some towns, he would find many open hearts willing to believe. He would find skeptics, scoffers, and sometimes vicious attacks in others. Paul would not abandon his efforts with the Jewish people in any given place until he had made what he felt was every reasonable effort to bring them the good news.

Romans 9:1-3 ESV
I am speaking the truth in Christ—I am not lying; my conscience bears me witness in the Holy Spirit—that I have great sorrow and unceasing anguish in my heart. For I could wish that I myself were accursed and cut off from Christ for the sake of my brothers, my kinsmen according to the flesh.

To understand how Paul would approach the Jews, awareness of one of the rituals of the larger Jewish traditions is essential. If you were in one synagogue reading the first part of the scroll of Isaiah on one Sabbath and then traveled to another synagogue prior to the next Sabbath, you could count on both synagogues continuing with the very next section of text in the scroll of Isaiah. This consistency assured traveling Jews were taught the Scriptures sequentially. It was considered of the utmost importance that Jews, whether literate or not, could hear the Scriptures read aloud, in order, and expounded upon by the rabbi. This tradition would assure that the Jews, and the believing Greeks, who regularly attended a synagogue, would be generally aware of the same Scriptures and theological concepts as the Jews of another region. Paul could count on this foundation when he began to make his case.

Acts 17:1-4, ESV

Now when they had passed through Amphipolis and Apollonia, they came to Thessalonica, where there was a synagogue of the Jews. And Paul went in, as was his custom, and on three Sabbath days he reasoned with them from the Scriptures, explaining and proving that it was necessary for the Christ to suffer and to rise from the dead, and saying, "This Jesus, whom I proclaim to you, is the Christ." And some of them were persuaded and joined Paul and Silas, as did a great many of the devout Greeks and not a few of the leading women.

As a traveling rabbi of the school of Hillel and thereby a man of notoriety, Paul would have often been welcomed to come and offer the weekly teaching or to speak when he arrived.

Acts 13:14-16, ESV

But they went on from Perga and came to Antioch in Pisidia. And on the Sabbath day they went into the synagogue and sat down. After the reading from the Law and the Prophets, the rulers of the synagogue sent a message to them, saying, "Brothers, if you have any word of encouragement for the people, say it." So Paul stood up, and motioning with his hand said:

"Men of Israel and you who fear God, listen."

He would typically move into showing how the passages he read in some way foreshadowed the coming of the Messiah, whom he intended to reveal to them was Jesus. As we can see from the selection above, Paul would teach authoritatively, but it would elicit multiple reactions. Some would be intrigued and want to hear more. Some would come to belief, and some would grit their teeth and argue until they were either in recognition of their defeat or so frustrated as to demand Paul not be allowed to return.

> *Romans 10:1-3, ESV*
>
> *Brothers, my heart's desire and prayer to God for them is that they may be saved. For I bear them witness that they have a zeal for God, but not according to knowledge. For, being ignorant of the righteousness of God, and seeking to establish their own, they did not submit to God's righteousness. For Christ is the end of the law for righteousness to everyone who believes.*

Paul would use his extensive knowledge of the Old Testament Scriptures to argue persuasively. His intention was not to argue for the sake of arguing but to argue for the sake of helping his fellow Jews see the truth. Paul did not apologize for what might offend his audience. Instead, he would layer on top of what they already knew well (the prophetic writings) the things they had previously never seen (i.e., how Christ fulfilled those writings). The Bereans are noted by Luke (the author of the book of Acts) as being noble because they were moved by what Paul taught them but quickly reverted to the Scriptures to verify those things before accepting them. We know that Paul had taught well as these critical skeptics returned with the verdict that Paul had taught them a greater truth. He had revealed to them what they could not previously see in the text by showing them those same passages in the light of Christ.

While not all Jews were well educated, most Jews were indeed profoundly familiar with the tenets of their faith as their culture and religion were one. Paul would not be able to win these Jews over with foolish arguments or clever devices. He would need to offer them specifics and enough solid examples to at least create a circumstantial case worthy of further consideration. By circumstantial case, we mean the modern legal definition. We may not be able to convict someone of murder simply by showing they had a means, motive, and opportunity. Still, we may be able to convict them if we can show they had all those things and a credible body of witnesses willing to testify that the individual also demonstrated intent. Similarly, Paul may not have been able to make the case by showing each of these groups some individual miraculous sign. Still, the overwhelming weight of so many fulfilled prophecies could be weighed together to make that circumstantial case.

Paul would make his case by reviewing the specifics of passages we have already covered in Chapter 3. By showing these remarkable things, passage after passage, that referred to the specifics that Jesus had already fulfilled, Paul would raise the eyebrows of the willing skeptics. As he began to reveal the types, shadows, and stories that clearly pointed to Christ, he would move the willing heart with the aid of the Holy Spirit. Paul was demonstrating a grander picture. God had now fully revealed His faithful character and love for mankind while putting the true evil nature of His enemy on full display for all to see. Many would come to understand.

Paul repeated this pattern in every town he went to because of his great love for the Jews. He rejoiced when they came to the knowledge of the truth, and we see that many who were once skeptics in his audience became his loyal friends and coworkers.

In summary, Paul's teaching to the Jews relied upon their knowledge of the Scripture to either persuade them to repentance and acceptance of Christ for their atonement with God or to reject the message so that he could move on, knowing he had done his best.

To the Gentiles

Paul used similar tactics with the Gentiles. After he had studied their cultures enough to determine how to speak to them in ways they could understand, he would use that foundation to build a bridge to General Revelation. That is the concept that God's invisible qualities can be plainly seen in all creation. This would serve as a starting point for the question, "But can this God I claim to bring to you prove that He is unique?"

Paul shows us the need for personal and culturally aware relationships with our would-be converts and the power of gaining enough insight to find and answer the gaps in their inferior systems of belief.

We can see from the example of Paul in Athens that his ability and willingness to examine and engage the culture made him more effective at reaching the Gentiles. By engaging them at a level and through topics they could relate to, he could engage them in a dialogue that would allow them to get to the first step of recognizing the one true God, which is accepting the obviousness of General Revelation.

General Revelation is well defined by Paul in Romans 1:

Romans 1:20-23, NIV

For since the creation of the world God's invisible qualities—his eternal power and divine nature—have been clearly seen, being understood from what has been made, so that people are without excuse.

This passage offers a definition that is about as clear as you can get. The Scripture articulates God's position that people who fail to see that God must exist are without excuse for that erroneous conclusion. The reason for God's position on this issue is stated in the same verse. Since the world's creation, God's power and nature can be clearly seen in all He has made. I recently heard a preacher articulate this in a way that I found quite useful. God communicates the following message to His skeptic through this passage: "I know… That you know… That I am real." God is stating that His existence and power are apparent and that even if we can convince others around us that God is not real, we still know deep in our hearts that He is.

John Lennox, the well-trained philosopher, and apologist was going to debate Richard Dawkins, the famous atheist, and denouncer of God. Dr. Lennox shared that he was contacted by a newspaper reporter who said, "We are covering the debate and would like to have a quote from you about it." As an example, the reporter shared that Mr. Dawkins, explaining his general thesis for the upcoming debate, said, "Christianity is a fairy tale for those who are afraid of the dark." The reporter asked Lennox if he couldn't also summarize his position in a similar short quip. Dr. Lennox said he wasn't completely comfortable summarizing his position that way. Still, as an example of how most arguments against the existence of God can be easily turned on their heads, he provided the following, "Atheism is a fairy tale for those who are afraid of the light."

Lennox's simple quip echoes God's statement: I know... that you know... that I am real.

Paul would leverage this concept of General Revelation, available to all men, to sober the soul into realizing, "this is a moment of truth." This realization alone did not mean that Paul would have the ultimate truth, but it at least engaged the higher intellect necessary to process that possibility as he continued. Paul was not just some foreigner, unfamiliar with their ways and unwilling to contemplate what they believed before speaking about what he believed. He was not claiming superior information without knowledge of their practices, as that would've simply come across as arrogant. Again, consider the culturally relevant way Paul engaged his gentile audience in Athens before directly confronting their beliefs.

Acts 17:16-34
Paul in Athens

Now while Paul was waiting for them at Athens, his spirit was provoked within him as he saw that the city was full of idols. So he reasoned in the synagogue with the Jews and the devout persons, and in the marketplace every day with those who happened to be there. Some of the Epicurean and Stoic philosophers also conversed with him. And some said, "What does this babbler wish to say?" Others said, "He seems to be a preacher of foreign divinities"—because he was preaching Jesus and the resurrection. And they took him and brought him to the Areopagus, saying, "May we know what this new teaching is that you are presenting? For you bring some strange things to our ears. We wish to know therefore what these things mean." Now all the Athenians and the foreigners who lived there would spend their time in nothing except telling or hearing something new.

Paul Addresses the Areopagus

So Paul, standing in the midst of the Areopagus, said: "Men of Athens, I perceive that in every way you are very religious. For as I passed along and observed the objects of your worship, I found also an altar with this inscription: 'To the unknown god.' What therefore you worship as unknown, this I proclaim to you. The God who made the world and everything in it, being Lord of heaven and earth, does not live in temples made by man, nor is he served by human hands, as though he needed anything, since he himself gives to all mankind life and breath and everything. And he made from one man every nation of mankind to live on all the face of the earth, having determined allotted periods and the boundaries of their dwelling place, that they should seek God, and perhaps feel their way toward him and find him. Yet he is actually not far from each one of us, for

> *"'In him we live and move and have our being';*
> *as even some of your own poets have said,*
> *"'For we are indeed his offspring.'*

Being then God's offspring, we ought not to think that the divine being is like gold or silver or stone, an image formed by the art and imagination of man. The times of ignorance God overlooked, but now he commands all people everywhere to repent, because he has fixed a day on which he will judge the world in righteousness by a man

whom he has appointed; and of this he has given assur-
ance to all by raising him from the dead."

Now when they heard of the resurrection of the dead,
some mocked. But others said, "We will hear you again
about this." So Paul went out from their midst. But some
men joined him and believed, among whom also were
Dionysius the Areopagite and a woman named Damaris
and others with them.

In verse 16, we see the word "provoked," which is worth contemplating. In the book of Ephesians, Paul articulates the difference between righteous anger and unrighteous anger. In one passage, he says, "Be angry, but do not sin." Suffice it to say that the summary is this: being angry about what has been done to you, inconvenienced you, or not met your expectations does not rise to the level of righteous anger. Righteous anger is that anger exercised at the injustice done to another. I believe that Paul was provoked in this instance because he was angry at seeing fellow human beings so deceived that they had come to think that something they had fashioned with their own hands could become Lord over them. It is the same anger that was experienced by Christian missionaries when they discovered the ritual of the funeral pyre in Hindu culture. If a man died and his wife was still alive, she was to be burned alive above him when his body was burned. Imagine the righteous anger they felt when they realized the extreme torture and agony experienced by an innocent person simply because of the cultural power of a false belief.

God instilled this passion within Paul and directed it toward the Gentiles. He loved them. He served them. He taught them, and he fought for them. Paul truly understood the message of grace and how imperative it was as a component of effective evangelism toward those without a prior relationship with God. Having not been called apart, as the Jews had been, many of the Gentiles had no former knowledge of God at all. God did not require that they become Jewish and then followers of Christ. The New Testament certainly tells us that He expected the Gentiles to honor the fact that they had been grafted into the Jewish tree, but that's not the same thing as requiring them to get circumcised and follow the laws of the Old Testament.

The city of Antioch was the site of an early outbreak of Christianity during the period covered by the book of Acts. This was the city where Barnabas had brought Paul so that they could help serve as leaders discipling this rapidly growing young Christian body. It was here, at this time, that the question of whether or not these new Gentile believers would need to live like Jews in order to become Christians would quickly come to a head. As the Church in Antioch grew, Peter had also come to spend time with them. Prior to the arrival of some that Paul described as being "from the party of James," Peter was enjoying non-Jewish delicacies and customs along with the locals.

We must remember that the early apostles, and Paul, were still wrestling with the inclusion of the Gentiles into an essentially Jewish tradition. While I will not cover the entire story here, we can see from the story of the Jerusalem Council, found in Acts 15, and the additional perspective that Paul provides about that story in Galatians 2:11-14 that Peter and others feared those who came from Jerusalem. We can roughly infer from what Paul tells us that Peter did the equivalent of spitting out whatever it was that they were not supposed to be eating (according to Jewish law) before running over to help point fingers at "those law-breaking Gentiles." Paul tells us that this fear got so bad that "even Barnabas" was drawn into the fray. Barnabas had already been on one missionary journey with Paul and heard him passionately and effectively teach the message of grace. However, he was now being led away from Paul's deep commitment to preserving the freedom that these new believers had received through grace.

Paul ultimately stood alone against the rest of the apostles. It was decided in Antioch that Peter and Paul and the others should travel together back to Jerusalem to argue their case before the Jerusalem Council. Their purpose was to determine whether the Gentiles could live within the grace that Paul was teaching them and be considered faithful followers of the Jewish messiah. The Holy Spirit ultimately softened Peter's heart on this issue, and he switched sides at the last minute, defending Paul's claim for grace. Remember that Peter was also known to the Jews in Jerusalem as Simeon.

Acts 15:13-18, ESV

After they finished speaking, James replied, "Brothers, listen to me. Simeon has related how God first visited the Gentiles, to take from them a people for his name. And with this the words of the prophets agree, just as it is written,

"'After this I will return,
and I will rebuild the tent of David that has fallen;
I will rebuild its ruins,
and I will restore it,
that the remnant of mankind may seek the Lord,
and all the Gentiles who are called by my name,
says the Lord, who makes these things known from of old.'

We can also see from the passage above that Peter's thoughtful change of heart moved James. James was the head of the church at this point, and he now joined Peter in this new position of fully embracing both the Gentiles and this profound message of grace and freedom that Paul was teaching them. It was neither Paul's effective words nor his cantankerous willingness to defend the message of grace, even if he had to stand alone, that persuaded others. It was the work that God had already done, gently teaching the apostles that He was serious about the expansion of the Good News and the offering of the Holy Spirit into the communities of the Samaritans and the Gentiles. The thesis verse of Acts is Acts 1:8, where Jesus said, "I will send you into Jerusalem, Judea, Samaria, and to the ends of the earth." The rest of the book is simply an account of the unfolding of that plan.

Paul knew how important it was to win the hearts and minds of the Gentiles, and as we see from our brief survey in this section, he did that by meeting them where they were and helping them connect general revelation to the truth of God. Once their hearts were opened, Paul led the Gentiles to see that God was not an unknowable entity but rather a personal God who was now inviting them to reconcile with Him. Paul wrapped that message in grace and freedom, empowering the Gentiles to respond out of love for God instead of fear.

If we follow Paul's pattern for introducing the Gospel, not all will accept what we offer. We can see from the book of Acts and Paul's letters that the same results were also typical for him. Yet we are called to share the same message of grace, and the hearer is called to respond. We cannot control or force them into accepting. We can only present the Good News and trust the Holy Spirit to do the rest.

As Paul said, one plants a seed and another waters, but it is the Holy Spirit who brings the growth.

The Style

Paul's teaching style was relevant, provoking, and unapologetically complete.

Acts 20:26-27, ESV
Therefore I testify to you this day that I am innocent of the blood of all, for I did not shrink from declaring to you the whole counsel of God.

When Paul was departing Ephesus for the last time, he told the Elders there that he believed he would never see them again. He was correct in that he would soon be jailed and make his way to Rome over many years, where he would ultimately be executed for his message and faith. In that final discussion, we have this sentence recorded above. Paul uses an interesting phrase in many of his writings, declaring that he taught "the whole counsel of God." While this could be interpreted in various ways, the most apparent meaning is often the right one. In other words, Paul said, I didn't just teach you about the things you wanted to hear; I taught you everything God wanted you to hear. But how could one make such a claim?

The answer is simple: Paul taught his disciples the entire Old Testament and how it all related to God's plan and pointed to God's Messiah. Paul followed the Jewish tradition of teaching passage by passage. Again, as we have discussed throughout this entire book, Paul would've been able to review these Old Testament passages "in the light of Christianity." We see many passages where it says that Paul "reasoned with the Jews week after week from the Scriptures" [para]. This demonstrates that Paul was teaching the newly revealed Gospel message that could now be clearly seen across the entire Old Testament.

We are not suggesting that Paul's introductory teaching for new believers would start with Genesis 1 and work its way through the entire body of Scripture. Instead, this is to suggest that when he would disciple people, he would take the time to go passage by passage with them until they could see how they were all woven together, forming a complete picture of the predicted and now risen Christ. With this knowledge in hand, his disciples were not only qualified to serve but also to teach. Remember, this passage records Paul speaking to the Elders at Ephesus, whom he had personally discipled. Paul's letters to Timothy and Titus argue that Elders should be able to teach, even being ready to "refute false doctrine" on the spot.

In short, Paul's style was scripturally based, methodical, and thorough. He did not avoid challenging topics. He did not avoid controversial issues. He did not dwell endlessly on his favorite subjects either. If God repeated something three times, so would Paul.

This is often missed in many modern churches. There is no specific rule against a preacher doing a five- or seven-part series on marriage, finances, or whatever else he feels his flock needs. However, there is inherent harm when long-term church attendees have never gained a foundational knowledge of the beauty, sophistication, and powerfully intricate credentialing work of the full counsel of God. Many churches I have visited will find a way to weave the things they find most important into every Sunday's message. This could lead the disciples in that church to believe that God cares most about that particular topic. For some churches, it may be tithing. For others, it may be speaking in tongues - with some vehemently against, and others teaching that it is required to prove that you have been saved. For another, it may be how the members of the church must keep themselves separate from the world, despite that being against the directives we are given in the New Testament. If these things are taught every week from the pulpit and not wrapped in the full counsel of God, they can end up displacing God's priorities at a high cost.

In Chapter 9: The Way That We should Teach, we will discuss this in more depth, but for now, suffice it to say that if God wants to repeat or emphasize something, we should do that as well when discipling others. If God only wants to mention something once in a great while, we should likewise feel comfortable following His lead. After all, God made us and knows us better than we know ourselves. He knows far better than us what matters to Him, to us, and to the watching world around us. Paul's teaching style emulated God's teaching style by simply sharing "the full counsel of God."

The Depth

A story in Acts tells us of a man falling out of a window when Paul had been teaching all day. That and a reference to his work at the School of Tyrannus show us that Paul spoke for many hours at a time, taking issues in depth. His new disciples were going to get equipped in short order. He wasn't settling for less.

Acts 20:7-12, ESV
Eutychus Raised from the Dead
   On the first day of the week, when we were gathered together to break bread, Paul talked with them, intending to depart on the next day, and he prolonged his speech

until midnight. There were many lamps in the upper
room where we were gathered. And a young man named
Eutychus, sitting at the window, sank into a deep sleep as
Paul talked still longer. And being overcome by sleep, he
fell down from the third story and was taken up dead. But
Paul went down and bent over him, and taking him in his
arms, said, "Do not be alarmed, for his life is in him." And
when Paul had gone up and had broken bread and eaten,
he conversed with them a long while, until daybreak, and
so departed. And they took the youth away alive and were
not a little comforted.

As we examine this Scripture, we have to ask ourselves,
could this potentially be the birthplace of the phrase "bored
him to death"? Respectfully, we can see a remarkable thing in
this passage: the depth with which Paul taught and the time he
invested. Paul was a busy man who accomplished much in his
life and often worked by day as a tentmaker while preaching at
night and on the weekends. Yet it was not out of character for
Paul to have dinner with a group of people and then teach them
for hours. It may have been another five, six, perhaps even seven
hours before this young man fell out of the window. In addition
to the reference to "until midnight," we see that Eutychus "sank
into a deep sleep as Paul talked *still longer.*" How late into the
morning had they gone? We don't know. We only know that
everyone was alarmed when Eutychus fell to his death and that
after his miraculous healing, Paul "conversed with them a long
while, until daybreak."

In the previous chapter of Acts, we also see reference to
Paul's teaching, in the same town, at the school of Tyrannus.

This would have been a public-school house, perhaps requiring facility rental.

Acts 19:8-10

And he entered the synagogue and for three months spoke boldly, reasoning and persuading them about the kingdom of God. But when some became stubborn and continued in unbelief, speaking evil of the Way before the congregation, he withdrew from them and took the disciples with him, reasoning daily in the hall of Tyrannus. This continued for two years, so that all the residents of Asia heard the word of the Lord, both Jews and Greeks.

We can quickly ascertain a few important points from this passage. First, we see a reminder that Paul had first spent time in the synagogue, surely harvesting new disciples from among the Jews and believing Greeks. When things began to turn badly there, he did not despair nor give up. Rather, he simply moved to another venue and continued discipling those who were willing. We can also see his level of commitment and the depth of teaching again in that Paul was reasoning with them "daily in the hall of Tyrannus." This also gives us insight into the length of time Paul invested in these future leaders of Ephesus and those he was going to send out from there to the surrounding region. The passage tells us, "this continued for two years."

We can see other scriptural references to Paul's expectation that just a few years was sufficient time for someone to go from being a new convert to being able to teach. He wrote to the Corinthians just a few years after being with them that "many of you still require milk," referring to their level of spiritual maturity and learning. James also supports this concept, writing in his letter that "many of you should be teachers by now" [para]. Can you imagine the panic that would ensue if you walked into many churches today and told the pastor that you would like people who came to Christ three years ago to take over and preach for him this Sunday?

The depth with which Paul taught was intended to help promote new believers into qualified Christian workers. Paul was not satisfied with simply getting a conversion decision out of someone who feared Hell or desired heaven. He knew that state of mind alone was insufficient, as Jesus' parable of the seeds shows us. Instead, he wanted to teach them how to have a fulfilled Christian life, where one understands who God is and can effectively fulfill their role as ambassador of reconciliation. Paul wanted them to be able to explain the nature of the one true God to those around them. This level of readiness to "give an answer for the hope that is within us" is still exactly what we are called to today. If we can find a way to return to that state, we would likely also find ourselves in the position where many—if not most—new believers would be able to stand up and effectively teach directly from God's Word within just two to three years. Lord, may that be so once again!

9

The Way That We Should Teach

Matthew 28:16-20, ESV
The Great Commission

  Now the eleven disciples went to Galilee, to the mountain to which Jesus had directed them. And when they saw him they worshiped him, but some doubted. And Jesus came and said to them, "All authority in heaven and on earth has been given to me. Go therefore and make disciples of all nations, baptizing them in the name of the Father and of the Son and of the Holy Spirit, teaching them to observe all that I have commanded you. And behold, I am with you always, to the end of the age."

BUT WHOM DID Christ commission? And what is the role of a disciple, once "made"? Paul would tell us that we are all called to serve as Ambassadors of Christ, as Ambassadors of the message of reconciliation. So, while not all are called to teach or preach in large settings, we are all called to share the Gospel's message and make disciples. Adam Clarke, a well-regarded but sometimes controversial theologian, seemed to understand the gravity of the situation when he wrote:

"Every scribe—Minister of Christ: who is instructed—taught of God; in the kingdom of heaven—in the mysteries of the Gospel of Christ: out of his treasury... A small degree of knowledge is not sufficient for a preacher of the Gospel. The sacred writings should be his treasure, and he should properly understand them. His knowledge does not consist in being furnished with a great variety of human learning, (though of this he should acquire as much as he can); but his knowledge consists in being well instructed in the things concerning the kingdom of heaven, and the art of conducting men thither. Again, it is not enough for a man to have these advantages in possession: he must bring them forth, and distribute them abroad. A good pastor will not, like a miser, keep these things to himself to please his fancy; nor, like a merchant, traffic with them, to enrich himself; but, like a bountiful father or householder, distribute them with a liberal though judicious hand, for the comfort and support of the whole heavenly family."

If new believers read that statement today, they might think themselves unqualified to share the Gospel. But there is a difference between being a teacher or preacher and being an ambassador to our neighbors. While I wholeheartedly agree with Clarke's statement, we must understand to whom it applies. It is also important that we understand how it can be applied incrementally. Theological expertise is not required for one to convince their friend or neighbor that they wholeheartedly believe what they are sharing. Consider someone convinced a new medication works. Do they need to be able to explain its molecular formula to convince a neighbor it has helped them?

The confident faith of a new believer alone may be enough to cause that friend or neighbor to want to inquire further, especially if, as advised by Peter, we live in such a way that our good deeds glorify God. But all of us, as Christians, should aspire to develop our knowledge of God to the point where we can personally disciple others. The purpose of a disciple (one who has been through the discipline of learning and submitting to the basic tenets of Christianity) is for that person to become a qualified Christian worker. A Christian worker is one who can do work in the name of Christ without causing undue scorn to the name of Christ. This requires that we have been at least sufficiently educated in the principles of Christ so as to understand what He would want us to do and how He would want us to do it in given situations.

Mentoring like it matters

Discipleship is not a process that happens overnight. However, it should also not take a lifetime. For those of us fortunate enough to have encountered Christ early in life, or perhaps when we've still got ten years left, why waste the remaining time being spiritually immature, ineffective, and unable to "disciple others"? Both James and Paul show us that there was an expectation on the part of the Apostles that "many of you should be teachers by now," or "many of you should be on to solid food, but you still need spiritual milk." This suggests, especially since we believe that Paul's writing on this topic can be dated to just a few years after he had been in Corinth to start that church, that the apostles believed this maturing of Christians was something that could happen within just a few years.

Having Christians mature, as the Apostles expected, would require a level of time commitment we are not familiar with in today's church experience. However, lest we think this to be impossible within the time pressures of modern life, let us assure you that there are examples of this working effectively today. What if new converts spent just a few hours a week with more mature Christians, studying the Bible together? Would that allow someone to gain a more excellent knowledge of the Scriptures in a shorter time? What if that "more mature Christian" also spent a few hours a week with an even more knowledgeable believer? And, what if all three of them could join together every week to listen to someone who God had clearly called to be a teacher or preacher, and that teacher or preacher were committed to opening, expounding, and meaningfully applying the same Scriptures?

All of this may sound very daunting. In fact, it would sound daunting to each of the folks in my example. To the new disciple, this might sound like a significant time commitment, but is it? What if the church they attended taught directly out of the Word of God, explaining it to the point where the average new believer could leave feeling like they fully understood that portion of Scripture? If I were then able to meet with someone more mature than I, asking them questions I might have about that teaching and how to apply it to my life, wouldn't that be effective reinforcement?

To that "more mature" believer, this might also sound daunting. "I'm going to meet with a new believer who has questions!" Let's say you've only been a Christian for a few years. Would you feel qualified to answer these questions? However, what if you met with an elder the day before to review the same passage in depth? You may not be an expert on the entire Bible. However, because you have now had a meaningful conversation with someone who explained why others might be confused about parts of this text, you can now feel confident in your knowledge of *this* passage. Perhaps they've demonstrated the logical arguments developed by learned theologians and how to explain this to the average person. Wouldn't you feel a bit more prepared for this Q&A with your new believer?

We have only asked the new believer for a few hours a week; regular church attendance, which most new believers are comfortable with, and a weekly meeting with someone to discuss what they have just learned, which most new believers also find quite helpful.

For the "more mature" believer, we have only asked for about an hour more. In their case, we have asked for regular church attendance, their weekly meeting with their assigned new believer, and a weekly meeting with an elder (or a team of spiritual workers within the church) to prepare for that time.

For the elder, we have only asked for a few hours. Regular church attendance is just a natural part of life in their role, and perhaps an hour or two a week to support those spiritual workers who want to make sure they are well prepared to serve the body of Christ.

The pastor may be meeting with a handful of elders, helping them reinforce the deepest and most important meanings of the passages they are working through. The pastor may spend an hour or two researching common arguments against the truth in those passages and how to respond to them, sharing those findings with the elders.

Everyone in this flow we have described is being blessed. The pastor is now following the Scriptures and "equipping the saints for the work of ministry." No longer is there a line waiting at their door with everyone who has a question about anything. No longer do these pastors despair at seats full of people with little understanding or commitment to the Gospel. Pastors are called to teach and preach. And now, they are doing that again while equipping the saints to disciple.

The elder may be called upon to teach, and by biblical definition, they should be ready for that. And instead of being overwhelmed with the work of the church, they now find themselves in a growing abundance of people who would meet the qualification of a deacon (a word that comes from the Greek word Diakonia, meaning servant or table waiter). The Bible tells us that deacons need to be qualified in ways that are very similar to the elders. The primary difference is that the elders must be able to teach and refute false doctrine. This is not required for deacons, who serve the body in more practical ways.

The deacons, or in my example, "the more mature believers" (and a formal appointment in this role is not always required), have the extraordinary opportunity to see themselves being used by God as they disciple new believers. And, as they succeed, they add to the number of qualified Christian workers helping to lighten their own load.

Everyone in this mix grows in their knowledge of God's Word at an accelerated pace, especially those who recognize the responsibility of learning for the benefit of others. After all, this leverages human nature. We all like to be needed. Most of us will find ourselves more motivated to study a passage again when we know we will soon meet someone who will have questions for us about it.

Results over appearances

The idea of a healthy cascading movement of organic discipleship is not some impractical Utopian fairy tale. I once shared thoughts with a friend about how disciple-making should be done. She asked, "But do you think this can really happen here today?" My answer is the same now as it was that day. "Yes!" In fact, I have already seen it work.

The example I'm about to give, briefly covered in Chapter 2, is not the only example, but it is undoubtedly the most striking I have seen in North America. That church in Columbus, Ohio, is now called "Dwell" but was formerly called "Xenos Christian Fellowship." That church is the one started by the author of the essay upon which this book is based.

I was struggling with doubts regarding their substantial claims of effective discipleship. I was skeptical of the idea that so many with no prior relationship to Christ were being deeply discipled and transformed into capable workers, especially in so little time "here today." I traveled out to visit the church and find out for myself, and as I mentioned previously, my friend and pastor at that time went along. I could fill an entire book with the things we learned on that trip, but I will point out a few salient examples.

We spent three days at Xenos shadowing people involved in numerous ministries throughout the church. One of the most striking things I remember experiencing was this: a young man about twenty years old leading a Bible study on a chapter within Philippians. The dissonance for me in processing this experience came from my own bias. This young man was explaining profound truths that I could not refute, and his teaching was a blessing to me, yet he was dropping "F-bombs" as he taught. He had only been a Christian for six months, and a lifetime of foul language had not yet worked itself out of his system. Yet, it was also evident that his newfound passion and love for the Scriptures and Jesus was causing his teaching to be quite effective despite his unintentional choice of words.

Earlier that evening, this group sat around in a circle and shared prayer requests. This was an experience I was very familiar with, or so I thought. I expected the usual, "My Aunt Sally is getting hip surgery." "My boss is being a jerk; please pray that he disappears." "I am hoping to get a spot on the soccer team. Can you guys pray for me for that?" In fact, when I would sit with older groups in regular church circles, the prayer requests would mainly be around medical procedures and parts of their bodies that I hoped to never see. If I sat in the circles among younger groups, the requests were often about boyfriends, girlfriends, college classes, jobs or tax refunds, and the like.

Nothing like what I was used to happened in this group. Roughly thirty people were sitting in a circle in a poorly maintained house near the campus of Ohio State. There was a large open area full of couches that looked like they must've been picked up from dusty yard sales. There was one familiar request. Someone made a request about a broken ankle. However, from there, everything changed. Every single request, every single one, was one of these young students (still comfortable with their F-bombs) asking for prayer on behalf of a family member, coworker, fellow student, roommate, friend, or someone else that they were trying to lead to Christ. They were praying that God would provide them with a better opportunity to witness, more clarity on what to say, or insight on how to be a genuine friend to the person, or that God would move on the heart of the person to make them more willing to hear the truth and change.

The caliber of these prayer requests, followed by the deep and meaningful Bible study, just wouldn't reconcile in my hypocritical head with their use of foul language. Imagine my further surprise when at the end of this powerful Bible study, one of the young men ran to the refrigerator and returned with two six-packs of beer. They hung around on the porch, smoking and dropping more F-Bombs while discussing how to win their friends and family for Christ!

It took me a while to process all of this, but in the end, I concluded that this church had it right.

- They were focused on discipling their youth, and they were intentional about it.
- They got together frequently, and they studied the Bible intensely.
- They encouraged every new believer to teach at least some small passage in the comforting support of their new peers within months.

What I had experienced was this gentleman's first time ever leading the study, and barring the language that tripped me up, it was excellent. He knew the passage and its meaning far better than I did. I thought I had been a Christian for more than 80 percent of my life, but I felt like the novice in the room as these relatively new believers discussed the Scriptures. By focusing on what mattered, the belief system these people had, and the confidence they had to defend it—not only to others but also to themselves—this body of believers was empowering new converts to aid in the work of ministry WHILE they were being discipled.

As I met people discipled in this same environment who were now well into their late twenties, thirties, or forties, and so on, I could see that meaningless behaviors just fell away. Their lives continued to develop more meaning as their confidence in what they had come to believe increased. In other words, by focusing on God's Word, they moved their disciples much farther forward than if they had just employed social pressures toward specific habits, attire, church attendance, or other outward behaviors. They were not focused on the behaviors. They were focused on the belief. As belief deepened, behaviors simply emerged to reflect those beliefs.

Isn't this the same in every other area of our life? If we believe we can sell, we are more likely to take a job in sales. If we think we can ride a bike, we are more likely to buy one. If we believe we will look good in that new outfit, we are more likely to buy it. Likewise, when we are seasoned in the rich evidence and truth that the Word presents and come to believe that Jesus is who He says He is, our choices will reflect what we now believe. Just as easy. Just as natural. No peer pressure is required.

Trying to do it the other way around, where we focus on the behaviors first, tends to create fake Christians. I doubt anybody would argue that fake Christians are attractive, effective, or productive at self-replication.

What we saw over the next few days, before we returned home, reinforced the power and effectiveness of focusing on belief. I remember visiting a coffee shop the church had set up near the university. High school kids were excited to show up, knowing they would get to meet with "cool college kids" who were willing to hang out with them, one-on-one, for an hour a week to study the Bible. You might not be surprised that the format was one book at a time, one chapter at a time, and one small passage at a time. They would go through the passage together and then discuss how it could be applied to their own lives. You might think this could be an error factory. "Dear Lord! Those young Christians, and even worse, young kids, will end up in horrible heresy!" Not so. As I experienced that night with the F-bombing study leader in training, I came to see that these kids knew the Bible far better than I did, and it humbled me. These same college kids were excited to go and meet one-on-one once a week with someone who had already graduated college and was willing to invest time in them.

This cascading mode of study was reaping a harvest of Christian workers who were organically learning to see the rich tapestry of the Scriptures. They were building relationships with mentors and learning to be mentored. Within those close relationships that naturally developed through the investment of time, these disciples were also experiencing personal accountability and motivation to apply the truths they were studying together.

Defining discipleship

Before we go on, let's ask the question: What is discipleship?

- **Discipleship is not always successful.** It is essential for anyone making a foray into discipling others to realize that even Jesus Himself, in the parable of the seeds, recognized that not all who come to believe end up staying the course. That can be disheartening, but it should not lead you to give up. Every success in this endeavor is worth innumerable failures. We can never know the impact of just one genuine disciple on the world. If we were to spend a lifetime trying to disciple people and only succeed once, but that person led a movement that led thousands of others to Christ, wouldn't that be a great success?

- **Discipleship is a shared effort.** Not everyone who starts out discipling someone will get to see the end of the course that person is on. Sometimes, someone will reject the Gospel only to come back later and recognize the truth, reengaging with someone else. Paul said, "One plants the seed and another waters, but the Holy Spirit provides the growth."

- **Discipleship is intentional.** Discipleship is not a self-help program where someone takes home a bunch of books from the church library. The willingness of the disciple alone does not facilitate discipleship. Discipleship is facilitated by the desire and intentional investments of disciple-makers. You must be willing to invest a significant amount of time, across an extended period, with a specific objective: equipping this new believer to do the same thing for others.

- **Discipleship is meaningful.** Discipleship is geared toward creating copies of ourselves in a spiritual sense, but it is not geared toward creating parrots that reproduce canned answers they previously learned. Instead, discipleship is meant to impact the life of the disciple profoundly. When the change they experience is personal and meaningful to their lives, their testimony will be meaningful as well. It's not about memorization. It's about deep organic change. A disciple will remember passages, but it will be because they helped them see the truth, empowering them to also share these Scriptures in a meaningful way.

- **Discipleship is deeply personal.** You cannot disciple someone effectively if you make it entirely about them. The most effective disciple-makers take significant risks in intentional relationships by revealing substantial past and present struggles with sin and how God has taught or rescued them. A relationship formed to facilitate discipleship that makes the disciple the sinner and the disciple-maker the saint is not only likely to fail but may incentivize the disciple to hide their sin to show false progress. When an intentional disciple-maker reveals who they really are, deeply and transparently, it creates a vulnerability that invites the disciple into that vulnerability as well. "We are not here to impress each other. We are here to share the truth about God so that we can understand that both of us, as sinners, can have confident hope in Him and His Grace and Mercy through His self-credentialing and authoritative word." From there, we can spur one another on to good works, not for the sake of works themselves but for the sake of the One who saved us to complete those good works.

- **Discipleship is Christ-focused.** We are not just seeking to make people better people. We are seeking to help them learn to see and take on the image of Christ.

- **Discipleship is identity-based.** When someone comes to faith, the moment they say, "Wow, I believe this and want a relationship with God!" they have been accepted into the family of Christ. They are also immediately imparted with a new identity. They are already a new person. One of the most excellent teachings I ever heard on this was an expository teaching on Ephesians 1. It presented the metaphor of a teenage child that had been accidentally separated from his family at birth. The story brought us to a moment where this child was now a long-lost teen. He was found by his estranged father, who had been searching for him the entire time. The teen, fully engaged with his identity as an orphan, was having trouble accepting that this was his long-lost father. The father was extremely wealthy, but the long-lost child was trapped in a life of poverty and crime. Until this teen was convinced of his new identity, his decisions would still reflect his old "orphan" mindset. Like us, this lost sheep would need to accept his new identity before it would affect his choices. Teaching a disciple to understand who they are now and how they can live differently because of that truth comes from getting to know the Father and learning to trust that He is who He says He is.

- **Discipleship is Scripture-based.** There is no better authority on God than the book that He wrote Himself, about Himself, through men. I am not against reading books about the Bible. I just believe that reading the Bible itself is better. Many will argue that we need help understanding it, like the Ethiopian eunuch. Still, the Ethiopian eunuch was reading a passage from the Old Testament and did not yet understand Christ's finished work. That understanding, the Mystery Now Revealed, allows us to interpret Scripture in a way our predecessors could not. We also have the presence of the Holy Spirit, who helps us understand. If our disciple-makers have been discipled themselves, then some of the challenging passages have already been explained to them, much as Philip explained difficult passages to the Ethiopian Eunuch, with immediate effect. It is a common belief that there was a significant outbreak of Christianity in Ethiopia after that time. Do we believe that the Ethiopian eunuch sent all of those new converts back to find Philip? No, the tough passages had been explained to him. With that mustard seed in hand, he returned to Ethiopia and shared the authoritative information he had with others, and the process of replication began. Why do we imagine we are incapable of the same, especially when we have so many great resources that the Ethiopian eunuch did not?

Build your own audience

But as an adult, you may ask, "But where will I find my new disciples?"

One of the Elders we spoke to at Xenos said that he had a group of about forty people who came into his home once a week and deeply studied the Scriptures together. That is sort of impressive on its own and might be the end of the story in many Christian circles. However, it was what he shared next that moved me more. The group had struggled with leading people to Christ. None felt gifted at turning conversations with coworkers, friends, or neighbors into spiritual conversations. A few of the men who enjoyed bicycling and needed to get in better shape decided to enter a bike race. This was partially an effort to reduce their waistlines but also a stealthy plan to increase their ministry. They agreed they would each be responsible for getting one coworker or friend to join their team.

What was the fruit of this? The four men got four other men to join them as they trained and prepared over nine months for their race. The investment of time in these four men had paid dividends in that three of them had joined the group, and two had led their entire families to Christ. They had fulfilled the great commission and "gone into the world and made disciples." All it took was the investment of time into something they already wanted to do and the welcoming inclusion of others who might share a similar interest. As those who had studied deeply, they were quite ready to turn conversations into spiritual ones. They just needed to spend time for the conversations to get to more profound matters naturally.

None of what I saw in Ohio would have been possible unless that church first committed, from the top down to the consistent teaching of God's Word. They were committed to explaining it in such a way so that new believers could understand. They were committed to establishing the processes and relationships necessary to reinforce this learning and provide ministry opportunities. While the bar for leading one of their "central teachings" was undoubtedly high (i.e., meeting the biblical test of eldership), the bar for discipling others was much lower. They simply wanted someone willing to learn, committed to giving their time, and willing to prepare for each meeting.

One page ahead

A man I worked for in a technology business once said, "You don't have to have read the whole book to be of value in the marketplace. You only have to be one page ahead of your customer." I chuckled at that in the moment, but as I processed it later, I realized there was great wisdom in what he said. When new technologies come along, you don't have to be an expert to deliver value to the marketplace. You only have to know more than your client and be willing to share that knowledge in exchange for payment. That isn't to say that there isn't more value in being a fully informed expert. Still, the truth of that example does handily refute the idea that I have to know everything about a topic before I can give correct answers about any part of it. Does the fact that a nurse lacks the title of doctor cause you to distrust what she does know? In the same vein, we can see that a college student being mentored by a young adult on a particular passage from the Bible would have no problem sharing that same information effectively with a high school student. That high school student would also have very little trouble (as we saw them doing) sitting down weekly with a middle school student to share that same information again.

1 Corinthians 3:5-9, ESV

What then is Apollos? What is Paul? Servants through whom you believed, as the Lord assigned to each. I planted, Apollos watered, but God gave the growth. So neither he who plants nor he who waters is anything, but only God who gives the growth. He who plants and he who waters are one, and each will receive his wages according to his labor. For we are God's fellow workers. You are God's field, God's building.

Paul reminded us that none of us are ultimately capable of making a convert or a disciple. In his example, he reminds us that one plants, another waters, but it is God who brings the growth. Ultimately, we may be one of many who plant seeds that do not take, but when the Holy Spirit has finally softened a person's heart, we come along with the seed that finally germinates. We may not have had every seed at our disposal (i.e., we are not yet experts at every biblical matter), but we cast the ones we do have. We may not have enough water to lead that person to maturity, but don't worry; God has that under control. He will appoint someone else to come along and water the seed we planted, and another, and another. But the seed and the water all came from God anyway. Likewise, His Holy Spirit, who helps us know what to say and when to say it, is also from God. If we only have one talent of knowledge, should we bury it? No, the Holy Spirit is looking for us to deploy whatever we have been given and trust Him for the increase.

1 Corinthians 3:10-15, ESV

> *According to the grace of God given to me, like a skilled master builder I laid a foundation, and someone else is building upon it. Let each one take care how he builds upon it. For no one can lay a foundation other than that which is laid, which is Jesus Christ. Now if anyone builds on the foundation with gold, silver, precious stones, wood, hay, straw—each one's work will become manifest, for the Day will disclose it, because it will be revealed by fire, and the fire will test what sort of work each one has done. If the work that anyone has built on the foundation survives, he will receive a reward. If anyone's work is burned up, he will suffer loss, though he himself will be saved, but only as through fire.*

This passage shows us that one man's work is layered upon another in the craft of discipleship. It also shows us that even the one whose work is worthless is still saved. Hopefully, we set the bar a bit higher for ourselves than that. However, it's still reassuring to know that God will burn away the worthless or temporal things (wood, hay, and straw) we have accomplished and reward us for what remains (the gold, silver, and precious gems). These are the things He accomplished through us. How much better to risk ending up producing some hay than for us to arrive empty-handed for failing to try at all.

The complete truth of the Gospel, or as Paul calls it, "the full counsel of the Gospel," is not required to have been entirely consumed for any part of God's Word to stand as truth. Now certainly, if we are not yet trained in the whole counsel of the Gospel, we may get questions we cannot yet answer. But my metaphor of the technology business still applies. If the client asks us a question we do not yet have the answer to, it is okay to say, "That's a great question, and we don't know the answer, but we will go back and find out for you." The kingdom variation of this would be, "That's a great question, and I don't know the answer, but I will go and talk to one of the elders, and we will find out together." This allows us to build disciple-makers and put them to work quickly. The work itself inspires them to want to develop more expertise. And as we continue, weekly, teaching them the full counsel of the Gospel, the Scriptures will thread themselves together in the believer's mind creating a strong and impenetrable tapestry sufficient for connecting the Scriptures and answering the most challenging questions of life.

Let's be honest; most pastors know that when they retire, a committee will need to "find our next professional." Wouldn't it be a beautiful thing if tomorrow's preachers and teachers simply organically emerged out of the bodies being served by today's preachers and teachers?

Expository Preaching

As we discuss elsewhere in the book, few seminaries prepare pastors for expository teaching. Many seminaries focus on:

- The administrative operation of a church.
- How to market and grow a church.
- The mechanics of three-point sermons and building an effective presentation.
- The history of the church.
- Greek and Hebrew.

All of these things are certainly useful for the aspiring pastor. However, if they are not stitched together to help that pastor see the critical importance of following the examples we see laid out by Jesus and the apostles, of scripturally based teaching, in-depth explanation, personal application, and a commitment to the "full counsel of the gospel," then are they really preparing these seminarians for New Testament success?

If pastors are not comfortable with expository teaching, many excellent resources are available. In fact, one can simply search for the phrase "expository teaching" online to quickly find a myriad of resources and advice, though certainly applying some discernment is advised. In other words, not every expository teacher or reference is a good source. But when we find a good one, we must remember that plagiarism is not only allowed in Christianity; it is welcomed. That is not to suggest that one should take credit for another's work, but that we can learn from the exposition already completed by others and verify it just as the Bereans did.

We need only look at Paul's writings to see him directing his disciples to teach just as they had seen and heard him teach. That begs the question, is it okay for a pastor to find someone who is a good expository teacher and follow their work, verifying then teaching roughly the same points and explanations? The answer is yes. Not only is it okay, but it is also biblically advised!

A natural question would emerge: How do I tell if someone is a "good expository teacher"? Well, there are a few simple rules from the concepts of hermeneutics that we can examine.

- **Harmonization.** The Scriptures will not conflict with one another. If you cannot get two Scriptures to harmonize, you have not yet correctly interpreted at least one of them.

- **Interpreting Difficult Passages.** An explanation of a difficult passage should never conflict with the obvious meaning of an easy passage. One of the rules of hermeneutics is that we can interpret and understand difficult passages by harmonizing them with easy-to-understand passages.
- **Historical Context.** The Scriptures should be interpreted through historical context. In other words, a promise made to an ancient Israelite tribe should not be read as a modern promise unless it is clear from the Scriptures that it was a general promise from God to all mankind. We can consider things like "first readership." Understanding the life and times of the first reader may help us understand the use of phrases that seem unfamiliar, and then the Holy Spirit can leverage our minds to translate those into modern examples (i.e., application).
- **Grammatical Context.** The Scriptures should be interpreted through grammatical context. It is an error to harvest a part of a sentence and build a theology on it without ensuring it resonates at various levels. In other words, if you read a passage and it has a clear meaning when read within the text that surrounds it, it should be interpreted to mean the same thing when recited on its own. That is the concept of grammatical context.
- **Original Meaning.** Further, the original meaning of a word or a phrase in its original recorded language is essential to consider. We can also refer to the use of a word or phrase elsewhere throughout the Bible or within other contemporary writings to inform us of the author's intent and the passage's meaning.

- **Divine Illumination.** Finally, it is critical to interact with the Holy Spirit, the comforter given to all of us who the Bible says "illuminates the Scriptures for us" to assure that we have found a good guide.

Men are flawed. Even if we find someone whose expository teaching inspires us 99 percent of the time, there will still certainly be a time that they have taken a liberty we may disagree with. There may also be a time that they teach something flat-out wrong. That is another reason we should be Berean whenever we are leaning on the teachings of another. Remember, in Luke's writing about the Bereans in the book of Acts; he referred to them as being "more noble" because they searched the Scriptures themselves to verify what they had heard Paul teach.

We hope that this brief survey of the power of expository teaching has met its goal. We are making the case that resources are available and that expository teaching does not need to be self-taught. It can be relatively quickly learned, one chapter at a time. We make the case that this can be replicated and cascaded down throughout a growing body and that the fruit is that each within the body grows as they serve others. We are making the case that moving people from new believers to Christian workers as quickly as possible benefits the whole body and each individual. We are also making the case that this is entirely possible and practical.

10

Failing Our Youth

ONE OF THE most heartbreaking trends I have observed is children raised in the church, schooled in Christian schools, ferried back and forth to youth groups, and sent off to summer and winter camps across their high school years who then head off to college and quickly abandon their faith. Sadly, I have observed this firsthand through friends of my children. Don't get me wrong; I think that if you were to interview most of these kids (when they were involved in the Christian community), they would've told you that they believed in Christ. However, it is my confident assertion that their beliefs lacked roots because they had neither faced nor been taught to answer tough questions.

It is not to suggest that this problem is unique to youth, but rather that they are about to head off into a most unfriendly territory, wholly unprepared for the battle ahead. The condition I see in the church at large that breaks my heart and leads to this sad state of affairs is a lack of in-depth learning or study. I believe this unfairly impacts youth because those already established in their lives will continue to enjoy the same community around them, making them "feel" like Christians. They can quickly return to that support system whenever life's inevitable challenges arrive. Additionally, many will simply learn to avoid the world around them instead of engaging "those heathens."

Conversely, youth will soon be packing their limited belongings into boxes and heading off to college or perhaps the big city to find their way. They will be separated from their community and quickly develop new communities. Even if they do manage to find a circle of "Christian" friends, all equally unprepared for battle, then they will fall as a group, concluding together that their previous beliefs were sadly untrue. After all, they have not withstood the test of fire.

I would argue that it is not the Gospel that has failed in this case, but their faith. The church and their parents who were called to disciple them should judge themselves accountable for that failure. That may sound heavy-handed, but the Bible tells us that this is our responsibility. We cannot control what adult children will do. We are not responsible for their salvation. Nonetheless, as parents and the church at large, we are responsible for planting and watering the seeds that God has given us. If our children decide to reject those seeds, we can take comfort in God's long view, a view that is in many cases longer than we will live to see.

Proverbs 22:6, ESV
   *Train up a child in the way he should go; even when he
   is old he will not depart from it.*

Our children are open-minded and impressionable. They are glad to believe what we believe. They are naturally accepting of what we tell them. They have learned that there is consistency in our words and trust that we have their best interests at heart. Not all homes are warm, safe, and loving, but most Christian homes have at least some of those attributes, if not all. Our homes are the cocoons in which our caterpillars become butterflies. Still, we often miss the day of opportunity for discipleship because we forget that the butterfly is going to fly away.

Do you see the pattern? When we explain the Gospel to our children, they are quick to accept it, at least most. This can insidiously lead us to a sense of accomplishment: we have led our children to Christ! However, this is the same shortsightedness that is hampering the church at large. Jesus did not tell us to go into all the world to make converts; He told us to go into all the world to make disciples. Do we think that we have less responsibility in this regard within our own homes? If we are not teaching our children about the lies the enemy will bring to undermine Truth, we are not preparing them for what life will be like when they leave the cocoon. It would be the same as never teaching our children how to safely cross a street because we live on a cul-de-sac, likely with similar results.

Some will find their own way to Christ, but that will lead to a much smaller harvest than if we were to fully prepare them for what we know lies ahead. Their faith will be assaulted. It will be assaulted in the workplace. It will be assaulted at school. It will be assaulted in their circle of friends. And unfortunately, it will also be assaulted in many churches that have strayed from the truth. If we have not firmly planted and rooted those deeper truths into their hearts, these shallow-planted truths will quickly be ripped away.

Consider the adage of taking candy from a baby. Innocent little children lack the strength and the foresight to see it coming. They lack the ability to quickly process what has happened or respond when the thief comes. The same is true in the realm of faith. Why do they think they are Christians? Is it because they said a prayer with Mom or Dad or their youth pastor, or because the majority of times they went to Starbucks, they went with their friends from the youth group? If so, they will be woefully unprepared for the vicious attacks of the God-hating world they are heading into.

Making it personal

Perhaps what I am writing will make some uncomfortable. Perhaps it even strikes close to home. Maybe your son or daughter is heading off to college or into their new and independent life, and what I have written resonates and worries you. Perhaps you think your kids are "good kids," and this won't happen to them. Maybe you think you're sending them to a "good college" and so this surely won't happen there. Perhaps you think you are sending them to a "Christian college," so the professors will finish what you should've done, and it will all be okay.

Let me tell you why I believe counting on Christian schools to outsource this for us may be an unwise hope. In my experience, the harsh and legalistic staff at a Christian grade school I attended pushed me away from Christ. Most staff struggled to feed and clothe their families due to meager wages, yet the principal and founder seemed to be living quite well. It turned out that funds were being embezzled. As mine was one of the families that felt the financial sting, can you imagine the impact? I do not impugn all Christian schools; I am simply saying they are run by people as broken as you and I. Perhaps most are excelling at teaching Christian principles, and I hope so, but not all.

But what about college? I won't name the college for the sake of their reputation. After all, I still hope this would be a minority experience. But again, speaking firsthand, my son came home and argued with me that I was close-minded for believing that God created the Earth, a view that, thankfully, he has now accepted. Imagine my heartbreak discovering he had gathered this new opinion at one of the more committed Christian colleges. A

Christian professor there had taught him that the best way to reconcile science and the Bible was to simply assume that the Bible was inaccurate in any areas where it appeared to conflict with science. This is an under-informed view, but it was taught as if it were a superior view. This kind of concession is more common than most would expect and can be more damaging coming from a "Christian" professor than a secular one.

I think this is an example of the generally lazy approach to the common claim of science and the Bible being in conflict. The work necessary to address this question head-on and to become confident in our ability to answer it is undoubtedly a big commitment. Still, it is also an important and worthy foundational stone for us to make sure we get laid in the hearts of our children.

Nothing in the observable universe undermines God's existence, preeminence, or sovereignty over all we can see. My intention here is not to make this book about creation. Creationism and all its various segments can be controversial. Many young-earth creationists conclude that old-earth creationists have abandoned the Bible. Many old-earth creationists judge that young-earth creationists have taken poetic passages too literally. Amidst these arguing sides arise the intelligent design creationists who offend both by leaving God out of their title. There are a handful of additional views we could unpack, but that isn't our point. The point here is that they all agree that God created the Earth and all of us who live upon it.

If we are unwilling to take on the tough issues our children will encounter, we are outsourcing the debate but will still be responsible for the unpredictable outcomes. This is a challenging thought if we felt safe that delivering our children to youth groups and sending them off to a Christian college had us covered. It may even be frightening.

Sometimes, when frightening thoughts challenge us, we want to attack the messenger. Please, don't attack the messenger. The topic is righteously uncomfortable and meant to call us into action for our children.

In many corners of the church, it is common to think that "the world" is a dangerous place we should keep our children away from. As a sinner, redeemed by Christ, who has been through many unprofitable periods, I could easily be tempted to hide all of that for my children and keep them away from anything that ever helped lead me astray. However, this would be an inferior approach to preparing my children for the inevitability of being tempted by the very same things themselves. The church (and that means us, parents and all) are, in fact, called to explain what we believe to our children and then to also go on offense proactively explaining how the enemy will distort God's truth. We need to sufficiently inoculate our children's minds with the Gospel so that they can withstand the onslaught of distortions. Our true call with our children is not simply to prepare them for defense but to prepare them as warriors ready to go into the enemy's domain and rescue others.

For instance, I will allow my children to taste alcohol in my home. I do not want beer to be a mysterious thing they cannot wait to try hidden in the corner of some basement with friends. I'd rather just let them have a taste of it and watch their face wince up as they discover that it is clearly an acquired taste and nothing like the orange soda they were probably imagining. I prefer to explain to them how Paul said, "all things are lawful, but not all things are profitable, and I will be mastered by none," and what that really meant. Paul was dealing with this topic in response to the crazy Christians in Corinth, who I often refer to as "Christians gone wild." They were questioning whether grace really covered their myriad of sins. Paul wanted to help them see that they now had freedom in Christ. Radical Freedom! They were no longer separated from God, living under the fear-threat relationship of the past, but as "the saints," they were now living under a love response relationship with God.

As adopted children, God is concerned with our freedom. I do not mean freedom to sin; I mean freedom from being mastered by it. One person may be unable to limit the quantity of something enjoyable and find that it begins to master them. If they feel the Holy Spirit counseling them to stay away from this, that is a wise directive for them to follow. Where pious individuals and the church-at-large often get into significant error is when they begin to apply these individual directives to everyone else. We can all think of groups that suggest that women's skirts must be of a particular length. Some have mandated that the consumption of any alcohol is an intolerable sin. But this thinking ignores the fact that in the New Testament, Jesus turned water into wine. In the Old Testament, God directed the Israelites to celebrate with the unequivocal inclusion of "strong drink."

For some, the use of any alcohol really is a sin because God has dealt personally with them, telling them to stay away from it. However, for others, it can be a source of relaxation at the end of a long day, and there is no risk that they will be mastered by it.

If we tell our children that anything that could master anyone is a sin for everyone, we constrain them by our own fears. We risk making these things magical to them or limiting their ability to relate to others in many areas where God has not expressly placed boundaries for all believers. Why do we do this?

Imagine the plight of a Christian teenager told by youth leaders that "secular movies are evil," and they want to comply.

Yet their secular friends say, "Hey, why don't we go and see a movie?" to which they respond, "I can't do that anymore. I'm a Christian."

"What about playing some cards?" They respond, "Sorry, that would be gambling, and that's another sin!"

How far will this list go on? Are these really the things that God most cares about? Again, if we are to be mastered by any of them, then God cares significantly about them because He cares significantly about us and our freedom. But if we are not going to be mastered by these activities, they are infinitesimally smaller than what He truly cares about, which is our relationship with Him. Our relationship with God is built upon our knowledge and understanding of Him. That knowledge comes from the Bible and from spending time with Him. As we have previously argued, leaning on the teachings of Jesus and the apostles directly, our relationship with God is not bolstered by works, nor can sin diminish it (for God's part). Rather, both works and our sanctification (the cleanup of our sinful ways) are fruit, organically born out of our love for Him as we get to know Him better.

The same is true of sexuality. Christian parents often think that ducking the topic altogether and just telling their children "Not to" will suffice. Nothing could be further from the truth. Sexuality is healthy, positive, and designed by God. We need to not only glorify it as a gift from God but also unapologetically explain it to our children in the context of its true purpose. Long-term relationships are exceedingly difficult to maintain. The initial attraction and euphoria of a new romance quickly fade. God knew (after all, He created us) that we would need a powerful reward system to help us stay engaged in long-term committed relationships. In this context, we can see sex as a reward and a relational glue intended to be released into a marriage as a powerful counter to the many divisive forces a married couple will most certainly experience.

When we correctly explain the power and benefits, even the enjoyment of sexuality to our children, it is certainly a bit uncomfortable, but it also seems necessary. It should be done long before they are tempted by sexuality. Likewise, we should also explain, especially if we've experienced it firsthand, the damage that can be caused by abusing this powerful God-given tool. One of the metaphors I have used to address this topic with my children is the idea of how I can use a circular saw to cut lumber and build useful things. I then ask if it would be wise for me to turn it on and play catch with a friend? The obvious answer is no. By relating sexuality to a tool God has given us for a specific purpose, with extraordinary power and benefits (when correctly used), the metaphor helps them see that when misused, it can also create incredible damage.

When two people who are not committed to remaining in a long-term relationship experience sexuality, they become one in ways God ordained, no matter their intentions. One of the most powerful metaphors I've heard to explain this was to imagine gluing two pieces of paper together and then trying to get them back apart. This is what it is like for a young couple who has inappropriately shared a sexual experience when they break up. If we wonder why people are so sexually damaged in the modern world, consider a piece of paper that has been glued to many other pieces and separated multiple times. The tears will now become visible. The original article is permanently damaged. Some of the paper has been left behind over and over.

In this metaphor, shared with me by Dennis McCallum, there is increasingly less material present when it is finally glued to the piece of paper it was originally meant for. This is a tragedy we should want our children to forgo, but avoiding the topic will not help us achieve that. If you are not the first to bring it up, then their friends will beat you to it and may even convince them that their paper will be the stronger one and the tear will not hurt them at all. Public schools will train them how to do it, and sex education teachers will teach them that sexuality is natural—a loose term devoid of "natural" bounds. Some of their peers will express curiosity. Some will share pornography. Some will even offer sexual intimacy. Telling your children that sex is evil is neither accurate nor effective.

When it comes to helping your children understand why what is bad for them is good for you, why not get ahead of the curve, and admit that it's incredible, beautiful, and powerful. Explain the danger and tell them to be careful, saving it for the time when they will be building something with saw and lumber, as opposed to tearing their life apart like sheets of paper glued to too many other hearts, too many times.

These issues we have surveyed are real issues, and there are many others, but let's dig into an even deeper problem, the issue of sending our children out unprepared for the defense of their faith. Aspiring only to the hope that they will avoid error is not our goal. Instead, God has ordained that they should be sent out as young warriors, ready for the world that fiercely opposes all that they believe.

Paul has told us that we are to be more than conquerors.

Romans 8:35-39, ESV
Who shall separate us from the love of Christ? Shall tribulation, or distress, or persecution, or famine, or nakedness, or danger, or sword? as it is written,

"For your sake we are being killed all the day long;
we are regarded as sheep to be slaughtered."

No, in all these things we are more than conquerors
through him who loved us. For I am sure that neither
death nor life, nor angels nor rulers, nor things present
nor things to come, nor powers, nor height nor depth, nor
anything else in all creation, will be able to separate us
from the love of God in Christ Jesus our Lord.

Most of us can easily apply this to ourselves, but what about the children we steward of in our homes, our churches, or our communities? Are we to prepare to be more than conquerors, fully grounded in the love of Christ, but then send our children out as lambs unprepared for the opposition they will experience? No, we are to prepare them to be overcomers. But how can they overcome what they have never been prepared for? How can they wield concepts or against counter-arguments they have never been exposed to?

Lambs to the slaughter

By foregoing our responsibility to teach our children the truths of God, we send them into battle unarmed and unprepared. And worse, they do not even realize they are heading into battle. Sadly, I believe that many parents, churches, and Christian communities are doing their best to attract their children's interest by being "relevant." They are trying to be "cool" or "hip." However, our kids both want and need to be called into the adventure of seeing how their Christianity can be applied to the world around them while learning how to be overcomers.

Most little boys grow up dreaming of being able to rescue others. You don't have to convince most boys to get excited at the idea of getting to wear a police badge or a fireman's helmet when they are little. Most little girls dream of being able to nurture others and make a difference in the world around them as they care for those they are closest to. We as human beings are naturally drawn into the adventure that God has already placed us into. He has saved us from being in the opposition force, which is destined to lose. He has appointed us to be His ambassadors of reconciliation and called us to go back into the same world we were rescued from as rescuers. Yet we fail to train for the job.

We train ourselves and our children to stay away from the world and keep clean from it. Rare is the teaching on how to return to it with a plan to rescue the captive inhabitants, calling them out for freedom. This uninspiring fortress mentality leaves our children, who are naturally curious about the outside world and inspired to help others, tired of living in the fortress and bored by the predictability. So they are both innately curious about "life outside the church walls" and totally unprepared for the opposition they will face when they eventually get there. The result? Our warriors-in-training, never truly trained, are quickly captured, turned against the little they were taught, and ultimately experience Stockholm syndrome coming to resent the place and ways they once called home.

What if instead of having a peacetime mentality, where we assume that the enemy will never come for our children, we had a wartime mentality, thinking that the enemy was coming for all of us? We need to prepare our children to be ready to defend their faith and defeat that enemy while advancing the cause of Christ as they grow into maturity. Would our young adventurers be more interested in that vision of their future? Would that challenge us to press harder and farther into the issues of our day? Would it require us to be more diligent in our study to be prepared to answer the onslaught of tough questions (the enemy's most predictable and reliable weapons) that our children will face? I think the answers to these questions are apparent. The real question is, when will we act?

The chasm between Christian and "science-based" worldviews is challenging to young Christians. Typically, we haven't even engaged or addressed their own intellectual and philosophical concerns regarding whether or not God actually exists. What will they do when a credible-sounding college professor proclaims their "naïve cartoon book vision of God creating the heavens and the earth can be disproven by 'science'?" We often fall into the same trap as the pure evolutionists. I have heard many an angry creationist tell an evolutionist: "You weren't there! How do you know it was billions of years ago!?" Can't a motivated evolutionist simply respond, "You weren't there either! How do you know it wasn't?" Large portions of the church will provide emotional arguments punctuated by, "You need to have more faith." In contrast, the college professor will provide hundreds of well-referenced textbooks and materials attacking a young person's faith.

What we should all be thoroughly convinced of is that God created the heavens and the earth just as He says He did. We can all see that creation displays logic, math, order, precision, and regulated systems that operate with extraordinary predictability. The idea that we could look at all this and imagine it happened as the equivalent of a series of heavenly lottery tickets is ridiculous. But likewise, the typical Christian dogmatic response is often just as hollow—for instance, Genesis 1 and 2 conflicts in the order of detail for the specifics of creation. One is written in a poetic style, and the other is a Hebrew acrostic. To read these poetic and acrostic texts without any openness to the idea that we don't know *exactly* how God accomplished what He is telling us He did is just as ridiculous as the evolutionist's proverbial lottery tickets.

Again, I am not attempting to take a position among the young-earth, old-earth, or theistic evolutionary dogmas. That's not the point of this book. Instead, I would argue that this topic is not as important as some in the church would make it out to be. By placing our immovable object at the entrance to our system of belief, we trip many people up on the wrong thing. Jesus did not say go into all the world and convince people of a young-earth creation, an old-earth creation, or a theistic-evolution model. He said to go into all the world and make disciples.

Disciples who come to know Jesus Christ through an in-depth study of who He is and the impact He has on all of us will gladly accept if He says the world was created in six days that it was created in six days. You may ask how I can reconcile that with the openness I inferred earlier. I will answer this way: I am not sure whether God designed the earth in six days and created it across a long period of time, whether God literally formed the earth and all we see in six days, or whether those six days were spread across time. While I wish I could answer that question without any doubt, I look forward to asking God exactly how He did it. I also know it will not be the criteria for entry into heaven. Entrance into heaven will be determined by whether I have accepted a relationship with Jesus Christ. In this atoning relationship, He has paid for my sin, allowing me to enter the throne room of God. I will enter that throne room as an adopted son, and as an adopted son, I will run right up to the Father and say, "Please tell me the rest of the creation story!"

At this time, we see through a glass dimly, but at that time, we will see clearly, and all will be revealed. In the meantime, it might be a good idea to focus on the irrefutable truth that God has incredibly and deeply credentialed Jesus Christ as God's one and only son. He was sent into the world to live as fully man and fully God. He came (though no man could see it coming) to be crucified to give us a path into reconciliation with the Father. True disciples who see this undeniable and fully credentialed truth, the Mystery of the Gospel Now Revealed, may disagree on exactly how they should interpret Genesis 1 and 2. Still, by focusing on first things first, they should now be discussing it as brothers and sisters in Christ.

Are we so arrogant as to believe that none of us will be surprised when God fills in the rest of the details on any number of topics we may have held so high as to place them above the core tenets of the Gospel itself? Is it right to think that our children have abandoned our faith if and when they question the details? No! The devil has observed this flaw in our priorities and uses it to leverage our children away from us.

I hope you now already see my more significant point. Suppose we taught our children how to confidently rationalize that God has used predictive prophecy to unquestionably credential Jesus Christ as His own Son. In that case, we also have a rational basis for expecting them to differentiate the verifiable uniqueness of Christianity. The lack of supernatural credentialing in all other world religions, or systems of belief, will stand out in clear contrast. This is the most salient point of this book and the foundational stone that we can lay before our children, our youth, the church, and the entire world. This foundational stone, the credentialed story of Christ Himself, is the one upon which a confident belief can be based. Jesus is the stone the builders rejected, and just as the Bible foretold, He is now the cornerstone. Jesus Christ has verifiably come as God and man to bring us back into reconciliation with our Heavenly Father. This is life and hope.

Confronting doubt

A weak church, not strengthened by generous interaction with the truth, finds itself fearful of confronting doubt.

We box doubt up. We put it away. We bury it deep, hoping that not even God will see it when we stand before Him. We have grown up taught that doubt is sin and that it should live in the dark, hidden away where no one else can see it, as they might judge us as defective Christians. Nothing could be further from the truth! Doubt is part of the natural human experience. Doubt is also part of the natural Christian human experience. God, who designed us, designed us to be skeptical. He created us to have questions. In fact, He designed the universe around us, making it uniquely observable from our location within the universe so that we could question everything. As we explore science and find more answers, we bring Him more glory, not less! The never-ending intricacy of discovery forces us to either recognize the Designer of this creation's order and elegance or reject Him. Do you think God designed us with this innate curiosity and skepticism but then expects that we should suddenly turn that off in the area of His claims about being our Creator, loving Father, and hope for eternal life? By no means!

God is so confident that He can overcome our doubts that He encourages and applauds those who pursue truth in the face of doubt. So why on earth would we scold our youth for asking challenging questions about the things we claim to know about God? When elementary school teachers tell their students that

God did not create the earth, why would a Sunday school teacher tell them that it is sinful to bring that question back into the church and repeat it? Isn't that the exact place we would want them to bring it and work it out? When their friends challenge them and ask, "Do you really believe in God, even with all the awful things that happen in this world?", should they wrestle with those questions alone? Wouldn't we rather they bring them to their Christian circles, youth groups, Sunday schools, and conversations with their parents?

If we treat rational doubts and questions as if they are sin, we are unlikely to continue getting the opportunity to help those who have doubts work through them. We may also be robbing ourselves. After all, if we have simply wished those same doubts away in our own minds instead of engaging them, maybe we too remain weak. Conversely, by openly digging in with our children and seeking answers to those tough questions, we might find what we need to help someone else.

1 Peter 3:15, NIV
"But in your hearts revere Christ as Lord. Always be prepared to give an answer to everyone who asks you to give the reason for the hope that you have. But do this with gentleness and respect."

God was comfortable enough with your doubts, as an adult, to take the time to build a case to prove that His Son was exactly who He said He was. He made that case over centuries. He made it through many prophets and through extraordinary complexity. He hid that message within the Scriptures, only to be seen by those present after Jesus' first coming. If God was willing to do all that for you to convince you that His Word is true, why would you be unwilling to do the same for children who have genuine doubts? We cannot continue to run away from doubt and expect our children to survive a world that is prepared to instantiate doubt, amplify it, and then drill into it repeatedly until all of the barriers of their faith are worn down.

Addressing this will take a seriousness that is lost for most of us in modern times. Sunday school is not a babysitting service. It is a school that happens to occur on Sunday, and it should be on par with or far superior to any other type of education our children encounter. Youth groups should not simply be groups that collect our youth and allow them to sit around in circles and talk about how they feel about God. Youth groups should be the next level of education, using fellowship to reinforce and work out what has been taught. Having taught our children the basic principles in Sunday school, they should start learning how to apply them. In kindergarten, our children stack blocks and learn the order of letters. We teach elementary school students to form the basics of sentences and learn simplistic geometry. Would it make sense to repeat this in high school and have them simply talk about how they feel about those things?

In secular education, we advance our students to classes where they are now expected to write papers using the early skills they learned. Why do we not teach our high school-age children how to prepare Bible lessons for their peers or the younger students? Why do we not have them practice making the arguments with each other that we think they will need to be prepared to make in the world? There is great hope in our youth. Modern secular research tells us frequently that our youth desire to be part of something larger than themselves. The massive amounts of research that can easily be found on millennials and generation Z tell us that they want to do something with their lives that makes a difference in the world around them. We have the answer to this desire, yet we fail to inspire them with it.

The world around us and all of its citizens desperately need our youth to leave our halls prepared for the war they find themselves trapped in. The war we send children into is waged between good and evil and between the truth of God and the lies of His enemy. When we inspire our youth to go into this high calling as rescuers, we give them something worthwhile to train for. We are connecting their human nature and desire to be part of something larger than themselves to their spiritual nature in the very way that God intended.

This concept is not unique to youth, but it is quite salient here. We must take preparing our children for what is ahead of them seriously, which means we as adults, the grown-ups in the room, will need to get serious about digging into the truth ourselves. Hiding from our opposition is no longer a viable option as peace-time has long expired. We are under assault, and we will either teach our children to be part of the responding force, or we will lose them, and there is little middle ground remaining.

A crisis of faith – research from the Barna Group

We do not want you to believe that the concerns we are addressing in this chapter are simply based on an idly formed opinion. Accordingly, we have decided to include the authoritative research of the Barna Group to help make the case. Per their materials, the Barna Group is a visionary research and resource company located in Ventura, California. Started in 1984, the firm is widely considered a leading research organization focused on the intersection of faith and culture. Over the years, I have found their groundbreaking research to be incredibly fruitful for faith leaders in various roles who want access to empirical data about the state of the modern church and its impact on the world around us and those we serve within the faith.

The following article, reprinted in its entirety, and a great deal of other valuable research, can be found on the Barna Group's website at www.barna.com. I would encourage you to read the entire article before pressing on, as the key findings relate to many of the concerns we are raising in this chapter.

Six Reasons Young Christians Leave Church

Many parents and church leaders wonder how to most effectively cultivate durable faith in the lives of young people. A five-year project headed by Barna Group president David Kinnaman explores the opportunities and challenges of faith development among teens and young adults within a rapidly shifting culture. The findings of the research are included in a new book by Kinnaman titled *You Lost Me: Why Young Christians are Leaving Church and Rethinking Faith*.

The research project consisted of eight national studies, including interviews with teenagers, young adults, parents, youth pastors, and senior pastors. The study of young adults focused on those who were regular churchgoers [Christian church] during their teen years and explored their reasons for disconnection from church life after age fifteen.

No single reason dominated the break-up between church and young adults. Instead, a variety of reasons emerged. Overall, the research uncovered six significant themes why nearly three out of every five young Christians (59 percent) disconnect either permanently or for an extended period of time from church life after age fifteen.

Reason #1 – Churches seem overprotective.

A few of the defining characteristics of today's teens and young adults are their unprecedented access to ideas and worldviews as well as their prodigious consumption of popular culture. As Christians, they express the desire for their faith in Christ to connect to the world they live in. However, much of their experience of Christianity feels stifling, fear-based, and risk-averse. One-quarter of eighteen- to twenty-nine-year-olds said, "Christians demonize everything outside of the church" (23 percent indicated this "completely" or "mostly" describes their experience). Other perceptions in this category include "church ignoring the problems of the real world" (22 percent) and "my church is too concerned that movies, music, and video games are harmful" (18 percent).

Reason #2 – Teens' and twenty-somethings' experiences of Christianity are shallow.

A second reason that young people depart church as young adults is that something is lacking in their experience of church. One-third said "church is boring" (31 percent). One-quarter of these young adults said that "faith is not relevant to my career or interests" (24 percent) or that "the Bible is not taught clearly or often enough" (23 percent). Sadly, one-fifth of these young adults who attended a church as a teenager said that "God seems missing from my experience of church" (20 percent).

Reason #3 – Churches come across as antagonistic to science.

One of the reasons young adults feel disconnected from church or from faith is the tension they feel between Christianity and science. The most common of the perceptions in this arena is "Christians are too confident they know all the answers" (35 percent). Three out of ten young adults with a Christian background feel that "churches are out of step with the scientific world we live in" (29 percent). Another one-quarter embrace the perception that "Christianity is anti-science" (25 percent). And nearly the same proportion (23 percent) said they have "been turned off by the creation-versus-evolution debate." Furthermore, the research shows that many science-minded young Christians are struggling to find ways of staying faithful to their beliefs and to their professional calling in science-related industries.

Reason #4 – Young Christians' church experiences related to sexuality are often simplistic, judgmental.

With unfettered access to digital pornography and immersed in a culture that values hyper-sexuality over wholeness, teen and twenty-something Christians are struggling with how to live meaningful lives in terms of sex and sexuality. One of the significant tensions for many young believers is how to live up to the church's expectations of chastity and sexual purity in this culture, especially as the age of first marriage is now commonly delayed to the late twenties. Research indicates that most young Christians are as sexually active as their non-Christian peers, even though they are more conservative in their attitudes about sexuality. One-sixth of young Christians (17 percent) said they "have made mistakes and feel judged in church because of them." The issue of sexuality is particularly salient among eighteen- to twenty-nine-year-old Catholics, among whom two out of five (40 percent) said the church's "teachings on sexuality and birth control are out of date."

Reason #5 – They wrestle with the exclusive nature of Christianity.

Younger Americans have been shaped by a culture that esteems open-mindedness, tolerance, and acceptance. Today's youth and young adults also are the most eclectic generation in American history in terms of race, ethnicity, sexuality, religion, technological tools, and sources of authority. Most young adults want to find areas of common ground with each other, sometimes even if that means glossing over real differences. Three out of ten young Christians (29 percent) said "churches are afraid of the beliefs of other faiths" and an identical proportion felt they are "forced to choose between my faith and my friends." One-fifth of young adults with a Christian background said, "church is like a country club, only for insiders" (22 percent).

Reason #6 – The church feels unfriendly to those who doubt.

Young adults with Christian experience say the church is not a place that allows them to express doubts. They do not feel safe admitting that sometimes Christianity does not make sense. In addition, many feel that the church's response to doubt is trivial. Some of the perceptions in this regard include not being able "to ask my most pressing life questions in church" (36 percent) and having "significant intellectual doubts about my faith" (23 percent). In a related theme of how churches struggle to help young adults who feel marginalized, about one out of every six young adults with a Christian background said their faith "does not help with depression or other emotional problems" they experience (18 percent).

Turning Toward Connection

David Kinnaman, who is the coauthor of the book *Christian*, explained that "the problem of young adults dropping out of church life is particularly urgent because most churches work best for 'traditional' young adults— those whose life journeys and life questions are normal and conventional. But most young adults no longer follow the typical path of leaving home, getting an education, finding a job, getting married and having kids—all before the age of 30. These life events are being delayed, reordered, and sometimes pushed completely off the radar among today's young adults.

> "Consequently, churches are not prepared to handle the 'new normal.' Instead, church leaders are most comfortable working with young, married adults, especially those with children. However, the world for young adults is changing in significant ways, such as their remarkable access to the world and worldviews via technology, their

alienation from various institutions, and their skepticism toward external sources of authority, including Christianity and the Bible."

The research points to two opposite, but equally dangerous responses by faith leaders and parents: either catering to or minimizing the concerns of the next generation. The study suggests some leaders ignore the concerns and issues of teens and twenty-somethings because they feel that the disconnection will end when young adults are older and have their own children. Yet, this response misses the dramatic technological, social, and spiritual changes that have occurred over the last twenty-five years and ignores the significant present-day challenges these young adults are facing.

Other churches seem to be taking the opposite corrective action by using all means possible to make their congregation appeal to teens and young adults. However, putting the focus squarely on youth and young adults causes the church to exclude older believers and "builds the church on the preferences of young people and not on the pursuit of God," Kinnaman said.

Between these extremes, the just-released book *You Lost Me* points to ways in which the various concerns being raised by young Christians (including church dropouts) could lead to revitalized ministry and deeper connections in families. Kinnaman observed that many churches approach generations in a hierarchical, top-down manner, rather than deploying a true team of believers of all ages. "Cultivating intergenerational relationships is one of the most important ways in

which effective faith communities are developing flour-
ishing faith in both young and old. In many churches,
this means changing the metaphor from simply passing
the baton to the next generation to a more functional,
biblical picture of a body—that is, the entire community
of faith, across the entire lifespan, working together to
fulfill God's purposes."

About the Research

This Barna Update is based on research conducted
for the Faith That Lasts Project, which took place between
2007 and 2011. The research included a series of national
public opinion surveys conducted by Barna Group.

In addition to extensive quantitative interviewing
with adults and faith leaders nationwide, the main
research examination for the study was conducted with
eighteen- to twenty-nine-year-olds who had been active
in a Christian church at some point in their teen years.
The quantitative study among eighteen- to twenty-nine-
year-olds was conducted online with 1,296 current and
former churchgoers. The Faith That Lasts research also
included parallel testing on key measures using telephone surveys, including interviews conducted among
respondents using cell phones, to help ensure the repre-
sentativeness of the online sample. The sampling error
associated with 1,296 interviews is plus or minus 2.7
percentage points, at the 95 percent confidence level.

The online study relied upon a research panel called
KnowledgePanel®, created by Knowledge Networks. It is
a probability-based online non-volunteer access panel.
Panel members are recruited using a statistically valid

sampling method with a published sample frame of residential addresses that covers approximately 97 percent of U.S. households. Sampled non-Internet households, when recruited, are provided a netbook computer and free Internet service so they may also participate as online panel members. KnowledgePanel consists of about 50,000 adult members (ages eighteen and older) and includes persons living in cell phone only households.

About Barna Group

Barna Group (which includes its research division, the Barna Research Group) is a private, non-partisan, for-profit organization under the umbrella of the Issachar Companies. It conducts primary research, produces media resources pertaining to spiritual development, and facilitates the healthy spiritual growth of leaders, children, families, and Christian ministries.

Located in Ventura, California, Barna Group has been conducting and analyzing primary research to understand cultural trends related to values, beliefs, attitudes, and behaviors since 1984. If you would like to receive free email notification of the release of each update on the latest research findings from Barna Group, you may subscribe to this free service at the Barna website (www.barna.org). Additional research-based resources are also available through this website.

Raising and educating our children is OUR responsibility! Abdicating this responsibility is inexcusable. Executing this responsibility necessitates that we know what is being taught and have sufficient knowledge to recognize and extinguish deception. It also requires that we are able to give an answer for the hope that is within us. That hope comes from our assurance, and our assurance comes from knowing God and knowing His truth. The formula is simple. Not easy, but simple.

Hosea 4:6a, NASB

My people are destroyed for lack of knowledge. *Since you have rejected knowledge.*

Ephesians 6:4, NASB

Fathers, do not provoke your children to anger, but **bring them up in the discipline and instruction of the Lord.**

Deuteronomy 4:10, NASB

Remember the day you stood before the Lord your God at Horeb, when the Lord said to me, **'Assemble the people to Me, that I may have them hear My words** *so that they may learn to fear Me all the days that they live on the earth,* **and that they may teach their children.'**

Deuteronomy 6:5-9, NASB

And you shall love the Lord your God with all your heart and with all your soul and with all your strength. These words, which I am commanding you today, shall be on your heart. **And you shall repeat them diligently to your sons and speak of them when you sit in your house,** *when you walk on the road, when you lie down, and when you get up. You shall also tie them as a sign to your hand,*

and they shall be as frontlets on your forehead. You shall also write them on the doorposts of your house and on your gates.

The point of this last passage was that God was underscoring the importance of His Word to His people. While the specifics are less important, the concept remains salient. We claim to be people of the Lord, but if we lack knowledge, can't we take the time to address it? With all our modern conveniences, can we not listen to great teachings on our way to work? Can we not listen to the Scriptures on our way to our vacation rental? What about while we cut the grass? Is our favorite music really a better use of time? What about when we are in the gym, falling asleep, or taking a shower? How much time do we fritter away in utter cluelessness while suffering the consequences of not having an answer for the hope that is within us? Want to save our youth from the hopelessness of lacking knowledge? Gain knowledge and be ready to share it.

11

The Unacceptable Loss of Our Neighbors

The irony of unauthenticated influence

TOM HOLLAND IS a modern historian and author raised as an Anglican Christian. Sadly, he later described himself as an atheist who has found nothing in the natural world that would convince him that the supernatural exists. As we have taken the liberty of including his story, perhaps we will send him a copy of the book, hope he reads it, and hope that he finds something within the Mystery Hidden for Ages Past to change that view. Nonetheless, he remains a fascinating character study because he believed his good morals were originally rooted in the advancements of human culture that had occurred since the ancient Roman and Greek periods. However, upon studying the ancient world, Holland's assumptions about the source of his good nature changed.

Simply put, he found that the ancients were cruel, and their values were utterly foreign to him. "The Spartans routinely murdered 'imperfect' children. The bodies of slaves were treated like outlets for the physical pleasure of those with power. Infanticide was common. The poor and the weak had no rights."

"How did we get from there to here? It was Christianity," Holland wrote. "Christianity revolutionized sex and marriage, demanding that men control themselves and prohibiting all forms of rape. Christianity confined sexuality within monogamy. It is ironic," Holland notes, "that these are now the very standards for which Christianity is derided. Christianity elevated women. In short, Christianity utterly transformed the world."

The irony here is that Holland can see the influence the Gospel has had on the world, but he is unable to see the One who exerts that influence. Holland is a man of substantial intellect with a predisposition toward morals. Still, he was unconvinced that God had crossed from the supernatural realm into the natural realm to reveal Himself. Is it possible that Tom needs to see God's credentialing work for himself?

Is it possible that our neighbors in the Western World are also retiring their faith due to a simple lack of understanding about how God has revealed Himself? Is it possible we have the cure?

A crisis of identity – a report from the Pew Research Center

Consider these elements of recent research from October of 2019, publicly available courtesy of the Pew Research Center.

The report subtitled "An update on America's changing religious landscape" reveals insights gathered across time that arguably reflect the decline of Christianity in a nation viewed by many only decades ago as "a Christian Nation."

Here are some of the key contrasting data points:

2009:   77 percent of survey respondents identify as Christian.

2018/19: 65 percent of survey respondents identify as Christian.

2009:   17 percent of survey respondents identify as religiously unaffiliated.

2018/19: 26 percent of survey respondents identify as religiously unaffiliated.

These numbers may have even more impact if you consider that the population of the United States was about 330 million people at the time of this survey. Each percent then represents about 3.3 million people. Now consider the idea that 12 percent no longer identify as Christian. The math leads you to a stunning realization. About 39.6 million people no longer wanted their names associated with Christ's name after just ten years. Ten years.

During the same period, we can see various forms of Christianity also surrendering their formerly faithful. Protestantism declined by about 15 percent (51 percent in 2009 vs. 43 percent in 2019). Simultaneously, Catholicism declined by about 20 percent (24 percent in 2009 vs. 20 percent in 2019). But lest we fear evangelism is dead, the atheists and agnostics have come to the rescue. They increased their numbers by 100 percent (2 percent in 2009 vs. 4 percent in 2019) and 66 percent (3 percent in 2009 vs. 5 percent in 2019) respectively. The "Nothing in Particular" movement has also grown by 41 percent (12 percent in 2009 vs. 17 percent in 2019). This is a seismic shift in the religious landscape of just one country in just one decade.

Connectedness to church bodies is also in decline. Consider the following contrast.

When asked, Pew's respondents answered, "I attend religious services,"

NET Monthly or more:

2009:   52 percent of survey respondents
2018/19:   45 percent of survey respondents

NET A few times a year or less:

2009:   47 percent of survey respondents
2018/19:   54 percent of survey respondents

The following graphic, gleaned from the same Pew Research, shows that our assumptions regarding who may be leaving (somebody else) are probably wrong. Neither ethnicity, political persuasion, geography, or generation have been immune, though there are clear trends. The younger generations are bleeding faster, as are those in the northeast.

Broad-based declines in share of Americans who say they are Christian

Percentage-point change between 2009 and 2018/2019 in the share who identify as ...

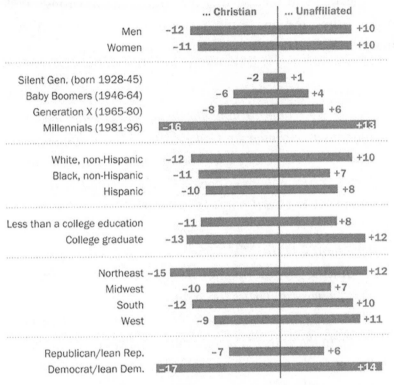

	... Christian	... Unaffiliated
Men	−12	+10
Women	−11	+10
Silent Gen. (born 1928-45)	−2	+1
Baby Boomers (1946-64)	−6	+4
Generation X (1965-80)	−8	+6
Millennials (1981-96)	−16	+13
White, non-Hispanic	−12	+10
Black, non-Hispanic	−11	+7
Hispanic	−10	+8
Less than a college education	−11	+8
College graduate	−13	+12
Northeast	−15	+12
Midwest	−10	+7
South	−12	+10
West	−9	+11
Republican/lean Rep.	−7	+6
Democrat/lean Dem.	−17	+14

Source: Aggregated Pew Research Center political surveys conducted 2009 and January 2018-July 2019 on the telephone.
"In U.S., Decline of Christianity Continues at Rapid Pace"

PEW RESEARCH CENTER

We have only surveyed the data available in this work from the Pew Research Center, but I suspect it resonates. Most of us know that these things are true. Christianity in the West is working ever harder to adapt to the perceived desires of the world they hope to reach. That makes the results even harder to swallow. The verdict is in. Even as the population of the United States increased, the number of Christians within it decreased. They are not only not reaching the world around them, but the world around them is siphoning off the faithful at alarming rates.

It leads us to ask, what is the church doing wrong? Well, perhaps the question we should ask before that is this: What is the church? The Bible tells us that the church is *us*.

1 Peter 2:4, NIV

As you come to him, the living Stone—rejected by humans but chosen by God and precious to him—you also, like living stones, are being built into a spiritual house to be a holy priesthood, offering spiritual sacrifices acceptable to God through Jesus Christ.

Ephesians 4:11-16, ESV

And he gave the apostles, the prophets, the evangelists, the shepherds and teachers, to equip the saints for the work of ministry, for building up the body of Christ, until we all attain to the unity of the faith and of the knowledge of the Son of God, to mature manhood, to the measure of the stature of the fullness of Christ, so that we may no longer be children, tossed to and fro by the waves and carried about by every wind of doctrine, by human cunning, by craftiness in deceitful schemes. Rather, speaking the truth in love, we are to grow up in every way into him who is the head, into Christ, from whom the whole body, joined and held together by every joint with which it is equipped, when each part is working properly, makes the body grow so that it builds itself up in love.

2 Corinthians 5 17-20, ESV

Therefore, if anyone is in Christ, he is a new creation. The old has passed away; behold, the new has come. All this is from God, who through Christ reconciled us to himself and gave us the ministry of reconciliation; that is, in Christ God was reconciling the world to himself, not counting their trespasses against them, and entrusting to us the message of reconciliation. Therefore, we are ambassadors for Christ, God making his appeal through us. We implore you on behalf of Christ, be reconciled to God.

We were designed to be built up as a body, organized under Christ, directed by His leadership, and equipped by the apostles, prophets, evangelists, shepherds, and teachers He provides. We are organized and prepared so that *we*, the interdependent body of Christ, can then function as the ambassadors of reconciliation, making our appeal to the world around us. Ambassadors travel to those they are sent to on behalf of those they are sent by. Ambassadors are not a local resource that people patronize like the post office; they are a resource that goes to where their assignments are like the postman himself.

When we tell our neighbors we are Christians, we need to consider that we are now the Ambassadors they will be observing because they are our assignment. However, none of us is up to the task, never were nor will be, so that is where things can get complicated.

Matthew 5:13-16, ESV

You are the salt of the earth, but if salt has lost its taste, how shall its saltiness be restored? It is no longer good for anything except to be thrown out and trampled under people's feet.

You are the light of the world. A city set on a hill cannot be hidden. Nor do people light a lamp and put it under a basket, but on a stand, and it gives light to all in the house. In the same way, let your light shine before others, so that they may see your good works and give glory to your Father who is in heaven.

Just prior to these verses, the Beatitudes list a series of attributes that few of us are likely to reflect on any given day. Jesus was not describing how we could be good enough to please God and have the men around us take notice that we are a "godly man or woman." Jesus was showing us the stark impossibility of the task. It gave hope to those who were already humble before God and took hope away from those who had placed it in themselves or their good works.

Matthew recorded this in the following passage:

Matthew 5:17-20, ESV

Do not think that I have come to abolish the Law or the Prophets; I have not come to abolish them but to fulfill them. For truly, I say to you, until heaven and earth pass away, not an iota, not a dot, will pass from the Law until all is accomplished. Therefore whoever relaxes one of the least of these commandments and teaches others to do the same will be called least in the kingdom of heaven, but whoever does them and teaches them will be called great in the kingdom of heaven. For I tell you, unless your righteousness exceeds that of the scribes and Pharisees, you will never enter the kingdom of heaven.

Jesus concludes with the shocking point that unless *we* exceed all that the Scribes and Pharisees did, we will never make it into the kingdom of heaven. It can be an incredibly discouraging passage if we do not understand the context of this statement. We can contemplate our behavior in the eyes of our neighbors, no less a perfect and Holy God, and realize that we are nowhere near as good as the Pharisees, and I speak from the human perspective here. After all, we do not hold ourselves accountable to all the rules of the Old Testament, do we?

We no longer value more minor matters like the Old Testament's precise directives on cleaning the house found to be infected with mold. Look it up sometime. You may be shocked to realize that when you see mold under the caulk in your shower or bathtub, the Old Testament would have directed you to burn down your house to assure that it didn't continue to spread. This may sound harsh, but remember, penicillin was still thousands of years away, and God was protecting His people as they were the time capsule appointed to bring us the Messiah. The point is this: if you think you can lean on rule-keeping to earn a relationship with God, then let's hope you don't have any hidden mold in your house.

Jesus said that you needed to exceed the righteousness of the law-keepers and the proponents of the law, or you didn't even have a chance. Let's put that in context again. Jesus was speaking to a crowd in the time before He was crucified. The law had not yet been fulfilled. He told them that it would remain in force until it was fulfilled. He Himself would soon fulfill it, and then He became the sacrifice needed to make a bridge from men (unable to keep the law) to reach God (who was unwilling to compromise the law). Jesus was teaching people that their works were worthless. Jesus was convincing people that works-based efforts were hopeless and that they needed a Savior. Jesus was showing people that running faster on the treadmill wouldn't get them anywhere. After all, the bar He was setting was not to run faster; it was to go faster than any human being will ever be able to run. Or in other words, this is not a race we can "win" by trying harder.

But what about Peter? Didn't he tell people to fight sin and do good works after the New Covenant was already in place?

1 Peter 2:11-17, NIV

Dear friends, I urge you, as foreigners and exiles, to abstain from sinful desires, which wage war against your soul. Live such good lives among the pagans that, though they accuse you of doing wrong, they may see your good deeds and glorify God on the day he visits us.

Submit yourselves for the Lord's sake to every human authority: whether to the emperor, as the supreme authority, or to governors, who are sent by him to punish those who do wrong and to commend those who do right. For it is God's will that by doing good you should silence the ignorant talk of foolish people. Live as free people, but do not use your freedom as a cover-up for evil; live as God's slaves. Show proper respect to everyone, love the family of believers, fear God, honor the emperor.

Peter was writing to Christians when the Roman government routinely persecuted them, yet he ends his writing by suggesting they honor the emperor. That is a challenging call! In this context, we might ask ourselves if Peter is suggesting that we are doing good works to lead our neighbors to Christ. While Peter has certainly written about the impact we can and should have on the world around us, that is not his point here. Let's examine the text at the end of verse 12. He expects accusations but expects that those accusations will be put to nothing on the day God visits us. That day is not expected to be a good day to be a pagan. God is not looking to receive glory at that final hour through people coming to Him, but through the exercising of His final judgment, long restrained. In verse 15, we can also see that Peter's intention is silencing the ignorant talk of foolish people. In context, Peter is asking us to honor the God who has first loved us by loving Him back through our behaviors. This is the love response that replaces the traditional religious fear-threat motive.

Things get slippery when we aspire to the hope that only our good should be seen by the world around us. Only when the work that Christ has begun in us is completed, when we enter our fully redeemed states (and as a hint, I do not mean in this life) will we be able to live a perfect life as Christ did. So, how are we to aspire to what the passages in Matthew and Peter are calling us to now if we know that these things are presently impossible? Let's look at an excerpt from 1 John and see if we can find the answer.

1 John 1:5-10, ESV
This is the message we have heard from him and proclaim to you, that God is light, and in him is no darkness at all. If we say we have fellowship with him while we walk in darkness, we lie and do not practice the truth. But if we walk in the light, as he is in the light, we have fellowship with one another, and the blood of Jesus his Son cleanses us from all sin. If we say we have no sin, we deceive ourselves, and the truth is not in us. If we confess our sins, he is faithful and just to forgive us our sins and

*to cleanse us from all unrighteousness. If we say we have
not sinned, we make him a liar, and his word is not in us.*

Here is where I hope I can bring home the point. God's recipe
for us having an impact on the world around us is incomplete
if we think it is only a show of good works. We can run endless
fundraisers. We can feed the homeless under a bridge. We can
provide clothing for the poor. We can visit the prisoner in jail.
We can mightily preach God's Word with great authority and
power. We can even speak in the tongues of men and angels, but
we are still at risk of being a putrid smell to the world around us
if we claim to be without sin.

**There is nothing less attractive or believable than when the
Gospel is shared by someone who claims not to need it for
themselves.**

If we approach the world as if we see ourselves as better than
them, we lose sight of our reality. We are losing sight of the truth
regarding what we still rightly deserve and would receive, but for
the Grace of God.

After all, salvation doesn't change what we deserve, only
who receives it.

Leading them home – transparently

I was once taken back by the lyrics of a song from a group
named Mars Ill. It had an impact on me when I visualized the
lyrics. The song, *Breathe Slow*, resonated with me even more as
I saw how it laid out a picture of how we can help lead others to
Christ.

From Mars Ill "Breathe Slow":

> Blessed is the head that shares the crown that he possesses
> Consider yourselves my brethren and this song is my confession
> 'Cause man shall not live by the bottle alone
> I keep a fist raised to the sky so you can follow me home...

The key point of the song is made in a few of the lines you can see above. "Blessed is the man who shares the crown that he possesses." The songwriter is trying to express a clear sense that we are not given salvation so we can hoard it, skulking off to the narrow gate. We are not given this gift so that we can despise the others who were not smart enough to grab the free gift that we now feel so proud of. Instead, he suggests that we model him by raising our fists to the sky, i.e., living our lives out in the open, so that others can also "follow us home." Jesus said, "Man shall not live by bread alone." The songwriter uses many controversial lines, such as "man shall not live by the bottle alone," to reference how in the modern vernacular, we may have replaced our need for bread (in such a prosperous society) with a desire for self-medication. He posits it is time for us to rise above the base, useless, and hopeless things and head toward something better, just as Jesus did.

So how does this metaphor relate?

When we try to convince our neighbors that we are better than them, that we are "good" or sinless, we attempt a fraud that no one has ever been able to pull off. After all, part of how human beings work is that we are exceptional at noticing the splinter in our neighbor's eye. Do we think that if we do good deeds, our neighbors will suddenly see the splinter in their own eyes but overlook the log in ours because of our good works? No. It is more likely they will begin to resent us, seeing us as goody-goodies who look down on them, or they will become ever more keenly aware of every speck of dust in our eyes. Rather, the point that the author of that song was trying to make is this: If we want to "live in the light" as the Apostle John calls us to, we have to do a terrifying new thing. We have to be willing to live in the light. We must be willing to "raise our fists to the sky so [they] can follow us home."

We are the Bibles the world is reading; we are the creeds the world is needing; we are the sermons the world is heeding. —Billy Graham

If we think living in the light means that we are the source of the light, we are not getting it at all. In Matthew, Jesus made the case that God examines the heart and the attitudes of the heart and that our works are insufficient unless we are significantly more righteous than those who pile good works and rule-keeping upon more good works and more rule-keeping. So how on earth can we possibly impact our neighbors for the kingdom of God? Who would ever have the courage to say, "Follow me home?"

The answer to this quandary is simple. We live in the light by doing good works to honor our God and openly admitting that we are still sinners on a long journey home. If we believe the gates will only be open to us because of God's grace, given to us through faith in Jesus Christ, we can share this as something we need, and they need, and we know where it can be found. This is transparent humility.

Living in transparent humility makes us authentic. It forces us to admit that it is not our good works giving us an in with God but testifies that we only have an in with God because it has been given to us as a gift. It also makes that gift something our neighbors can now see as also being within their grasp. It shows that our good works are a love response, not a fear-threat response, and not part of a contest to see who can do enough good to earn God's favor.

That is the message of the Gospel. Man has no way of pleasing God on his own, but Jesus Christ has made a way. If we find it, shouldn't we live in the light as we walk home? Shouldn't we hold our "fists to the sky" so our neighbors can follow us there too?

Living this way will require a fair understanding of grace and its extraordinary riches. You may not be surprised that I will return here to the need for discipleship. Immature Christians are easily led astray by the doctrine of works. They are easily led into feeling that they are closest to God when practicing formalism. They are easily drawn into circles where people pretend to be good and then fellowship as they compare their good works. Welcome back to the competition. Welcome back to a dead end. Welcome back to fruitlessness in your neighborhood.

Fruitlessness is not where we want to end up, and it's not where we want new Christians to end up. We want their joy to grow as they come to genuinely understand just how deeply God loves them despite their historical and present sin. We do not rejoice because we can sin, but we rejoice because we are free from the power of sin. We are no longer inclined to hide it from ourselves, neighbors, or God. That is what our neighbors are looking for: to see us living in the light and seeing what it brings.

12

Empowering the Body of Christ

Equip the saints

THE PURPOSE OF the church and its leadership is to equip the saints. Having been equipped, the saints go out into the world to do the good works "prepared for them in advance." These include the practical things the Bible calls us to, like caring for the poor. Most of us agree this is what we are called to do. But that is not the end of our commission. We (the body of Christ) were also clearly commissioned, by Jesus Himself, to go into all the world and make disciples. There is no greater cure for what ails the world than for the number of those who call Jesus Lord to increase within it.

> **"Never doubt that a small group of thoughtful, committed citizens can change the world; indeed, it's the only thing that ever has." —Margaret Mead**

Margaret Mead, a twentieth-century anthropologist, may not have realized that she perfectly described what Jesus did when He discipled a small group of men who then went and turned the world on its head. But what exactly is it that makes the difference between a small group of citizens and a small group of committed activists? Simple. The latter have been instilled with a confident belief that the future they are working toward is worthy of necessitating action now.

In the paradigm of Christianity, this also requires preparation. And surprisingly, it is not the new convert who lacks the motivation to invest in their newfound treasure.

The reality is that people are busy, and... people are lazy, aren't we? We have to push ourselves to do almost anything even if it will be directly beneficial to us, no less the things that are primarily beneficial for others. But an investment in the discipleship of another is not a one-way investment.

"Most people want to change the world to improve their lives, but the world they need to change first is the one inside themselves." —John Maxwell

If we want to change the course of the world through Christianity, we are going to need to start with ourselves, not with the world. Yes, we need to serve and disciple the world to see it change, but that is a job that deserves and requires at least as much training and preparation as working at a sandwich shop. Imagine going into a Subway "sandwich shop" and asking for the Turkey Club, only to have the employee respond, "Okay, I can probably do that. What should be on it?" Unfortunately, the experience of many new believers can be just as disappointing. They expect that other believers will be able to answer the question, "So what do I do now?" Far too often, they receive empty platitudes like "stop smoking," or "start buying Christian bookmarks," or worse, "I have no idea!" Some will suggest reading the Bible or going to church regularly. But how many will excitedly offer to study the Bible with that new believer for an hour a week? Will they offer to help the new believer find a local church that teaches the full counsel of God's word?

Indeed, many churches still do discipleship and biblical teaching quite well, but the vast majority do not. For most, and the evidence presented in previous chapters indicates that Christianity has largely become a dusty old lifestyle of behaviors, attendance, modest offerings, and looking down on our neighbors for not being in the "good people's club." Occasionally, an outsider may be attracted to this and willing to join, but most (like the parable of the seeds) will fail to develop roots in this environment and will be quickly carried away by the cares of life.

Education is the most powerful weapon which you can use to change the world. —Nelson Mandela

Nelson Mandela is correct here. Economic education teaches people how to build up capital and create businesses. That network of companies can then support a growing economy, enabling parents to provide the means for their children to learn to read as well. Let that soak in for a generation, and you will soon have people debating philosophy and being inspired by the great works of literature.

Why is it that we can all see the power of education so clearly when we consider the plight of those trying to escape poverty in the third world but fail to see the far greater power of this same truth when it comes to helping our own neighbors, friends, and coworkers escape the spiritual poverty of their pre-Christ state? Imagine how short-sighted it would seem to distribute a truck full of Snickers bars in a ghetto, then claim that we had solved hunger in that community. Do you see the parallel? Simply leading the world to accept the free gift of salvation is not enough. Without the education necessary to confidently understand their newfound status as sons and daughters of the Living

God shows the same short-sightedness. We have satisfied their momentary desire but left them vulnerable to their pre-existing plight of ignorance.

The ones who are crazy enough to think that they can change the world, are the ones who do. —Steve Jobs

Imagine if we had a complex technical product and wanted to hire people to sell it. What if we hired them, told them it was an excellent product, and asked them to commit to telling others about it, and they agreed. Would it then make sense for us to send them out and expect them to get results, having never been trained in-depth regarding what the product does, who it could help, or what problems it solves? What if we never took the time to explain the objections they would get when they tried to convince someone of the good it could do? What if we never told them about competing alternatives and why we were better, or how the competing product's sales people might try to confuse the market or even lie about our advantages? Would those new salespeople be effective? The obvious answer to most, if we are being intellectually honest, is, of course not.

The solution to the metaphor about equipping salespeople is the same as the solution for the church. We need to equip the disciple-makers:

- They need to know what they are offering (i.e., how does salvation work?).
- They need to understand how to determine when someone is ready to receive the Gospel and how to present it to them.

- They need to have thought through why their target market actually needs what they have to share.
- They need to know what the objections might be and how to help someone overcome them.
- They need to know about competing worldviews, their flaws, and why Christianity is superior.
- They need to be familiar with marketplace distortions their hearer will encounter and be prepared to refute them soundly.

Many churches have become a collection of programs and ministries, but few of these programs are designed to equip and train believers (i.e., the saints). Men are especially attracted to rescuing others. Instead, we often plan another men's fishing fellowship where they are encouraged to expose their weaknesses and sing together. What they want, by their very nature, is to test out their newfound hunting skills in debate, evangelism, service, hospitality—and ultimately, the rescue of others as ambassadors of reconciliation. But deep inside, we know we can't have them go and do that yet, because even after thirty years or more, they aren't ready. Perhaps another fishing outing?

Consider Paul's letter to the Ephesians, where he looked over at the Roman praetorian guard assigned to detain him in his home in Rome. Paul observed his uniform and equipment and related this as a metaphor for our spiritual equipping. This section is commonly referred to as "The whole armor of God."

Ephesians 6:10-20, ESV
Finally, be strong in the Lord and in the strength of his might. Put on the whole armor of God, that you may be able to stand against the schemes of the devil. For we

do not wrestle against flesh and blood, but against the rulers, against the authorities, against the cosmic powers over this present darkness, against the spiritual forces of evil in the heavenly places. Therefore take up the whole armor of God, that you may be able to withstand in the evil day, and having done all, to stand firm. Stand therefore, having fastened on the belt of truth, and having put on the breastplate of righteousness, and, as shoes for your feet, having put on the readiness given by the gospel of peace. In all circumstances take up the shield of faith, with which you can extinguish all the flaming darts of the evil one; and take the helmet of salvation, and the sword of the Spirit, which is the word of God, praying at all times in the Spirit, with all prayer and supplication. To that end, keep alert with all perseverance, making supplication for all the saints, and also for me, that words may be given to me in opening my mouth boldly to proclaim the mystery of the gospel, for which I am an ambassador in chains, that I may declare it boldly, as I ought to speak.

Paul wanted the saints to be equipped and used the metaphor of the armor of God to describe the necessary components and his own desired outcome. He asked them to pray that he would be given words to boldly proclaim the Mystery of the Gospel.

Equipping is about the provisioning of the armor and weapons. It is worth noting that the only offensive weapon listed in this passage is the sword of the Spirit, which Paul defines as the Word of God. If men and women want to be prepared to battle against the lies of the enemy, they must be trained to use the only offensive weapon we are given because it is the only offensive weapon we require. It is the same weapon that Jesus used against the devil when tempted in the desert. If we want to take ground from the enemy, if we're going to free captives, and if we want to win the world around us, we must be able to wield God's Word. Christian leaders are called to equip the saints as an advancing force so that those saints can be sent into the lost and waiting world around them as rescuing ambassadors. How could we live with ourselves if we sent them into that battle with only their defensive weapons? Equipping the saints necessitates diligent training.

Training is about how to use those weapons, or more precisely, how to "give an answer for the hope that is within us."

1 Peter 3:14-16, ESV
*But even if you should suffer for righteousness' sake, you will be blessed. Have no fear of them, nor be troubled, but in your hearts honor Christ the Lord as holy, **always being prepared to make a defense to anyone who asks you for a reason for the hope that is in you**; yet do it with gentleness and respect, having a good conscience, so that, when you are slandered, those who revile your good behavior in Christ may be put to shame.*

We are called into battle (i.e., risking that we will "suffer for righteousness' sake"), and we are even told how the battle will go down. We will be tempted to fear those who will call us out for what we believe, but the advised response is to be "prepared to make a defense to anyone who asks you for a reason for the hope that is in you." And this directive is modified with the directive to deliver it with gentleness and respect.

We are not called to tell the world how we are better than them. Rather, we are called to share how we are like them, also having a desperate need for the Savior and having found Him, we are now willing to share. Peter also advises that handling this in a way that leaves us with a clear conscience will increase the probability of the desired effect, whereby they choose to follow us home.

At the risk of some repetition, training, as we discussed in the metaphor about hiring a sales team, is not just about telling that team the attributes of our faith. It is not just about telling them the story of Jesus Christ. It is about the students having considered and contemplated how the Gospel answers the hard questions that life brings more effectively than its counterfeit alternatives. It is about having practiced how to answer the challenge of competing narratives. Preparation is about having readied ourselves for an inevitable onslaught of accusations from our marketplace enemies and learning how to defeat them with the verifiable truth that we are righteously, intellectually, and most importantly, now defensibly confident in. Ultimately, that is one of the main points of this book, to shore up a foundational element of our Christian faith by laying out a clearer picture of the Mystery Hidden for Ages Past. This mystery, far too often overlooked, is an intricate and powerful revelation of God by God. It is intended for use by redeemed men and women, as His appointed ambassadors, to deliver that supernaturally credentialed message with boldness, gentleness, and respect.

It is critical that these foundational truths, purposed to make us confident in our faith, are taught just as God intended them to be taught and repeated just as often as God intended them to be repeated. These truths must be made available to the saints in ways that prepare them to wield the truth as that "defense for the hope that is within us."

Ours is a wartime mission, so the church can no longer abide with a peacetime mentality. The equipping and training of warriors have for far too long been ignored while the enemy of our souls has waged an active war. Imagine if our nation was being attacked and TV stations were showing video of a fleet of ships coming toward our shores. Imagine the other nation boldly proclaiming that they are coming to wipe us out and enslave us all. It would seem ridiculous if our nation's leaders were to tell us, "Everything will be fine, and we should focus on unemployment legislation and long-term healthcare, or perhaps a stimulus check."

We should be shocked at the dissonance between our urgent reality and the lack of urgency expressed in many Christian circles. Nonetheless, many of us spend week after week, month after month, and year after year sitting in churches and so-called Bible studies that utterly lack the urgency of the reality we face. We are unprepared for the imminent arrival of our enemy and his intended slaughter of our friends and neighbors. We are the ambassadors appointed by Christ to save those in the lands around us, and we have not even begun to take the advancing force seriously, no less to prepare for their onslaught. The real tragedy is not that we are unprepared for our defense but that we are far too often unaware of our desperate and urgent need to be on offense, especially for the sake of our neighbors.

It's time for Christian men and women who are leaders to rise up and serve the church with passion and vigor as they refocus on discipling the saints, readying them to do what God has actually called us all to do.

Prepare for the harvest

God originally designed us as the caretakers of His garden. The earth was designed to provide everything we need, and we were intended to keep it in order. When sin came into the world and broke that relationship, God, masterful at orchestrating alternative paths to His intended outcomes, repurposed our nature.

First, through the saints of old, men carried the story of God down through the ages. Later, as Abraham and his offspring became the nation of Israel, they kept traditions and operated as a distinctive culture making it increasingly easy for others to see God in contrast to the world around them. God had allowed the nature we had, first intended to clarify His created order, now to be used as a means to display His nature to the world around us through our lives.

Once Christ ascended and sent us His Holy Spirit, those of us who have come to faith continue this modified journey as His appointed Ambassadors of Reconciliation.

> *1 Corinthians 5:18-20, NIV*
>
> *All this is from God, who reconciled us to himself through Christ and gave us the ministry of reconciliation: that God was reconciling the world to himself in Christ, not counting people's sins against them. And he has committed to us the message of reconciliation. We are therefore Christ's ambassadors, as though God were making his appeal through us. We implore you on Christ's behalf: Be reconciled to God.*

We are the salt of the earth. We are called to cover, preserve, protect, and influence it in godly ways. However, with God's spiritual workers so woefully undertrained, we find ourselves collectively unable to lead and, even worse, easily misled. Consider this short article on a troubling survey released in 2020 by Dr. Barna, the Director of Research at the Cultural Research Center at Arizona Christian University:

New Barna Poll: The Christian Church is Seriously Messed up.
August 12, 2020, News Division American Worldview Inventory 2020

A new poll *last week* released by George Barna's Cultural Research Center shows that professing Christians are developing more and more decidedly unchristian beliefs, demonstrating that many of these professing Christians are in fact un-professing pagans.

According to the American Worldview Inventory 2020, syncretism rules the day, with the majority of Christians having fundamental, troubling, primary belief problems.

56% of respondents who identify as Christian and who attend Evangelical churches, or 62% of Christians who say they attend Pentecostal churches, profess that having "some type" of religious faith is more important than which faith a person aligns with. Unsurprisingly, Mainline Protestants churches were at 67% and Roman Catholic at 77%

When asked if one could qualify for heaven by being good or doing good, compared to the belief that salvation comes ONLY from embracing Christ as Savior, 41% of professing evangelicals said that if a person is generally good, or does enough good things in their life they will earn a place in heaven, a view shared by 77% of Roman Catholics.

Dr. George Barna, CRC Director of Research and one of the authors of the survey, called the results of this latest survey discouraging.

"If you step back and look at the big picture painted by all of the outcomes in this research project it seems to suggest that people are in an 'anything goes' mindset when it comes to faith, morals, values, and lifestyle," Barna commented. "Americans appear to be creating unique, highly customized worldviews based on feelings, experiences and opportunities rather than working within the boundaries of a comprehensive, time-tested, consistent worldview.

Views on Faith, Sin and Salvation											
		Type of Church You Attend Most							Political Ideology		
Perspective	All Adults	Evan	Pent	MLP	Cath	BAC	Other	Skep	Con	Mod	Lib
Having faith matters more than which faith you have	63%	56%	62%	67%	77%	62%	61%	45%	59%	63%	69%
You consciously and consistently try to avoid sinning because you know your sins break God's heart	56	85	82	58	65	82	36	16	75	49	41
You have a personal responsibility, in appropriate situations, to share your religious beliefs with people who believe differently than you	49	74	74	48	54	71	38	20	67	43	38
A person who is generally good, or does enough good things for others, will earn a place in Heaven	48	41	46	44	70	38	54	32	42	49	54
You consider yourself to be a Christian; and when you die you will go to Heaven only because you have confessed your sins and have accepted Jesus Christ as your savior	33	72	55	41	28	100	0	0	52	28	16

Abbreviations:
Evan – attend evangelical church
Pent – attend Pentecostal church
Cath – attend Catholic church
BAC – born again Christian
Other – faith other than Christianity
Skep – Spiritual Skeptic
MLP – attend mainline Protestant church
Con – politically conservative
Mod – politically moderate
Lib – politically liberal

Source: American Worldview Inventory 2020; Cultural Research Center at Arizona Christian University; N=2,000 adults 18 or older.

If you look at some of the dominant elements in the American mind and heart today, as illuminated by the Inventory, we find that most people say that the objective of life is feeling good about yourself; that all faiths are of equal value; that entry into God's eternal presence is determined by one's personal means of choice; and that there are no absolutes to guide or grow us morally.

Reference: https://pulpitandpen.org/2020/08/12new-barna-poll-the-christian-church-is-seriously-messed-up/

Dr. Barna described the results of this survey as discouraging. I agree!

Is this the fruit of science, or is it the fruit of our unwillingness to engage when the high calling of science is misused as a weapon against the one who gave us science? Is this the fruit of modern philosophy, or is it the fruit of the modern church's lack of readiness to engage when philosophy is wielded like an ax in self-defiance against philosophy's own roots of logic and reason? Is this the fruit of churchgoers unwilling to study, or is it the fruit of leaders refusing to train them to be effective spiritual salt, or in this case. is it both? I think the answers are apparent. There is powerful truth in the Scripture. If we teach that truth, its power will be reflected. If we ignore that truth or fail to teach it, that will also be reflected in our lack of power and influence.

Imagine keeping your fertilizer in the bag and then being surprised it didn't have the desired effect on your garden.

The weapons we must take to battle

The battle between good and evil is a battle between truth and lies. It really is as simple as that because the war is between the source of all truth and the source of all lies. Some say it was in the days before men, and some say it was in the early days of creation, but regardless we are told of a rebellion in the heavens. In Ezekiel 28, we are told that Lucifer was once both "the signet of perfection, full of wisdom and perfect in beauty" and "an anointed guardian cherub." He was a created being, lofty in position and power, who allowed corruption to enter his heart. Ultimately, as John recorded for us in Revelation 12, he brought war to the heavens.

Revelation 12:7-9, ESV
Now war arose in heaven, Michael and his angels fighting against the dragon. And the dragon and his

angels fought back, but he was defeated, and there was no longer any place for them in heaven. And the great dragon was thrown down, that ancient serpent, who is called the devil and Satan, the deceiver of the whole world—he was thrown down to the earth, and his angels were thrown down with him.

We also know that one-third of the angels were cast down with Satan based on an allusion provided earlier in Revelation 12. In the book of Daniel, also very vividly in Ezekiel 28, and in various other places throughout the Scripture, we are given veiled insights into a shadowy spirit kingdom set up around the physical realm of the earth by these fallen spiritual beings.

Daniel 10:12-14, ESV

Then he said to me, "Fear not, Daniel, for from the first day that you set your heart to understand and humbled yourself before your God, your words have been heard, and I have come because of your words. The prince of the kingdom of Persia withstood me twenty-one days, but Michael, one of the chief princes, came to help me, for I was left there with the kings of Persia, and came to make you understand what is to happen to your people in the latter days. For the vision is for days yet to come."

I can assure you that "the prince of the kingdom of Persia" was not a mortal man that had somehow learned to restrain the angels. If we doubt this, we can look into the Scriptures of Ezekiel 28, where Ezekiel is given twin laments to record for **the prince of Tyre** (accurately forecasting the unexpected defeat and death of **the King of Tyre** at the hands of Alexander the Great) and then another for **the King of Tyre**, the clearly unhuman figure behind the Prince of Tyre:

Ezekiel 28:11-15, ESV

*Moreover, the word of the Lord came to me: "Son of man, raise a lamentation over **the king of Tyre**, and say to him, Thus says the Lord God:*
"You were the signet of perfection,
full of wisdom and perfect in beauty.
You were in Eden, the garden of God;
every precious stone was your covering,
sardius, topaz, and diamond,
beryl, onyx, and jasper,
sapphire, emerald, and carbuncle;
and crafted in gold were your settings
and your engravings.
*On **the day that you were created***
they were prepared.
***You were an anointed guardian cherub**.*
I placed you; you were on the holy mountain of God;
in the midst of the stones of fire you walked.
You were blameless in your ways
from the day you were created,
till unrighteousness was found in you.

The passage above shows us a government behind the earthly government. Still, it would also appear to even the most casual observer to be a reference to the father of lies himself.

The argument this insidious character first made, and has always made, is that God is not good. He argues that God does

241

not have our best interests at heart. He wields accusations that God cannot be trusted and is trying to keep us from something better. Satan seeks to divide us from God first through distrust, then through envy, then through deceiving us into acting upon the deception until we find that we have betrayed our Creator, Friend, and God. Then, he can use the fear of that division multiplied through our shame to further separate and isolate us from our Protector until we become his playthings.

If we are willing to accept our isolation from God and all that God provides, we will need another system for our provision. Satan is all too glad and quite ready to provide this alternative. However, he is not God, and his system is not godly. No matter how much we put into that system, it always delivers diminishing returns. We are offered very much for very little in the beginning. Still, eventually, the world's system requires that we give it everything in return for very little, including, across time, our very lives.

As a means of vicious and hurtful revenge against the One who cast him down, Satan desires to use us as pawns. His goal is to isolate us from God. Then, he means to deceive us into committing eternal suicide by convincing us to join his foolish rebellion against living life within the confines of safety laid out for us by the God who created us. We can see this same pattern even in the original narrative in the garden of Eden.

Genesis 3:1-8, ESV
Now the serpent was more crafty than any other beast of the field that the Lord God had made.

*He said to the woman, "**Did God actually say, 'You shall not eat of any tree in the garden'**?" And the woman said to the serpent, "We may eat of the fruit of the trees* *in the garden, but God said, 'You shall not eat of the fruit of the tree that is in the midst of the garden, neither shall you touch it, lest you die.'"* **But the serpent said to the woman, "You will not surely die. For God knows that when you eat of it your eyes will be opened, and you will be like God,** *knowing good and evil." So* **when the woman saw that the tree was good for food, and that it was a delight to the eyes, and that the tree was to be desired to make one wise, she took of its fruit and ate, and she also gave some to her husband who was with her, and he ate.** *Then the eyes of both were opened, and they knew that they were naked. And they sewed fig leaves together and made themselves loincloths.*

And **they heard the sound of the Lord God walking in the garden in the cool of the day, and the man and his wife hid themselves from the presence of the Lord** *God among the trees of the garden.*

We have been up against deception from the very beginning. Hollywood has programmed us to perceive the influence of our spiritual enemy as a dark presence with the penchant to spin people around. We expect him to throw them through the air, burn them alive, contort them into demonic creatures, and extend their lives across centuries if only they will avoid the sun. But there are powers he has not actually been granted. This is not to say that the enemy's influence has never been unleashed in remarkable and visible ways. Rather, it is to say that the power to do visible things is far less meaningful than his power of deception. Further, that latter and more likely means of assault is the one we are more woefully underprepared for.

When we are deceived, we become willing to do evil and unwise things to ourselves and others. Think of the great wars in our history. Did supernatural forces kill millions of Jews during World War II? No. Men, deceived by supernatural forces, did it themselves. We can see the rule of diminishing returns. Hitler's evil empire grew in might and power at a pace that almost none before it had ever been able to accomplish. The shadow of the rise of the Third Reich hung heavy over the entire world. It began to embolden other tyrants around the world as well. In the beginning, it took little more than powerful speeches and subtle subversion to organize an advancing army that seemed unstoppable. However, by the end, Hitler and his human allies were pouring in their young, their stolen treasure, and all of their passions and energy, yet none of it was enough. The Allied forces were coming for the Germans. Those not killed were brought to trial and humbled before those they had once thought themselves to be above.

Satan's methods and outcomes are not new. We are relatively young in contrast to him. By the time we gain seventy or eighty years of wisdom and experience, the strength of our bodies wanes. In contrast, the enemy of our souls has had many thousands of years to study the patterns and vulnerabilities of humans. He wasn't bad at deception from the start, and while he has undoubtedly advanced his methods across time, they remain based on the same routine principles that we see in the Genesis account:

- First, instill doubt in what God has said.
- Second, suggest that following God's plan will limit your human potential.

- Third, suggest that you set up a new kingdom under his auspices and system.
- Fourth, once you have taken hold of the act of betrayal, he will shower you with guilt and shame to assure you remain isolated from God.
- Fifth, use you for his own designs, including giving you access to the power and wealth he wished he could wield if only he had a physical form.
- Finally, when you are no longer useful, he discards you to the ash heap of history and moves on to repeat the plan with his next unwitting victim.

All the while, he has leveraged your influence and actions to lead others away from God as well, and he delights as they unwittingly join the dead-end rebellion of the big lie.

The weapons we must wield against this lie are not natural weapons. The weapons we need to combat deception are the weapons of truth. But even if we have the truth, we still must recognize the weapons of deceit. When they are raised against us, we must immediately recognize them as counterfeit so that we also instinctively counter them with the truth!

The US Treasury first teaches its agents every fine detail of genuine currency. There will always be new and innovative attempts to create counterfeit money. If you train new agents to recognize a particular pattern of counterfeit but fail to teach them to instinctively recognize the genuine article, they will be ill-prepared for the next innovation of counterfeit. Let me explain the metaphor if I haven't already made it clear enough. If we teach new Christians the truth about God so thoroughly that they understand it, as well as treasury agents understand the material, printing, and details of US currency, then they will also spot counterfeits immediately.

We need to be armed with a thorough understanding of who God is, confident that what He says is true, and aware enough of the patterns woven through His Word that we can instinctively spot an imitation as easily as a treasury agent would spot counterfeit currency. When he sees it, even in a casual moment, he knows it is time to act. The foundation of the economy he protects relies on people's faith in their currency. So then, how should we react when we see a lie that undermines the hope of all mankind? Likewise, we are called to spring into action with the truth.

2 Corinthians 10:3-5, ESV

*For though we walk in the flesh, we are not waging war according to the flesh. For **the weapons of our warfare are not of the flesh but have divine power to destroy strongholds. We destroy arguments and every lofty opinion raised against the knowledge of God, and take every thought captive to obey Christ***

Just as our proverbial treasury agent would show his identification and immediately ask to examine the rest of the money, we have the power of The Holy Spirit enabling us to freeze deception in its tracks. As Paul said, we have the power to "destroy arguments and every lofty opinion raised against the knowledge of God." We may not believe that we have this power, but we do, and it is incredibly fearsome when God's people have been equipped to recognize counterfeit and respond to it with the truth.

Ephesians 4:11-21, ESV

And he [Jesus] gave the apostles, the prophets, the evangelists, the shepherds and teachers, **to equip the saints for the work of ministry,** *for building up the body of Christ, until we all attain to the unity of the faith and of the knowledge of the Son of God, to mature manhood, to the measure of the stature of the fullness of Christ,* **so that we may no longer be children, tossed to and fro by the waves and carried about by every wind of doctrine, by human cunning, by craftiness in deceitful schemes.** *Rather, speaking the truth in love, we are to grow up in every way into him who is the head, into Christ, from whom* **the whole body, joined and held together by every joint with which it is equipped, when each part is working properly, makes the body grow** *so that it builds itself up in love.*

*Now this I say and testify in the Lord, that you must no longer walk as the Gentiles do, in the futility of their minds. They are darkened in their understanding, alienated from the life of God because of the ignorance that is in them, due to their hardness of heart. They have become callous and have given themselves up to sensuality, greedy to practice every kind of impurity. But that is not the way you learned Christ!—***assuming that you have heard about him and were taught in him, as the truth is in Jesus***

But lacking understanding, we are "tossed to and fro by the waves, and [we are] carried about by every wind of doctrine." We are "deceived by human cunning" and "vulnerable to the craftiness of deceitful schemes." We think "speaking the truth in love" ends with the word truth. We are very comfortable telling the world and its people how evil they are. There, we have spoken our truth! But speaking the truth *in love* is modified by the word love. It's the difference between throwing down the life ring and throwing it down with the rope still connected. If we see people who have fallen into a sea of deception as people that God loves, and if we see that as a common occurrence, we will be inspired to train ourselves up for the work of rescue. That requires we do more than tell the world and those in it how evil they are. We need to respond to the enemy's lies with the better truth and a willingness to help them see it deeply.

> *Luke 4:1-13, ESV*
> *And **Jesus, full of the Holy Spirit**, returned from the Jordan and was led by the Spirit in the wilderness for forty days, being tempted by the devil. And he ate nothing during those days. And when they were ended, he was hungry. The devil said to him, "If you are the Son of God, command this stone to become bread." And **Jesus answered him, "It is written**, 'Man shall not live by bread alone.'" And the devil took him up and showed him all the kingdoms of the world in a moment of time, and said to him, "To you I will give all this authority and their glory, for it has been delivered to me, and I give it to whom I will. If you, then, will worship me, it will all be yours." And **Jesus answered him, "It is written**,*
>> *"'You shall worship the Lord your God,*
>> *and him only shall you serve.'"*
> *And he took him to Jerusalem and set him on the pinnacle of the temple and said to him, "If you are the Son of God, throw yourself down from here, for it is written,*

"'He will command his angels concerning you,
to guard you,'

and

"'On their hands they will bear you up,
lest you strike your foot against a stone.'"
And **Jesus answered him, "It is said,** *'You shall not*
put the Lord your God to the test.'" *13 And when the devil*
had ended every temptation, he departed from him until
an opportune time.

One disheartening thing I hear far too often from people
who have spent their lives in church is some form of the statement, "I don't need to be an expert in Scripture. I've got the Holy
Spirit." What saddens me about this is that people do not realize
that Jesus Himself, as we can see in the passage above, from Luke
4, who is also God Himself, still quoted the Scripture to respond
to the enemy's innovative distortions of it. It is why Paul says
that he taught the "whole counsel of God."

Acts 20:26-32, ESV

Therefore I testify to you this day **that I am innocent**
of the blood of all, for I did not shrink from declaring
to you the whole counsel of God. *Pay careful attention*
to yourselves and to all the flock, in which the Holy Spirit
has made you overseers, to care for the church of God,
which he obtained with his own blood. I know that **after**
my departure fierce wolves will come in among you, *not*
sparing the flock; and from among your own selves will
arise **men speaking twisted things, to draw away the**
disciples after them. *Therefore be alert, remembering that*
for three years I did not cease night or day to admonish

every one with tears. ***And now I commend you to God and to the word of his grace,***

Paul knew that after he left, men would come in looking to distort the Gospel, hoping to pick off those who had not paid attention to what Paul had shared with them passionately. They would show them partial truths and then lead them astray into partial lies; thus, the atrophy would begin. However, if we teach the Word of God, the illuminating power of the Holy Spirit will support our efforts. We are not encouraged to focus on one part of the Bible that we find particularly powerful but instead to emulate what Paul did by teaching "the full counsel of God." In other words, going through passage-by-passage and explaining each part whether we are comfortable with that part or not.

When those new treasury agents, whom we discussed earlier, first start their careers, they may be imagining chasing bad guys with guns blazing. So, it must be a bit of a letdown to find out that they will first spend a fairly long time studying the currency they have been hired to protect. How tiring it must be to learn each detail of the 3D ribbon embedded in modern currency. How uninspiring it must be to examine and memorize how many lines there are in the brow of Thomas Jefferson on bills that bear his likeness. Yet, when they are finally presented with a variety of counterfeits, they will be able to demonstrate with confidence that these cannot be the genuine article. Metaphorically, this is what the saints are called to as well.

13

Go and Do Likewise

He's coming again!

THE MAIN TOPIC of this book has been the remarkable credentialing of Jesus' first visit. We have gone into detail about how God masterfully placed a steganographic message across the entire Old Testament that could only be seen after Christ had fulfilled it. By itself, this is an extraordinary thing. In fact, it is the hope of all mankind. However, what we have examined up to this point is not the fulfillment of all messianic prophecies.

One of the primary reasons the Jews of Jesus' time had trouble accepting Him as the Messiah is that they were looking for Him to fulfill the prophetic passages that are still going to be fulfilled in His second coming. The Bible describes this as the 'great and terrible day of the Lord'. This is a weighty thing to consider. On the one hand, all will finally be set right. On the other hand, for those still rebelling against Him, there will be no time left to turn, and the outcome of that day of cleansing will be horrific but necessary as it leads to something just and pure and beyond our ability to imagine.

2 Peter, Chapter 3, ESV
The Day of the Lord Will Come
This is now the second letter that I am writing to you, beloved. In both of them I am stirring up your sincere mind by way of reminder, that you should remember the predictions of the holy prophets and the commandment

of the Lord and Savior through your apostles, knowing this first of all, that scoffers will come in the last days with scoffing, following their own sinful desires. They will say, "Where is the promise of his coming? For ever since the fathers fell asleep, all things are continuing as they were from the beginning of creation." For they deliberately overlook this fact, that the heavens existed long ago, and the earth was formed out of water and through water by the word of God, and that by means of these the world that then existed was deluged with water and perished. But by the same word the heavens and earth that now exist are stored up for fire, being kept until the day of judgment and destruction of the ungodly.

But do not overlook this one fact, beloved, that with the Lord one day is as a thousand years, and a thousand years as one day. The Lord is not slow to fulfill his promise as some count slowness, but is patient toward you, not wishing that any should perish, but that all should reach repentance. But the day of the Lord will come like a thief, and then the heavens will pass away with a roar, and the heavenly bodies will be burned up and dissolved, and the earth and the works that are done on it will be exposed.

Since all these things are thus to be dissolved, what sort of people ought you to be in lives of holiness and godliness, waiting for and hastening the coming of the day of God, because of which the heavens will be set on fire and dissolved, and the heavenly bodies will melt as they burn! But according to his promise we are waiting for new heavens and a new earth in which righteousness dwells.

Final Words

Therefore, beloved, since you are waiting for these, be diligent to be found by him without spot or blemish, and at peace. And count the patience of our Lord as salvation, just as our beloved brother Paul also wrote to you according to the wisdom given him, as he does in all his letters when he speaks in them of these matters. There are some things in them that are hard to understand, which the ignorant and unstable twist to their own destruction, as they do the other Scriptures. You therefore, beloved, knowing this beforehand, take care that you are not carried away with the error of lawless people and lose your own stability. But grow in the grace and knowledge of our Lord and Savior Jesus Christ. To him be the glory both now and to the day of eternity. Amen.

Being ready

If you have made it this far through the book and are not sure this matter is resolved for you personally, i.e., that you are certain of your eternal reconciliation with God, then please let's take a moment and get that straightened out. If you have examined the Great Mystery of the Gospel and come to the obvious conclusion that Christ is exactly who He says He is, then it's time to acknowledge Him, accept the free gift He has offered you, and join the family of God. It can be as simple as speaking so quietly that no one can hear you except God and saying something like:

"Dear God, I admit that You are who You say You are and that I am a sinner in need of salvation. I now see that I have been deceived into joining a rebellion against You, and I don't want to be a part of it anymore. I want to come home. I want to be accepted into Your family again and accept Jesus' offer to pay for my sins. I want to turn away from my sin and call Jesus Lord and receive my salvation."

God has promised that if we confess our sins, He is faithful and just to forgive them and that He will cleanse us of all unrighteousness and come and live within us. That doesn't mean we won't still sin. It means that sin will no longer have the same power over us and that God will send His Holy Spirit to live within us as He transforms us into the image of Christ Himself over time.

Once we are members of the family of Christ, we are also immediately in training to serve as His ambassadors.

The Ambassadors

A Masters of Divinity is not required for one to absorb and proclaim the truth of the Gospel. After all, as the angels proclaimed:

Luke 2:10, ESV
*And the angel said to them, "Fear not, for behold, I bring you good news of great joy that will be **for all the people**."*

We do not need to be trained pastors or to become an expert in every area of the Bible before any change can begin. No, we simply need to dive into God's Word one passage at a time, asking for exactly what He promised us, the illuminating power of the Holy Spirit that helps us understand. But wherever possible, it is of the highest benefit for a new believer to get ingrained into a believing body of Christ and seek formal discipleship. However, if you cannot find such a local group, do not despair. Just start digging in and trust God to bring the counselors you need in time!

If all the expert teachers at the US Treasury were to be on a bus trip together and suddenly be no more, would the agency still be able to teach young agents to spot counterfeits? Of course, they would! They would sit them in a room and have them study the genuine articles together, to the nth level of detail, and they would find along the way they were becoming the experts themselves. This is not to reduce the value of theology or theologians. God has gifted some to be able to interpret the Scripture at an even deeper level, and He has gifted some to teach at that deeper level—even if they must lean on others for their original understanding. Many have written trustworthy resources to help us understand the difficult passages.

Many are called to pastor small flocks and serve them in this way—simply examining the genuine article together until it becomes intimately familiar. We should be thankful for people who are gifted and called in these ways. But consider the old adage, as it is true, that God does not have any grandchildren. We are each accountable for accepting His gift of reconciliation, paid for by Christ. When we have done so, we are also given the Holy Spirit to help illuminate God's Word to us, but that can only happen if we open our Bibles.

Do not be concerned if you lack confidence as to which biblical reference you should trust as you begin to dive in. The Bible itself is your most trustworthy reference. The simple and straightforward passages can be reliably used to interpret the difficult or challenging passages. Remember, the Bereans were considered more noble because they tested everything they heard. And what resources did they have for that testing? The Bible itself. At that time, "The Bible" was what we would now refer to as the Old Testament. We not only have the same resources at our disposal as the Bereans did, but we also have more.

The truth is available to us, and it is not hard to find if we are willing to invest time. The weapons of our warfare are the weapons of truth, and these are the weapons we should most desire because they are powerful and entirely within our grasp. Therefore, not being ready to use the weapon of truth after being Christians for many years should be considered wholly unacceptable, especially when we know that it is available to us if only we will invest the time.

If we are of the family of Christ yet feeling unprepared, all we need to do is to repent and ask boldly of Him who gives wisdom generously and gives it without prejudice. And here's more good news as we take on the Ambassador's adventure… God is with us!

Ephesians 2:8-10, ESV

For it is by grace you have been saved, through faith— and this is not from yourselves, it is the gift of God—not by works, so that no one can boast. For we are God's handiwork, created in Christ Jesus to do good works, which God prepared in advance for us to do.

2 Corinthians 5:16-21, ESV

From now on, therefore, we regard no one according to the flesh. Even though we once regarded Christ according to the flesh, we regard him thus no longer. Therefore, if anyone is in Christ, he is a new creation. The old has passed away; behold, the new has come. All this is from

God, who through Christ reconciled us to himself and gave us the ministry of reconciliation; that is, **in Christ God was reconciling the world to himself, not counting their trespasses against them, and entrusting to us the message of reconciliation. Therefore, we are ambassadors for Christ, God making his appeal through us. We implore you on behalf of Christ, be reconciled to God.** *For our sake he made him to be sin who knew no sin, so that in him we might become the righteousness of God.*

1 Corinthians 1:20-25, ESV

Where is the one who is wise? Where is the scribe? Where is the debater of this age? Has not God made foolish the wisdom of the world? For since, in the wisdom of God, the world did not know God through wisdom, it pleased God through the folly of what we preach to save those who believe. For Jews demand signs and Greeks seek wisdom, but we preach Christ crucified, a stumbling block to Jews and folly to Gentiles, but to those who are called, both Jews and Greeks, Christ the power of God and the wisdom of God. For the foolishness of God is wiser than men, and the weakness of God is stronger than men.

Key Takeaways

Let's review some of the key points that we've established so far:

- God's written Word is superior, by orders of magnitude, to the basis of any other system of belief.
- God has big shoulders. He is not afraid of our skeptical questions.

- God credentialed His plan to save mankind and demonstrate His love assuring that the supernatural nature of His rescue plan would be evident for all to see once Christ had completed it.

- God recorded that plan, in advance, in writing, in plain view, for all to see, using advanced steganographic techniques. Therefore, no one, including the prophets, understood it until it had been revealed.

- We know Satan accused God of being self-serving and continuously tells mankind that God cannot be trusted.

- We also know that God's superior intellect easily outwitted satan walking him into a trap of his own making, and

  o Satan's true nature as a murderer and liar was put in plain view while

  o God's true nature as creator, rescuer, and faithful friend was also put into plain sight.

- We can ascertain Satan's shock when he realized he had been exposed at the very moment he believed he was about to defeat the Son of God.

- We know that the disciples were not clear about what was happening until Jesus explained it to them, disproving the idea that this was a complex plan to fulfill Old Testament Scriptures and create a Messiah myth.

- We know that the learned Jews did not perceive Jesus as the Messiah because they did not realize that the prophecies credentialing Him were also about the Messiah. These prophecies were previously considered to be about a mysterious figure known to the Jews as "The Suffering Servant".

- We have shown that the missing key was that God had built a plan for Jesus to come twice.
  - o Once to fulfill the sacrificial system satisfying God's righteous demand for justice, and
  - o once (yet to come) to establish His heavenly kingdom on earth and bring the peace that all men sincerely hope for.
- We have examined the way Jesus revealed the truth about Himself to the apostles, and it was through
  - o examining the predictive prophecies and convocations and
  - o correlating them to the events of His life.
- We have examined the way the disciples and apostles taught.
  - o They were able to reach some of the Jews. They accomplished this by reasoning with them (an intellectual exercise) from the Scriptures.
  - o They were able to reach some of the Gentiles. They did this by first appealing to the sense that all men have that we are created beings and that we can see a divine nature in everything around us. Then they also appealed to God's credentialing work regarding Jesus as the Christ.
- We have examined the style of teaching that the disciples practiced.
  - o They dug deeply into the message of the gospel.
  - o They credentialed it with the message of the Old Testament.
  - o They brought it to a crescendo of clarity around our need to accept God's free gift of grace through faith.
- We have examined the depth of the apostle's teaching.

    o We have seen that they would teach deliberately and persistently, working to fully develop new converts into effective Christian workers through the impartation of the wisdom of God, facilitated by God's Word.

- We have examined the benefits of expository teaching and its approachability.
- We have reviewed the importance of serving our youth through biblical education and confidence building.
  - o We have also examined the high cost of failing to do that.
- We have looked at practical models for serving our neighbors through
  - o the sharing of The Gospel of truth and
  - o by living lives that make it clear that we are recipients of grace, eager to share in the abundant gifts we have been given.
- We have examined the critical nature of equipping the saints to do the work that God has called them to do within His garden, the garden of souls.
- We have examined how we can practically prepare new converts to become competent and confident Christian workers.

Conclusion

To borrow an idea from the Apostle John, I believe that we could fill 10,000 books on any of the topics we cover and still not do justice to the amazing things that God has done before a watching universe. His plan to rescue us is extraordinary, and His execution is worthy of study and confident proclamation. But we are not on our own. God has left us His Holy Spirit, who enlightens our minds and shows us how we can make a difference to the watching world and lead that world into reconciliation with Him one soul at a time.

God desires neither a faithless justice nor a justice-less faith. —Stephen Um

When we arrive commissioned to serve as Jesus' Ambassadors, conveying and carrying out God's rescue plan, it will get noticed. Sometimes we'll be thanked and lauded as heroes, but sometimes we'll be reviled and face persecution. Regardless, we are called to love those around us just as God first loved us while we were yet His enemies.

We are made in God's image. That means the closest many will ever come to seeing God in this life is when they see us serving as His Ambassadors. Like political ambassadors, and in the path of Jesus Himself, we come not speaking our own words but speaking the Father's words, carrying the Great King's letters, and executing the instructions God Himself has given us.

American president John Quincy Adams, previously ambiguous about slavery, had seen the light. He was the only president to ever return to a lower role in U.S. government by returning to Congress after his term as president was complete. His highest goal for that time in congress was to get a bill to the floor that would outlaw slavery in the United States. However, Adams died on his congressional desk, having never seen his goal completed. Thirteen times, his effort to put his bill before Congress was rejected with open ridicule. Once asked if he was tired of his unfruitful efforts to introduce legislation to free the slaves, Adams answered, "To do what is right is mine. The results are up to God." Adam's young mentee, a political disciple if you will, Abraham Lincoln, eventually used roughly the same text to pen the now-famous Emancipation Proclamation. John Quincy Adams left the results to God, and God came through by way of his impact on others. Do we doubt that leaving God's credentialing and guiding words behind as our legacy should have any less profound an impact?

We have gone from being rebels against God, indifferent to our sin and doomed to a bitter end, to being His appointed Ambassadors now running for "an imperishable crown." We are not guaranteed the results we might want, nor that they will come in our lifetime, but we are guaranteed by God Himself that His Word never returns void. We have seen how truth can be revealed to the dying. We carry the hope of eternal life by sharing that cognitively verifiable truth with confidence and using it to extinguish the enemy's lies.

You are now hereby challenged to "Go and do likewise."

Appendices

Appendix 1

The embarrassing riches of supporting evidence

HENRY COMSTOCK IS controversially credited with discovering the famous Comstock Lode, a massive silver ore deposit that created fortunes in Nevada and surrounding areas. However, Comstock did not understand what he truly had. For example, Comstock traded a significant portion of what he called "fearsome mud" for an old donkey and a bottle of whiskey, unaware that the area would be worth hundreds of millions later. And while he did receive $11,000 for a half share of another mine, a sizable amount of money then, he failed to realize that the entire area was chock full of silver. When more sophisticated miners realized what they had, they realized Comstock was likely one of the wealthiest men alive, but he never understood the riches he owned and squandered this great asset, leaving it to others.

How tragic it is when believers or would-be believers are like Comstock in the spiritual sense, unaware of the great riches at their disposal.

If we doubt the veracity of the Bible, we are very much like Comstock. God has left us abundant treasures, even embarrassing riches from which we can extract the truth about the greatest gift of all. But this is not a patch of fearsome mud with silver in it, rather the all-important truth about our relationship with God and the pathway to eternal and abundant life.

In this appendix, we will briefly survey a few examples of the great riches we have at our disposal.

The embarrassing riches of Predictive Prophecy

As an example, far too often ignored by the modern church, of how God provided a detailed and precise system of verification for His one true Messiah, Daniel 9 is probably the most remarkable chapter of the Bible. Daniel 9 accurately predicts Jesus' arrival in Jerusalem. Luke records Jesus Himself calling out "the time of your visitation" and that Jesus challenged those He was addressing for not recognizing the day. Consider that almost 500 years in advance, Daniel forecasted the exact year and day that Jesus would ride into Jerusalem on the foal of a donkey. It was right there for them to see, if only they could.

Daniel's writings were included in the Dead Sea Scrolls, hidden away when Israel was under attack during the period between the Maccabeans and the arrival of Christ. Even the more recently copied scrolls in that collection were dated to be at least 100 years before the arrival of Christ, with many dating 300-400 years prior. Carbon dating efforts were repeated from time to time as carbon dating methods were updated. Efforts completed in Zurich and the University of Arizona at Tucson generally confirmed that Daniel's writings pre-dated Christ, showing they had withstood the rigorous process of canonization (i.e., inclusion into the trusted Jewish Scriptures) by that time.

Here are several resources that provide details on that prophecy, articulating how we can use Daniel's writings to reliably and authoritatively resolve the specific day of Christ's arrival:

Author:

Robert Clifton Robinson

Book: *The Prophecies Of The Messiah*
https://www.amazon.com/gp/product/B00UA7Q6VA/

Article: The Key to all Bible Prophecy: Daniel Chapter 9
https://robertcliftonrobinson.com/2014/09/13/
the-key-to-all-bible-prophecy-daniel-chapter-9/

Teacher:

Dennis McCallum

Online Video Teaching on "The Intersection of Luke 19 and Daniel 9"

- o Includes a downloadable presentation with detailed references and sources for corroborating this remarkable claim
- o Includes a step-by-step buildup (in chart/timeline form) to show to-the-day prediction of the day of Jesus' arrival

https://teachings.dwellcc.org/teaching/3548

Many other resources are worth exploring on this topic, and many are referenced within these two recommendations.

We have referred to many other predictive prophecies regarding Jesus' first coming in Chapter 3: The incredible hidden story, in the section titled Old Testament Prophecies of Jesus. Many great works expand upon (as well as numerous efforts to debunk) the specific prediction and event pairs that show Christ is who He says He is. Don't be discouraged by the debunkers. We know that scrolls have been found predating Christ. We know that Christ fulfilled, by some accounts more than 400 specific prophecies, and even if someone can make a good argument that one may be misunderstood, sleep well on the improbability alone of Daniel's precision, and take the other 398 as a bonus.

The embarrassing riches of Archeology

Psalm 22 is another passage whose existence predates Christ. That pre-existence is also validated by its inclusion within the Dead Sea Scrolls we discussed above. It is a passage we have already covered in far more detail in Chapter 5: The Big Reveal – Part 1, in the section titled: Satan's Aha Moment. While there is controversy over the translation of verse 17 (much can be found about this with quick research), it is a trivial matter when viewed against the remarkable clarity of the text as a whole, clearly representing a view from the cross.

In fact, I would liken the argument to a lawyer attempting to invalidate a guilty verdict by arguing that someone remembered and recorded the wrong color shirt that a murderer wore when the testimony of ten eyewitnesses and a video of the crime were the cause for conviction. The argument is that interpreters chose the phrase "they have pierced my hands and feet" when the text found in the scrolls simply says, "lions at my hands and feet." Yet the controversial verse read under the "light of Christianity" is just as clear in the original phrasing as it is under the interpreted text.

Many discounted Psalm 22, claiming it had been injected into the Scriptures *after* Christ's death by those hoping to fabricate a prophetic connection. When archeologists discovered the dead sea scrolls, this weak argument had to be reduced. Nit-picking about the translation of an individual verse was all that was left. The pre-existence of this passage and its clarity of thought is a gift from God. For those who want to see what it holds, it brings confidence. And for those who prefer not to see it, a stumbling block.

Sir William Ramsay

Sir William Mitchell Ramsay (March 15, 1851 – April 20, 1939) was raised by atheists. He had a strong personal bias and a clear intention toward debunking the Bible through his work. Ramsay originally traveled to the Middle East to do archeological work, funded by the Queen of England. He believed (as did many of the British historical scholars of his time) that Luke was an inaccurate historian who should be disproven so that people would stop taking the Bible so literally. However, Ramsay's discoveries discredited his own disbeliefs, leading him to become a fierce advocate for the historicity and authority of Luke and his writings.

Ramsay wrote more than twenty books, including *St. Paul the Traveler and Roman Citizen* (1895), many of which detailed his archeological findings. His significant contributions to the field of archeology ultimately led to him being knighted by the Queen. When he passed in 1939, he had gone from being a passionate skeptic to one of the world's foremost authorities on Asia Minor. Ramsay was also regarded as one of the leading scholars of the New Testament.

While Ramsay initially saw Luke as a potentially mythical character or, at best, a real person who was loose with the details of history, he later wrote that Luke was "a historian of the first order." This and many other of Ramsay's 180-degree reversals can be found within the first few pages of his book, as noted above. And Ramsay "brings the receipts." He had personally made many of the discoveries that upset the previous view that Luke had made numerous errors regarding locations and the contemporary governance of various regions he described as background to the Apostle Paul's travels.

Ramsay later concluded that further study "…showed that the book [Acts] could bear the most minute scrutiny as an authority for the facts of the Aegean world, and that it was written with such judgment, skill, art and perception of truth as to be a model of historical statement" (*The Bearing of Recent Discovery*, p. 85). On page 89 of the same book, Ramsay explained, "You may press the words of Luke in a degree beyond any other historian's."

Luke also wrote a summary account of Jesus' birth, life, death, and resurrection. Consider that Ramsay, the skeptic, referred to Luke as a genius of detail and a historian of the first order. Consider that the story we have of Jesus' life was not only provided as three first-hand accounts in Matthew, Mark, and John but also provided in summary form, to include details of location and contemporary governance by the very same author that Ramsay set out to debunk.

Ramsay's many books are a treasure. Several have been updated to use more modern language and are easy to find through many popular book sellers.

Another well-regarded resource is the *Zondervan Handbook of Biblical Archaeology: A Book-by-Book Guide to Archaeological Discoveries Related to the Bible* (J. Randall Price, H. Wayne House, ZONDERVAN ACADEMIC, 2017). This comprehensive work provides numerous proof points arranged to match their references within the Bible.

There are many other resources, such as videos, lectures, and authoritative teachings, to be found by the avid seeker. Our riches in this area are an embarrassment and nullify any excuse we might make for being uninformed about the verifiable historicity of God's Word.

The embarrassing riches of Teleology

Teleology comes from the Greek root Telos which means "end or purpose." However, the modern definition of The Teleological Argument is more about the obviousness of beginnings that can be ascertained from the apparent end or purpose of a thing. For example, if we were to observe Eli Whitney's cotton gin, it would be evident that it was designed. It had the purpose of processing cotton in a way that was faster than the preceding method that relied entirely upon human labor. The obvious purpose of the machine's design necessitates a designer.

But let's take this a layer deeper than the cotton gin. Many still assume that the cotton itself emerged from a long series of accidents (i.e., evolution) versus being designed. This complex and self-replicating natural material, with an obvious purpose, is no more likely to have arisen by chance than the cotton gin itself. A staunch proponent of random origin might argue that a series of branches may have fallen to the ground near a deposit of iron ore until a combination of these materials was perhaps struck by lightning, yielding both the cotton gin and the cotton.

The random chance argument sounds ridiculous when applied to complex machinery. For example, I once asked someone how many billions of years you think we would need to allow hurricanes to traverse a junkyard before we end up with a properly operating Lamborghini—or, for that matter, any properly functioning machine? I asked this in response to his statement that I "didn't understand the potential for genetic variations across billions of years." Some will also argue that if you just add energy, the magic will happen. Have you ever left something out in the sun for too long? Did the addition of energy cause it to become something more complex or useful, or did the second law of thermodynamics diminish the order, usefulness, and lifespan of your object? Your item was designed for some purpose, yet the random application of energy will not improve it, and we all know that. As we can observe with endless consistency, the addition of energy itself is not a solution for the apparent presence of a design unless that energy is applied under a designer's control.

The teleological argument is simple. It focuses on the idea that the obviousness of a thing being designed obviates the existence of a designer. However, the argument against this is a painfully detailed claim of randomness throughout the universe resulting in all we can observe across creation. Yet Paul boldly claims in the first chapter of the book of Romans that the invisible attributes of God are plain to see in all creation so that all men are without excuse. Which argument is true?

The argument for randomness as a cause has many supporters, unfortunately including most of our modern "educational" institutions and resources. Many charts and graphs have been developed to convince young minds of the progression of random chance across divided pathways. Many of those charts and graphs have had critical elements debunked. Many fossils used to support the idea of transitional creatures have long since turned out to be frauds—yet the charts and images still include them, even when published today. Many books and websites are available to explore this topic, so I will not attempt to detail those many shortcomings here. Instead, we are focused on the obviousness of the problems with this argument of chance over design and creation.

It has become popular to suggest that birds are the modern descendants of dinosaurs. Never mind that this theory suggests that reptiles became mammals, ending up looking similar to other branches of creation, a thing that a full-blown evolutionist would never want to discuss. Still, it also leads to another massive problem, the problem of the commonality of design.

Consider the problem of the Hummingbird moth. Suppose we believe that billions of years and billions of small genetic accidents led to completely divided branches of development. How then would we explain the Hummingbird moth? If you have never seen one, search for a video of one and prepare to be astounded. This is an insect, 100 percent insect, that looks, flies, and feeds like a hummingbird. In fact, you may have seen one and never realized it because you thought it was a hummingbird. This is just one example of the commonality of design. And these creatures with strikingly common attributes live on different branches of evolution's divided tree. How could this be?

When I see two cars going down the road from the same manufacturer, I can recognize the commonality of design, and so can you. Sometimes if they are many years apart, I will need to see the logo to recognize them as being from the same company. However, when they are from the same period, it is much easier to recognize that they are from the same company because of the increased probability of them sharing the same designer, or at least the same design theme.

Consider the complexity of your immune system and your ability to see, hear, and speak. Which core abilities or attributes could a single member of our supposed early ancestors have done without yet still survive long enough to evolve and become our ancestors?

The frame we are built on is also similar to many of the creatures around us, yet the Bible tells us that we are made in the image of God. We can think, speak, and even create. Doesn't this suggest that we are also far more than a series of accidents?

There are many excellent resources available to expand upon the teleological argument. The Christian community has an embarrassing wealth of resources in this area. John Lennox is one of the most profound speakers, debaters, and authors I have ever encountered on this topic. I highly recommend researching him and his writings, perhaps starting with finding some of his now-famous debates. He is a winsome apologist, able to point out the emptiness of one's arguments against design and the existence of God, yet he delivers it without being offensive. He leads those he counters to think and has left many of the world's most famous atheist debaters and teachers speechless yet smiling at the same time.

The embarrassing riches of Language

We wrapped up the concept of teleology with the fact that humans are created in the image of God and that we see that demonstrated through our ability to think and communicate as part of our creative capacity. Engineers see something in their minds and draw it out into blueprints to communicate to others the things they are imagining and want to see become real. We can describe things to each other that can then become the basis of things yet unseen. Isn't this like the way that God spoke things into existence? When Chuck and I talked about writing this book, not a single bit of it existed. It began with an idea that turned into a conversation that eventually became a tangible and physical thing now in your hands.

One of the most remarkable things God gifted us with is the ability to communicate through the richness of language. Not only does it enable us to convey complex ideas to each other, but language is also the means God uses to convey powerful ideas and truth to us.

Many studies have been done on the communication abilities of other creatures within creation. I remember in my early twenties watching a nature program where scientists delightedly spoke about the early discoveries of the communication capacity among a group of dolphins they were studying. The Dolphins conveyed information with a series of clicks and various forms of physical expression. I was struck by irony as I watched. One of the scientists physically expressed a smile, then used several thousand words to explain the amazement and wonder she held at discovering that dolphins could warn each other of danger through sounds and actions. She added several hundred more words to discuss their abilities to coordinate their hunt for fish. The irony is that she also downplayed being human versus "the hidden communications of these amazing sea creatures." It was clear that these scientists saw what they were discovering as a miracle of evolution. Yet they had failed to observe the amazement and wonder also due their own ability to communicate so much more information through just a series of sounds (words) and physical expressions. Further, that information had reached so many at one time due to the creation of television, something no dolphin could ever imagine, no less create.

While animals can certainly express fear, anxiety, delight, and affection and coordinate their efforts, they will never describe to each other a concept they have in their head for the development of a machine. They will never record their history for future generations. They will never develop TV cameras or produce TV programs to explain their excitement about discovering the communication abilities of humans. They were not designed to do these things. We were, and it is this highest gift of language that most separates us from all that is around us.

Language gives us the ability to communicate concepts that transcend the physical. We can discuss the possibility of the spiritual realm. We can question the meaning of life. We can speak inspiration to one another. We can abuse language to abuse others. We can create through our words. We can destroy through our words. We have been given an extraordinary power unlike anything else in the universe. As already stated, it is also how God has chosen to convey His truth to us. It is also how God has chosen to work through us to share that truth with others.

Language separates us from all that is around us and underscores the previous discussion of the teleological argument. The end and purpose of language is the communication of high-level information. The fact that information can transcend the physical obviates the idea that there is a realm that transcends the physical. As you read these words, your mind can process the exact information I intended to convey. The ink and paper that this book is printed with are a highly advanced combination of chemicals, but they have no meaning.

Language is the expression of meaning, and it conveys purpose. Whether it honors God or not, every word we speak brings Him glory because it proves that we were created in His image and that we are separate from all creation by our ability to communicate to others just as God has spoken to us.

The embarrassing riches of Philosophy

Regardless of philosophy's roots, it can be defined as the study of the thing that remains when you remove the tangible. And what is it that remains when you remove the tangible? Ideas, concepts, and questions or statements about the meaning and purpose of life and all that we observe within it... that is what remains.

For example, suppose you were to exhaustively document and categorize every tangible thing in the universe. Then, what if someone walked up to your impressive library of everything and asked the question "why"? Would all of your collected knowledge of the "what" suffice to answer the question of why?

Philosophy without God is meaningless and leads to nothing. But when God is added, the answers to the all-important question of "Why?" becomes visible. The meaning of life is owned by God, and so, therefore, is philosophy itself owned by God, as Philosophy itself is merely the outcropping of a system of belief. So as the Author of Truth, God, should also be the author of our system of belief.

Great philosophers effectively argue that these things that remain once the tangible is removed are the most important things to consider. What is the point of a life full of material blessing that ends without meaning? What is the point of a life full of accomplishments if those accomplishments are without meaning? In fact, why are we here? And what comes after that?

The great debater, John Lennox, whom I mentioned in previous sections, was once arranged to debate Richard Dawkins, a famous and outspoken atheist. The local newspaper had reached out to Dawkins in search of a quote about the upcoming debate. The reporter, seeking a response from Lennox, taunted him with Dawkins' quote, "Christianity is a fairytale for those who are afraid of the dark." The reporter said I am doing an article on your upcoming debate and wonder how you would respond to that quote. Lennox resisted, not wanting to be petty, but being pressed by the reporter that "in the absence of a response, the article might seem one-sided," he begrudgingly responded. He used a device he wields quite effectively, turning the phrase around in simplicity. His response? "Atheism is a fairytale for those who are afraid of the light."

The truth is that we all have a philosophy (a system of belief about what remains when all the tangible is gone). For those without God, their philosophy leads them to answer that question with a horrific response of "nothing." After all, if we are just an accidental combination of chemicals, then once the magic of life escapes a person, our personhood, since it is not a tangible thing, will also become "nothing." This is both the impetus and urgency behind so many efforts among "elites" to wield science as a means to separate the human consciousness from it's physical form. A most salient example being the wealthy inventor Kurzweil's ongoing and incredibly costly effort to extend his life by attempting to transfer his consciousness into a machine.

The *Christian philosophy* is a worldview and system of belief based upon a verifiable confidence that we were created in the image of God. And, though deceived into joining a rebellion against Him, we were rescued by the selfless act of God's Son. Jesus presented us with the opportunity to be reconciled back to God through His saving gift. This is superior to the "nothing" philosophy in that it is full of meaning and purpose and answers the most challenging questions, like "Why?" Christianity, properly understood, provides a philosophy where what remains when all of the tangible things are gone is more significant than what we had with all of the tangible things present, and resolves our deepest fears about our own futures.

Consider an alternative philosophy known as collectivism. In the view of collectivism, there is no eternal purpose for our unique personhood. Instead, our individuality must be subjugated to the collective, and our lives only have a purpose if we contribute to the collective, as that entity is all that will remain of humanity when we are no longer a part of it. But collectivism cannot answer the question: "Why?" Collectivism abandons the individual at the same "nothing" that the atheist's chemical-based worldview leads us to. But the argument here is not that we want to feel better about a philosophy that has a future for us, but that the Christian-based philosophy is truly superior because of its ability to be fully reconciled to our God-given abilities of reason and logic.

Dr. Lennox has several excellent books, and they are rich with philosophically and intellectually satisfying arguments that support the superiority of God's truth. His book titled *God's Undertaker* is one that I highly recommend reading.

Another of our time's most brilliant minds who covers the topic of Philosophy well is Dr. William Lane Craig. William Lane Craig is a well-educated and accomplished author, speaker, and debater on this subject that matters most. He has authored or edited over thirty books (including *The Kalam Cosmological Argument*; *Assessing the New Testament Evidence for the Historicity of the Resurrection of Jesus*; *Divine Foreknowledge and Human Freedom*; *Theism, Atheism and Big Bang Cosmology*; and *God, Time and Eternity*), and over a hundred articles in professional journals of philosophy and theology. His work is easy to find, and I would suggest starting by hunting down videos of some of his past debates.

The point here is this. What would your life mean when all tangible things are gone, including your physical form? If you don't know the answer, I encourage you to get to know the One who does. He is God, and He has made an open offer to you. All that is required is to accept the free gift of His Son's death in exchange for your eternal life, and His Word promises that those who ask Him for wisdom receive it generously and without prejudice.

The embarrassing riches of Science

Have you ever considered the striking fact that the word *universe* can be broken down into its root parts, "Uni" (a single item) and "Verse" (a spoken sentence), and then recombined in that way to show us that the universe is a single spoken sentence?

We not only see this in math, where long equations can be written to describe every force, movement or pattern we discover consistently, but we also see it within our bodies. Dr. Francis Collins, a controversial character who recently stepped down from leading the National Institute of Health, believed by many to be a non-Christian, wrote a book titled, *The Language of God*. Dr. Collins led the human genome project. That project was responsible for decoding the entire human genome sequence and disassembling the DNA to its meaningful parts. This groundbreaking research has led to many advances in medicine and science, but it also led to Dr. Collins having to admit that he could see language in our DNA.

You will notice a pattern if you have read these last few sections together. Language, and our ability to understand it, makes us unique. Math is a language of proportions, motions, and forces. Words convey ideas, concepts, meaning, and philosophies. And one of the most brilliant minds of our times, in the course of disassembling the root instructions held within ourselves, could not help but observe... Language.

While I do not subscribe to many of Dr. Collins' conclusions, I would still recommend reading the book. It lays out the case for the necessity of wonder. The Bible describes it this way; we are "fearfully and wonderfully made."

We have also referred to Dr. Lennox enough that it should not seem the least bit out of form to let him conclude our discussion on the embarrassing riches of evidence available to the believer and those who desire to believe.

—◦◦◦—

The following article is an extract from "Can Science Explain Everything?" by John C Lennox, published by The Good Book Company, January 2019.

Another way of looking at this is to think once more about explanation. We are often taught in science that a valid explanation seeks to explain complex things in terms of simpler things. We call such explanation "reductionist", and it has been successful in many areas. One example is the fact that water, a complex molecule, is made up of the simpler elements hydrogen and oxygen.

However, reductionism doesn't work everywhere. In fact, there is one place where it does not work at all. Any full explanation of the printed words on a menu, say, must involve something much more complex than the paper and ink that comprise the menu. It must involve the staggering complexity of the mind of the person who designed the menu. We understand that explanation very well. Someone designed the menu, however automated processes led to the making of the paper and ink and carrying out the printing.

The point is that when we see anything that involves language-like information, we postulate the involvement of a mind. We now understand that DNA is an information-bearing macromolecule. The human genome is written in a chemical alphabet consisting of just four letters; it is over 3 billion letters long and carries the genetic code. It is, in that sense, the longest "word" ever discovered. If a printed, meaningful menu cannot be generated by mindless natural processes but needs the input of a mind, what are we to say about the human genome? Does it not much more powerfully point to an origin in a mind—the mind of God?

Atheist philosophy starts with matter/energy (or, these days, with "nothing") and claims that natural processes and nature's laws, wherever they came from, produced from nothing all that there is—the cosmos, the biosphere and the human mind. I find this claim stretches my rationality to breaking point, particularly when it is compared with the biblical view that:

In the beginning was the Word ... the Word was God ... All things were made through Him... John 1 v 1,3.

This Christian worldview resonates first with the fact that we can formulate laws of nature and use the language of mathematics to describe them. Secondly, it sits well with the discovery of the genetic information encoded in DNA. Science has revealed that we live in a word-based universe, and we have gained that knowledge by reasoning.

C.S. Lewis argues this point saying that "unless human reasoning is valid no science can be true." If ultimate reality is not material, not to take this into account in our context is to neglect the most important fact of all. Yet the supernatural dimension has not only been forgotten, it has been ruled out of court by many. Lewis observes: "The Naturalists have been engaged in thinking about Nature. They have not attended to the fact that they were thinking. The moment one attends to this it is obvious that one's own thinking cannot be merely a natural event, and therefore something other than Nature exists."

Not only does science fail to rule out the supernatural—the very doing of science or any other rational activity rules it in. The Bible gives us a reason for trusting reason. Atheism does not. This is the exact opposite of what many people think."

Appendix 2

The Mystery Hidden For Aeons Past

by Dennis McCallum
Reprinted with the Author's Permission

The Mystery Hidden for Aeons Past
Dennis McCallum

Considering Anomalies in Messianic Prophecy

ANY CAREFUL READER of Old Testament messianic prophecy quickly becomes aware of the two portraits of Messiah found there. On the one hand, we have the picture of the reigning Messiah, who banishes his enemies and lives forever. On the other hand, we have the portrait of the suffering servant. This one "has no stately form or majesty," lives in obscurity, is rejected by the people, and dies badly. But his death is redemptive like a guilt offering, and he is raised from the dead to lead many to God and to glory.

Christians are well aware that these two portraits correspond to the two comings of Christ: the first to suffer and atone for sin, and the second to reclaim the world for God and banish evil. Regardless of our millennial views, these two comings satisfy the Old Testament predictions in a very similar way.

While Christians feel this is a settled issue, Jewish interpreters reject the argument, not without cause. Their problems fall into three very good objections:

- Passages on the suffering servant never say they refer to Messiah, and in some cases, seem to refer to someone else.
- The Old Testament never teaches that Messiah will come twice.
- The Christian understanding of messianic prophecy requires acceptance of the so-called "prophetic gap" which, they argue, is unprecedented in the Bible.

Most Christian commentators give little attention to these objections, and actually try to downplay their importance, because Christ and the apostles explained both. (Indeed, I have done this as well in my book on the subject.) Yet, I think they are very important, because once we admit these three facts, the prophetic material becomes not only difficult to understand at the time of Christ, but actually impossible to understand.

This in turn leads to other questions. What use is a prophetic message that can only be understood after the fact? Also, if God wanted to pre-authenticate Christ through prophecy, why would he fail to link the portrait of the suffering servant to the Messiah? Why would he fail to mention that there are two comings?

While these deficiencies have occupied little thought from Christian readers, I will argue that they were of much more interest to New Testament authors. In fact, I think that by failing to focus on these very problems, Christians are missing a key aspect of God's plan for the world. They also miss the point of a number of key New Testament passages that explain the obscurity in messianic prophecy as well as the reasons for it.

Let's begin by examining how the three objections mentioned above work out in several of the clearest messianic prophecies in the Old Testament.

Is the suffering servant the Messiah?
Isaiah's Servant Songs

Probably the best body of prophecy concerning Christ's first coming is found in the "Servant Songs" of Isaiah. The passages are Isaiah 42:1-9; 49:1-13; 50:4-11; and 52:13-53:12 Isaiah portrays the servant is as follows:

A savior will one day come who will be filled with the Spirit of God. He will begin his ministry in obscurity rather than with the majesty people would expect of such a savior. Indeed, his own people will reject him. He will suffer persecution and torture, his body marred horribly. Although he teaches the Word of God, his contemporaries will believe that he is against God. Finally, the servant will be killed, but in dying, he will pay the price that the human race should have to pay for sin. After a period of time he will be raised from the dead, and multitudes will be brought into close relationship with God because of his work. Eventually, he will be crowned as a king, and even the other kings of the earth will be subject to him.

This description conforms to Jesus' life to an amazing degree. The New Testament makes it clear that early Christians knew these passages referred to Christ (see Matthew 8:17; 12:17-21; Acts 8:32-33). However, a number of objections can be raised against this Christian reading.

The passages never call the servant Messiah.

The four passages are spread out in a section of Isaiah dealing with God's faithfulness to Israel and his future dealings with her. When cut out of the text and stacked next to each other, a remarkably consistent picture emerges. But when viewed in the original context, these passages are far less clear. Jewish readers argue that Christians are performing a cut and paste surgery of the text that ignores the context.

In the same section of Isaiah, Israel herself is called "my servant Jacob" and "my servant Israel." It seems natural to Jewish readers to see these passages as also referring to Israel as the servant of the Lord. Even within one of the servant songs, the term "my servant Jacob" is used, referring apparently to the "anonymous" servant. Christians reply that these passages can't be about Israel as the servant of the Lord, because the career of the servant is completely different from that of Israel. Also, in more than one case, Israel is contrasted over against the Servant of the Lord (Isaiah 53:2, 3, 4, 5, 6).

All of these problems result in considerable confusion, especially to anyone who doesn't already know the history of Jesus' life. Scholars declare that no Jewish reader before the time of Christ ever interpreted these passages as referring to the Messiah. For instance, George Ladd says,

> ". . . it is of greatest importance to know that Judaism before Christ never interpreted this passage [Isaiah 53] as referring to the sufferings of the Messiah. An expert in Jewish literature [Joseph Klausner] says, 'In the whole Jewish Messianic literature of the Tannaitic period [before 200 AD] there is no trace of the 'suffering Messiah.'"

And,

> "This is the point: it was completely hidden from the disciples that the Son of Man must fill the role of the suffering servant of Isaiah 53 before He comes in the

power and glory of God's kingdom . . . a suffering and dying Messiah or Son of Man was unheard of and seemed to be a flat contradiction to the explicit word of God." (George Ladd, I Believe In The Resurrection Of Jesus, p. 66)

This, of course, is in contrast to clear predictions of the Messiah as reigning king. Such predictions, which, according to Christians, refer to the Second Coming, were universally recognized as referring to Messiah before the time of Christ.

Why would God break the servant prophecies into four pieces and intersperse them with passages about a different servant? If they were all together, the pattern would be so much clearer! Surely God would realize the confusion that had to arise as a result of this strange layout.

We can see that identifying the suffering servant with Messiah would be difficult, especially when we remember that the Old Testament never teaches that Messiah will come twice. Therefore, readers who knew that Messiah would live forever, that he would destroy his enemies, that he would have both stately form and majesty, were compelled to see some different person in these descriptions.

How odd it is that God would fail to mention that the servant is Messiah! How odd that he would leave out the crucial detail that Messiah will come twice! Without these two missing pieces of information, the whole section becomes difficult, if not impossible to understand for readers before and during the life of Christ.

Psalm 22:6-18

This passage describes in detail Jesus' death by crucifixion centuries before crucifixion had been invented! The details include the fact that his hands and feet were pierced, that he was naked, that his bones were being pulled out of joint, that his thirst was so intense that his tongue stuck to his jaws, that he was encircled by taunting persecutors as he died, and that men gambled for his clothing while he watched. Note that Jesus quoted the first verse of this psalm while on the cross: "My God, my God, why have you forsaken me?" No doubt he was calling people's attention to the fact that the well-known psalm was being fulfilled in their presence. Also, he literally was being forsaken by God at that moment as the judgment for human sin fell upon him.

We can only marvel at such a remarkable prediction today, especially in light of our knowledge of Christ's crucifixion. However, if we imagine ourselves reading this Psalm before, or during Jesus' life, we would get quite a different picture. The Psalm uses poetic language, and speaks in the first person. It seems to describe the miseries of the author in metaphorical terms. One would hardly conclude that this refers to the fate of King Messiah until after Jesus called attention to it on the cross. Messiah is never mentioned in this Psalm. Further, since it says the victim is laid in "the dust of death," a pre-Christian reader would hardly conclude that it refers to Messiah, since passages on Messiah make it clear that he lives forever (Is. 9:7, etc.) The missing point, that there are two comings of Messiah, compels any reader to conclude that this is about someone other than the Messiah.

Zechariah 11:12-14

The betrayal of Christ by Judas Iscariot is predicted in one passage where God is portrayed as a "foolish shepherd." For the purpose of communication, Zechariah the prophet enacted the betrayal and, remarkably, actually mentions the figure of "thirty pieces of silver." God remarked with sad irony that this "magnificent sum" (the price of a slave) was the value the people placed on him.

The New Testament teaches that this divine drama was referring to the betrayal of Christ by Judas (Matt. 26:15). Notice the passage also predicts that the money would finally be thrown into the temple and given to a potter. This was fulfilled when Judas's money was used to buy land from a local potter after Judas's death.

This is a remarkable prediction, but it is not without problems. First, the highly metaphorical nature of the foolish shepherd requires interpretation—a careful study of the context reveals that the shepherd is really God, and therefore in a way, Christ as God was sold for thirty pieces of silver. However, this would in no way be clear before the event actually occurred. Certainly, the passage mentions nothing about Messiah.

Micah 5:2

We all know this passage from Christmas readings:

But you, Bethlehem Ephrathah, though you are small among the clans of Judah, out of you will come for me one who will be ruler over Israel, whose origins are from of old, from ancient times.

This passage was known to be referring to the Messiah in the time of Christ as witnessed by the fact that the scribes quoted it to Herod when arguing that Messiah would be born in Bethlehem

(Mat. 2). But have you ever wondered why we only focus on the first part of the verse (his birth in Bethlehem) and not on the fact that he is to be ruler in Israel? This passage is clearly referring to a reigning king whose throne lasts forever and is worldwide, as the context makes clear:

> 5:4 He will stand and shepherd his flock in the strength of the LORD, in the majesty of the name of the Lord his God. And they will live securely, for then his greatness will reach to the ends of the earth.

None of this fits Jesus' first coming, so it's not surprising that Jewish interpreters refuse to see this passage as referring to Jesus. This passage is also an example of what some call the "prophetic gap." Messiah's birth in Bethlehem occurred during his first coming, according to Christians, while the rest of the passage refers to his second coming. The problem is that nothing is said of the gap of time between the two parts of the prediction. We are expected to believe that the passage would skip over 2000+ years without a word. Skeptics would argue that this is nothing less than a clear break in historical context, which renders the interpretation suspect.

Isaiah 61:1,2

Jesus quoted this passage during his first public sermon in Luke 4. The passage says:

> 1 The Spirit of the Sovereign Lord is on me, because the Lord has anointed me to preach good news to the poor. He has sent me to bind up the brokenhearted, to

proclaim freedom for the captives and release from darkness for the prisoners,

2 to proclaim the year of the Lord's favor and the day of vengeance of our God, to comfort all who mourn,

3 and provide for those who grieve in Zion—to bestow on them a crown of beauty...

Unlike some earlier examples, this passage was well known as a messianic prediction long before the time of Jesus. When Jesus read the passage, he stopped reading in the middle of verse 2 where it refers to "the year of the Lord's favor." He left out the part about "the day of vengeance of our God." Rolling up the scroll, he said, "Today this passage has been fulfilled in your hearing." (Luke 4:21)

How odd that he stopped reading in the middle of a rhyming couplet! The rest of the passage goes on to predict that Messiah will bring lasting peace and blessing to Israel. Today, we realize that he didn't read the rest, because that part hadn't been fulfilled yet. However, it will be fulfilled at the second coming.

The problem here is again, the prophetic gap. Why would God craft a prediction of Messiah in a way that suddenly skips from one coming to another without mention of the intervening millennia? (Even in the same rhyming couplet!) Even if he did inspire such a prophecy, why wouldn't he at least mention somewhere that there are two comings of Messiah? With all his omniscience, God would surely know that such omissions could only cause confusion. No wonder Jewish interpreters scoff at this reading, when it involves a break of context without any textual cue.

We should realize that these omissions were universal. Although the list of messianic predictions could go on and on, the pattern remains the same. In every single case, the passages either do not mention Messiah, are metaphorical and obscure, contain misleading prophetic gaps, or in other ways require two comings of Messiah in widely different roles. Yet, nowhere in the Old Testament do we find any teaching to the effect that Messiah should come twice. In every case, this missing information compels the reader to reach the wrong conclusion.

What are we to conclude?

Honest reading of the prophecies concerning Messiah reveals a very clear pattern of missing information, confusing contexts, and hard to interpret language. But this lack of clarity is not universal. Actually, many predictions of the Messiah are crystal clear. A closer look reveals that all the clear predictions refer to the second coming of Messiah as a ruling king. All the obscure or confusing predictions refer to the first coming. This is not just a generalization. In fact, all of the predictions of the second coming are clear. All of the predictions of the first coming contain one or more of the problems mentioned above, with the resulting difficulty in interpretation.

This pattern is so consistent, so lacking in any exception, it demands an explanation. Jewish interpretation (as well as other perspectives sharing their skepticism about Jesus) have a ready explanation. They feel this is clearly a case of Christians wanting to believe that the Old Testament predicted Jesus, even though it did not. In their desperation, the early Christians "read in" their interpretation, forcing the meaning into passages that were never intended to say what they claimed. The results were predictable: broken contexts, bizarre leaps in chronology, and assumed material that simply is not found in the text.

I was aware of this critique as an atheist raised in a Bible believing home, and became more aware of it as a young Christian. It lay in the back of my mind, a troublesome stumbling block. As a student of the Bible, I would look up from time to time in my reading, profoundly troubled by the realization that it would be all too easy to see these predictions as forced reading after-the-fact by Christians who needed a justification for their new faith. I could only wonder how Paul "proved from the scriptures that Jesus was the Christ." (Acts 17:2,3) I never had the time to resolve this hanging question when I was an undergraduate student.

When I went to seminary, I finally had the time to do lengthy research on messianic prophecy. Through my own reading, I became convinced that the predictions of Jesus' first coming were not mistaken readings. They are amazing confirmations of the authenticity of Christ. Passages like the servant songs in Isaiah must refer to Jesus, and to no one else. And while some predictions could be read in more than one way, they certainly can be seen in the Christian light without distortion.

But this conclusion leaves key questions unanswered. Why does God often present predictions in a confused context? Why does he omit any mention of Messiah? Why isn't there even a single reference to two comings?

I think there is one, and only one, answer to these questions: God created this situation deliberately. A large view of the complex of predictions of the first coming of Messiah crystallizes into a single picture: These predictions are written in such a way that they cannot be properly understood until after the life of Jesus. The author of these predictions was very purposeful in omitting the key information that would have made them easy to understand in advance. The passages never say anything untrue. It's what they don't say that makes them ambiguous.

If God wanted people to recognize Jesus' coming and mission, there's no way he would have left out the part about two comings. This omission makes one passage after another incomprehensible, while knowing that there are two comings makes them suddenly as clear as day. In fact, the conflation of the two comings into a single passage (the prophetic gap) seems to be calculated to lead to the impression that there is only one coming. At the same time, we notice it's always the first coming that is obscure, never the second coming.

Yes, this could be because the first coming is not really predicted, but is an invention of wishful early Christians. But I think there is another explanation that accords with the text in an incredibly convincing way. In fact this answer opens the door to understand not only Old Testament prophecy, but also New Testament teaching in a new and marvelous way, as I hope to show. I believe the resolution to this problem includes information Paul had that made it all too possible to demonstrate from the scriptures that Jesus was the Christ.

Jesus and Predictive Prophecy

In Jesus' preaching and discussion, we see many comments that seem to perpetuate the confusion. For instance, when he appeared, Mark says:

And after John had been taken into custody, Jesus came into Galilee, preaching the gospel of God, and saying, "The time is fulfilled, and the kingdom of God is at hand; repent and believe in the gospel." (Mark 1:14,15)

Anyone familiar with Jewish theology of the time sees that this could mean only one thing to his audience. They would see this as Jesus proclaiming himself King Messiah, and the kingdom would be the one promised in messianic prophecies of the second coming. Although Jesus later qualified his proclamation of the kingdom as being different than the Old Testament picture of a world-wide compulsory rule of God, he did so in a veiled way.

The best known discussion on this is in Mat. 13. There, Jesus gave the parables of the kingdom—each one stressing the difference between what they were expecting, based on Old Testament prophecy, and what he was actually here to begin. Instead of a sudden takeover, there would be gradual growth from obscure beginnings (parable of the mustard seed, and the leaven). Instead of "ruling the nations with a rod of iron" and banishing all sinners, believers and non believers would live side by side (parable of the soils, dragnet, wheat and tares, etc.).

In his comments to the disciples on these parables, Jesus made it clear that he didn't expect his audience to understand them. In fact he indicates that he was deliberately speaking in a way that they could not understand:

And the disciples came and said to Him, "Why do You speak to them in parables?" And He answered and said to them, "To you it has been granted to know the mysteries of the kingdom of heaven, but to them it has not been granted... Therefore I speak to them in parables; because while seeing they do not see, and while hearing they do not hear, nor do they understand." (Mat. 13:10,11,13)

We see here an ongoing effort to keep the nature of his mission veiled to the public. In other places, it seems like he wanted the disciples to understand the nature of his mission as the suffering servant:

Jesus took the Twelve aside and told them, "We are going up to Jerusalem, and everything that is written by the prophets about the Son of Man will be fulfilled. He will be handed over to the Gentiles. They will mock him, insult him, spit on him, flog him and kill him. On the third day he will rise again." (Luke 18:31-33)

This was clear enough. However, we also read in verse 34,

The disciples did not understand any of this. Its meaning was hidden from them, and they did not know what he was talking about.

Why didn't the disciples understand? Was it because they couldn't break out of the paradigm of the eternal Messiah who cannot die? Or was it God himself who "hid" the meaning from them? We don't know. But if we study all of the similar disclosures Jesus made, we see sixteen passages where Christ told his disciples what he was going to do (although some are referring to the same discussion). The list is as follows: Mark 8:31*; 10:45*; 9:9,10,12*; 10:32-34; 9:31-32; Matthew 20:17-19*; 17:22,23; 16:21; Luke 9:22*; 9:44,45; 18:31-34; John 3:14*; 10:15-18,20; 12:32-34; 16:17-18,25. In each of the starred passages, it records the disciples reaction, and makes it plain that they did not understand what he was saying.

It seems they never did understand. Right up to the end of his ministry they were asking him, "So is this the time when you will reveal your kingdom?" Even the question they asked at the Mount of Olives, "What will be the sign of your coming?" may be misleading to modern readers. It sounds to us like they now knew he would leave and come back. But the term "coming" may have meant a triumphal entry, or presentation of himself as king. It's entirely possible that they were still thinking that the coming might happen any day.

Notice the paradigmatic thinking of the crowd in John 12:34. After Jesus mentioned being "lifted up" on the cross, "The multitude therefore answered Him, 'We have heard out of the Law that the Christ is to remain forever; and how can You say, "The Son of Man must be lifted up"? Who is this Son of Man?'" Since they couldn't conceive of a Messiah that would die, they tended to shift the identity of the Son of Man in order to compensate. This must have been the norm throughout Jesus' life.

At the last supper, Jesus makes a series of significant statements. After dinner Jesus said, "Little children, I am with you a little while longer. You shall seek Me; and as I said to the Jews, I now say to you also, 'Where I am going, you cannot come.'" (John 13:33)

Then we read, "Simon Peter said to Him, 'Lord, where are You going?'" (36) Clearly, Peter still didn't know what was about to happen. This confusion is echoed by Thomas as well. (14:5) Then, when Jesus promises that those who receive the Spirit after his departure will receive revelation of Christ, Judas Alpheus asks, "Lord, what then has happened that You are going to disclose Yourself to us, and not to the world?" (14:22) Clearly, they were incredulous that he was not going to reveal his true identity to the world. Remember, this conversation occurred the night before the cross. Even at this late date, none of his disciples realized that he intended to die, rise, leave, and come again.

Later in that same conversation, Jesus said, "These things I have spoken to you, that you may be kept from stumbling." (16:1) Later, he expanded, "But these things I have spoken to you, that when their hour comes, you may remember that I told you of them. And these things I did not say to you at the beginning, because I was with you." (4) and, "A little while, and you will no longer behold Me; and again a little while, and you will see Me." (16)

Again, dismay and confusion reigned: "Some of His disciples therefore said to one another, 'What is this thing He is telling us, "A little while, and you will not behold Me; and again a little while, and you will see Me"; and, "because I go to the Father"?' And so they were saying, 'What is this that He says, "A little while"? We do not know what He is talking about.'" (17,18)

Jesus' only response was "These things I have spoken to you in figurative language; an hour is coming when I will speak no more to you in figurative language, but will tell you plainly of the Father." (25)

As we read this exchange, we get the strong sense that Jesus was pursuing a course identical to what God earlier did in the Old Testament. He was telling them things they did not understand, but which they would remember after the events occurred. How similar to God's apparent strategy of predicting the first coming in a way people would miss until after it happened! Once the cross and the resurrection occurred, these statements all made perfect sense, but beforehand, Jesus himself acknowledges that they couldn't grasp what he was saying.

After the resurrection, Jesus met with the disciples again. In Luke 24, we read, "Then he opened their minds to understand the Scriptures, and He said to them, 'Thus it is written, that the Christ should suffer and rise again from the dead the third day; and that repentance for forgiveness of sins should be proclaimed in His name to all the nations, beginning from Jerusalem.'" (45-47)

What a Bible study this must have been! Notice that what he "opened their minds" to were the Old Testament predictions of the suffering servant. Now they understood that the suffering servant and King Messiah were one and the same, but revealed in two separate comings.

Why did Jesus wait until after his resurrection to tell them these things? Why couldn't he open their minds earlier? Why did he speak in "figurative language" earlier, but plainly now? It seems clear from these passages, and many others we don't have time to cover, that Jesus was intentionally veiling his mission up until a certain point in time. Like God in the Old Testament, Jesus seemed to want a situation where he could say, "I told you so," but at the same time, he didn't want people to know what he was doing until after he did it.

Satan's Strange Role

Nobody behaved more strangely during this time than God's enemy, Satan. We read in John 13:2 that at the last supper, "the devil had already put into the heart of Judas Iscariot, the son of Simon, to betray Him." What an odd thing for Satan to do! If Jesus had come to die for human sin, why would Satan actively cooperate in his death? Hadn't Jesus just warned that the cross would be the undoing of Satan? (John 12:31,32) Wasn't it the cross that made it possible for Paul to say, "When He had disarmed the rulers and authorities, He made a public display of them, having triumphed over them through Him." (Col. 2:15)

This part of the story is like a poorly written novel where people's motivations don't line up with the action. Why would a creature as brilliant as Satan, not just acquiesce, but actually assist in doing the very thing that would be most destructive to himself?

Several answers have been advanced.

One suggestion is that Satan was compelled to do what he did, because God sovereignly made him. Since the cross was God's plan, Satan was made to play his part in that plan. This suggestion is certainly possible, although it is speculative. The Bible never claims Satan was acting under compulsion, only that the cross was part of the "predetermined plan and foreknowledge of God." (Acts 2:23) Certainly God knew Satan would do what he did, as he also knew the other players, like Pilate and Herod would do what they did. But unlike the human players, Satan had everything to lose from the cross.

Others have argued that Satan was so arrogant that he thought he could hold Jesus in death after the cross. Again, this is possible, although speculative. Certainly, Satan is arrogant, but would he be this stupid? He certainly knew who Jesus was. And we see him backing down from God's power in cases like that involving Job.

Others argue that Satan knew the cross would destroy him, but he couldn't resist the sadistic pleasure of watching Jesus suffer. Again, we can imagine this, and we do know that Satan is irrationally hateful at times. But it seems to me like quite a stretch to see the anointed cherub behaving in such a self-destructive way.

Maybe Paul offers us another explanation in 1 Cor. 2:6,8:

Yet we do speak wisdom among those who are mature; a wisdom, however, not of this age, nor of the rulers of this age, who are passing away; but we speak God's wisdom in a mystery, the hidden wisdom, which God predestined before the ages to our glory; the wisdom which none of the rulers of this age has understood; for if they had understood it, they would not have crucified the Lord of glory.

Could it be that Satan, the great adversary, didn't know that Jesus actually wanted to die? If so, it would perfectly explain why he helped orchestrate his death.

Many feel this passage is not referring to Satan, but to the human rulers who put Jesus to death. That's possible, although Paul uses the term "God of this world" to refer to Satan. (2 Cor. 4:4) Also, the "world rulers of this darkness" refers to demons (Eph. 6:12) the term here is kosmos, rather than aeon, but the sense is similar). Also, if he was referring to Pilate, Herod, and Caiaphas, why would he use the present tense "who are passing away" when all of them were now dead or at least no longer in power?

I will argue, based on this and other passages in the New Testament that this is exactly what happened: The brilliant, bitter, and arrogant enemy of God acted freely, thinking he was disrupting God's plan to take over and rule the world through Jesus. But instead he played directly into Jesus' hands, doing exactly what Jesus wanted him to do, and proving in the process, his own character as hate as well as God's character as true, self-giving love.

Did Satan Know Jesus Planned to Die?

Some readers find it difficult to believe that Satan would have made such a colossal blunder when all the information was right there in front of him for hundreds of years. But let's think about it. How would he have known what Jesus was doing? He would have had the same information everyone else had—the predictive scriptures. But we have seen that God crafted those in such a way that a reader before the time of Christ could not have discovered the plan for two comings. The missing information made it impossible to reach this conclusion. Why would Satan be any different than anyone else?

Again, if we accept the premise that God was intentionally veiling his intentions in the first coming, the hanging question remains: Why would he do so? Here, we may have an answer. Perhaps in God's eternal plan of salvation, he was also putting the permanent smack-down on Satan and his accusations.

We know that the devil (diabolos = slanderer) gets much of his power from his ability to create suspicion about God. His accusations are not just directed to us and about us, but about God. From his first appearance in Genesis we see him implying that God can't be trusted—that he is self-serving and oppressive. This fallen angel was so persuasive that not only the first humans, but much of the angelic host followed him into rebellion in spite of the fact that these creatures must have actually seen God.

This accusing of God is interesting to consider in light of the dilemma it creates for God. Each part of this carefully crafted lie contains self-validating implications that would seem to prevent God from opposing the lie effectively.

For instance, Satan claims that God is self-serving when he calls on his creatures to follow him. We know God's counter claim that he calls on the creation to follow him for their own good. But to fallen creatures, a God who enforces a rule to follow his will may indeed seem self-serving. Satan's picture of a God duping his creatures into thinking that he is self-giving, when he is actually self-serving has been very persuasive in the history of the universe. Millions have bought into this suspicion.

Secondly, Satan postures God as mean, oppressive, and unfair. We see this claim implied when he told Eve that the real reason God didn't want her to eat the forbidden fruit was because it would result in her gaining wisdom and becoming like God. This pictures God as willing to oppress people in order to keep them from attaining to all they could be. God declares that he is love, that he is compassionate, and that he is always perfectly fair. But how can he punish rebellious creatures (which is fair) without seeming to confirm the suspicion that he is mean? How can he spare any rebellious creature from punishment without becoming unfair?

Satan continually tries to play off God's love against his justice. Any God who would judge cannot be loving, he argues. A judging God is vindictive and hateful, according to Satan. Satan must advance a form of permissiveness as love. Again, if God destroyed Satan, wouldn't that suggest that Satan was right after all, and that God is vindictive and hateful?

This cosmic dilemma is the background for the Bible. Satan is a careful student of Scripture (Luke 4) and was well-aware that God was developing a plan of salvation. He has opposed that plan at every point, as he still does today.

Suppose, for the sake of argument, that when Jesus came, Satan, like everyone else, concluded that he had come, not as a suffering servant, but as reigning king. King Messiah is said to destroy his enemies, and rule the world with a "rod of iron." This picture of dominance fits all too well with Satan's concept of God as the mean, vindictive destroyer of freedom. Aside from anything in prophecy, Satan would be inclined to see Messiah this way because of his prejudice against God.

I will argue that Satan did, in fact, make this mistake. He thought Jesus had come to rule, not to suffer. Jesus' self-effacing behavior must have been confusing, but most people thought he was going to unveil his power any day. Satan may have thought this as well. In one instance, some demons cried out to Jesus, "have you come to torment us before the time?" They were apparently surprised to see him there earlier than expected, but saw his mission only as one of torment. How typical this is of demonic thinking.

If Satan was mistaken about Jesus' intentions, he would naturally conclude that arranging to kill him would short-circuit the planned kingdom. Suddenly, his actions with Judas make sense. But what was the outcome? Too late, he would realize that he had actually facilitated not the destruction of the kingdom, but the salvation of humankind. At the same time, his greatest weapon, his accusations of God, were now useless. The cross demonstrated in an undeniable way the loving and sacrificial nature of God. Instead of God being vindictive and cruel, it was Satan who was unmasked as utterly vindictive and cruel.

Perhaps this is what Paul alludes to when he says in Colossians 2:15, "When He had disarmed the rulers and authorities, He made a public display of them, having triumphed over them through Him." The cross forever disarmed Satan by striking down his main contention: that God is self-serving, mean, and unfair.

This would account for Jesus' declaration that "now is the judgment of this world, now is the prince of this world cast out." (John 12:32) Paul seems to echo this explanation in several places:

> Now to Him who is able to establish you according to my gospel and the preaching of Jesus Christ, according to the revelation of the mystery which has been kept secret for long ages past, but now is manifested, and by the Scriptures of the prophets, according to the

commandment of the eternal God, has been made known to all the nations... (Rom. 16:25,26)

In this remarkable passage, Paul reveals that God was, indeed, keeping something secret for aeons—something that had recently been revealed. This "mystery" or secret is tied up with Paul's gospel. I believe the cross and God's whole redemptive intent in the first coming of Messiah, are the mystery to which he refers. It was secret because, although predicted, it was predicted in a way that was undecipherable until too late, as we have seen. Only after Satan had made his violent and hateful move against Christ did the truth emerge.

In another passage, Paul says,

By revelation there was made known to me the mystery, as I wrote before in brief. And by referring to this, when you read you can understand my insight into the mystery of Christ, which in other generations was not made known to the sons of men, as it has now been revealed to His holy apostles and prophets in the Spirit... (Eph. 3:3-5)

Apparently, Paul was given a special revelation about God's plan. He clearly states that this mystery was not revealed to people. The particular aspect of the mystery of interest in this passage has to do with the universality of the redemptive work of Christ, in that it included gentiles as well as Jews. But we know that Paul's mystery extends well beyond this point, as we shall see. But here in Ephesians, Paul goes on to draw out cosmic significance of the secret plan of God:

To me, the very least of all saints, this grace was given, to preach to the Gentiles the unfathomable riches of Christ, and to bring to light what is the administration of the mystery which for ages has been hidden in God, who created all things; in order that the manifold wisdom of God might now be made known through the church to the rulers and the authorities in the heavenly places. This was in accordance with the eternal purpose which He carried out in Christ Jesus our Lord. (Eph. 3:8-11)

Several points are interesting here. For one thing, he says the mystery has for aeons been "hidden in God." Apparently, God alone knew what he was intending to do. Here is clear confirmation that God was actively veiling his intentions in Christ from the whole world, and even from the angelic hosts.

Also, he points out the result of the mystery: that the "rulers and authorities in the heavenly places" (angels and perhaps demons) will learn something about God. Is it that they now see God's character of love and self-sacrifice for what it is? Isn't it plausible that the cross, a unique event in the history of the universe, has laid to rest any possibility of suspicion about the character of God?

We see that the church plays a key role in this revelation to the heavenly hosts. As recipients of grace, we forgiven humans are in a unique position. We know what it is like to live apart from God, to harbor suspicions of God, and even to hate God. But we also know what it is like to experience his grace and love; an incredible gift that cost him everything and us nothing.

This mystery is central to what Paul calls God's "eternal purpose." God planned this whole thing out from eternity and for eternity. Never again will there be a revolution against God, even though free-will creatures populate the universe. That is because all will remember what happened last time. They will remember how God demonstrated his nature as good, loving, and fair, while his accusers revealed their character as evil, bitter and deceptive.

This idea of a demonstration appears also in Romans 3.

God displayed [Jesus] publicly as a propitiation in His blood through faith. This was to demonstrate His righteousness, because in the forbearance of God He passed over the sins previously committed; for the demonstration, I say, of His righteousness at the present time, that He might be just and the justifier of the one who has faith in Jesus. (25,26)

The cross was a public demonstration of God's goodness, according to this passage. What does the phrase "the just and the justifier" mean? At the cross, God demonstrated his justice, because the sins of his favorite humans was not ignored, but punished fully. At the same time, he is the justifier, because he paid that penalty himself at incredible cost. How perfectly these stand as antitheses to Satan's lies mentioned earlier!

Paul brings the mystery up again in Colossians 1:

Of this church I was made a minister according to the stewardship from God bestowed on me for your benefit, that I might fully carry out the preaching of the word of God, that is, the mystery which has been hidden from the past ages and generations; but has now been manifested to His saints, to whom God willed to make known what is the riches of the glory of this mystery among the Gentiles, which is Christ in you, the hope of glory. (25-27)

This passage is very similar to some cited earlier. Again we see that the mystery "has been hidden from the past ages and generations." Yes, it was there, right in front of them in the prophets, but because of the key omissions, no one could see it. Recently, he says, it has been manifested, or brought to light. The content of the mystery according to this passage is, "Christ in you, the hope of glory." Of course it is the cross that opens the door to the new intimacy between us and God; an intimacy so deep that he actually indwells us through the Holy Spirit.

Again, this passage makes it very clear that God was keeping a secret, a mystery, that has only recently been revealed. Unless my theory about Old Testament prophecy is right, what would that secret be, and why was he keeping it? I must confess, I have never heard an adequate explanation to this question.

I think the notion that God purposely veiled the Old Testament prophecies of the first coming is confirmed in an interesting passage in 1 Peter:

As to this salvation, the prophets who prophesied of the grace that would come to you made careful search and inquiry, seeking to know what person or time the Spirit of Christ within them was indicating as He predicted the sufferings of Christ and the glories to follow. It was revealed to them that they were not serving themselves, but you, in these things which now have been announced to you through those who preached the gospel to you by the Holy Spirit sent from heaven—things into which angels long to look. (10-12)

According to this passage, even the prophets who wrote the predictions didn't know who the predictions referred to. Notice it is the first coming of Christ ("the sufferings of Christ and the glories to follow") that confused them. Even after careful search and inquiry, it never says God told them who the suffering servant was. Peter only says God revealed to them that a later generation would be served by these predictions, and therefore they didn't need to know who it was. That must be the case, since Paul says the mystery was a secret "hidden in God" in Ephesians 3.

The last phrase is interesting as well. We notice that the angels are astonished by what they see in this revealed mystery. Like the passage in Eph. 3, Peter seems to imply that the entire universe is learning a lesson they will never forget from the work of the cross and its result in the church.

The Big Picture

As we ponder the mystery hidden for aeons past, the multitude of information begins to congeal into a marvelous picture.

I would suggest that God wanted to create personal beings, and personal beings by definition, must be un-programmed, free-choosing moral agents. Anything less is a machine, not a person. Yet, the creation of freedom inherently entails the possibility and indeed, the likelihood that eventually someone would use their freedom the wrong way.

We know this happened when Satan rebelled against God. And that rebellion has spread to our world, nearly ruining it. Of course God saw all of this coming, and he had a plan. He laid down a well-attested scriptural tradition that promised he would one day intervene to return the world to its proper state with him as its leader. But inserted into this same predictive material was another message—a message that was clear in one way, but hidden in another way, almost like it was in code.

Then, at the right time, Christ came, and basically laid a trap for the enemies of God. As they pitted their limited wisdom against his infinite wisdom, they were completely out-classed, and ended up proving how good God is, and how bankrupt was their own revolution.

The outcome is clear. The Cross has silenced for all time the ravings of Satan and his ilk. In light of what has happened, the universe can feel an amazing level of confidence in God and his character, a confidence so complete that revolution will never again taint the course of eternity future.

Objections to This Theory

I hope this very brief explanation of the mystery has been persuasive, although the subject clearly deserves a lot more thought. Already a number of objections and questions have been raised, which I will share along with possible responses for interested readers.

It's one thing to see that the disciples didn't perceive or understand what Jesus was saying when he clearly announced his intention to die, but how could Satan have missed such clear declarations?

Response: We should remember that Satan is not omniscient like God. Even though he is probably far more intelligent than humans, he is limited in knowledge and understanding. There is no proof he can tell the future, or read people's minds. Neither is he omnipresent, even through the agency of his many demons. These limitations raise at least two possibilities:

First, Satan may have made the same mistakes, for the same reasons, everyone else did. Whatever the reasons the disciples failed to comprehend what Jesus was saying, Satan may have failed for the same reasons. Whether it was God actively blocking his understanding, or simply paradigmatic thinking, he must not have grasped the meaning of Jesus' words.

Or, perhaps Jesus only gave these disclosures when he discerned that Satan was not around. When talking to the disciples in the upper room, Jesus says, "I will not speak much more with you, for the ruler of the world is coming, and he has nothing in Me." (John 14:30) It sounds like Jesus only talked about confidential information when no demons were listening.

If nobody knew what the predictions of the suffering servant meant, why does Simeon cite one of the servant songs when he sees Jesus as a baby? (Luke 2:25-32)

Response: It seems like Simeon is speaking a prophetic word, since he speaks in verse, similar to that found in the prophets. If so, he was inspired to say what he did, but perhaps without realizing the full implications. He would have been like the Old Testament prophets who predicted "the sufferings of Christ" without knowing who it referred to. (1 Pet. 1:12) Prophets definitely utter things they, themselves, don't always understand. Daniel states this when he says after one of his prophetic visions, "As for me, I heard but could not understand..." (Dan. 12:8) and on another occasion, "I was astounded at the vision, and there was none to explain it." (Dan. 8:27) Our best evidence is that nobody, including Simeon, understood the mystery because it was "hidden in God." (Eph. 3:9)

If nobody was able to know what the predictions of the first coming meant, why does Jesus chide the men on the road to Emmaus saying, "O foolish men and slow of heart to believe in all that the prophets have spoken! Was it not necessary for the Christ to suffer these things and to enter into His glory?" (Luke 24:25,26)

Response: Note that this incident occurred after the resurrection. Jesus apparently expected people to connect the dots once the cross and his resurrection occurred. It should have been obvious by this time that recent events conformed, not only to prophecy, but to the verbal warnings Jesus had given earlier. Notice how the angels reproved the women at his tomb with the words, "Why do you seek the living One among the dead? He is not here, but He has risen. Remember how He spoke to you while He was still in Galilee, saying that the Son of Man must be delivered into the hands of sinful men, and be crucified, and the third day rise again." (Luk. 24:5-7) They like Jesus seem to feel that after the cross the whole puzzle should have snapped into focus.

If Satan thought Jesus was here to begin his kingdom, why would he try to tempt him? Wasn't this done so he could disqualify Jesus from being a spotless lamb?

Response: Satan may have had this motive, although this is speculation. The text nowhere gives his motives. Clearly, committing sin would have disqualified Jesus from being King, just as it would from being sacrificial lamb. Many passages like this would have to be re-thought if we accept that nobody knew Jesus planned to die for sin.

If nobody knew Jesus was the suffering and atoning servant, why did John the Baptist declare, "Behold the lamb of God." (John 1:36)

Response: Again, John may have been speaking under prophetic inspiration, rather than from his own understanding. Jesus said John was a prophet, so the same argument would apply as that for Simeon above. We know John's understanding was not complete because he later even had to send messengers asking whether Jesus was the Messiah at all. (Mat. 11:2,3)

If we accept this theory, when do we suppose Satan and others finally grasped what Jesus had come to do?

Response: We don't know the answer to this question, but I imagine Satan may have realized his error while Jesus was still on the cross. Jesus cried "My God, My God, why have you forsaken me?" which comes from Psalms 22:1. This Psalm goes on to describe the crucifixion in considerable detail. Of course, like other predictions about the first coming, it was veiled, failing to mention who it referred to, and even given in the first person, making it seem like it refers to David in metaphorical terms. This was probably the first time people realized it actually referred to Christ. As Satan watched his handiwork and heard Jesus make this cry, he would have no doubt immediately drawn the connection, and, no doubt from memory recalled the rest of the Psalm. With a growing sense of horror, he would realize that he had unwittingly done exactly what God wanted! Instead of the excitement of winning, he would have quickly realized that he had been defeated by his own hand, but it was already too late to do anything about it.

Contact the Authors:

Web: www.exposition.media
EMail: mysterybook@exposition.media

CPSIA information can be obtained
at www.ICGtesting.com
Printed in the USA
JSHW020516270523
42345JS00004B/8